Contents

Assessment
in Schools

David Satterly

BASIL BLACKWELL

14498

First published 1981
Reprinted 1985, 1986

Basil Blackwell Ltd
108 Cowley Road, Oxford OX4 1JF, UK

Basil Blackwell Inc.
432 Park Avenue South, Suite 1503,
New York, NY 10016, USA

British Library Cataloguing in Publication Data

Satterly, David
    Assessment in schools. – (Theory and practice
    in education. no. 1).
    1. Students, Rating of – Great Britain
    I. Title   II. Series
    371.2'64   LB1117
    ISBN 0–631–11151–4
    ISBN 0–631–12564–7 Pbk

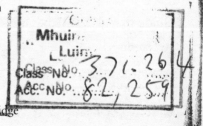

Typesetting by Freeman Graphic, Tonbridge
Printed in Great Britain by
Billing and Sons Limited, Worcester

Editor's Preface

Very few, if any, educational problems are straightforward enough to have simple answers. Therefore, in so complex a human activity as educating, it should be no surprise that yet another series can still have a vital and significant contribution to make to our understanding of educational problems. Theorists and practitioners in the many developing interests in education quite properly continue to want to share their views and findings with others.

Theory and Practice in Education attempts to present, in a readable form, a range of issues which need to be considered by serving and student teachers in their roles as practitioners. Wherever formal, organized learning exists in our schools and colleges, there will always be questions relating, for example, to the effectiveness of teaching and children's learning, the preparation and adequacy of what is taught, the processes of assessment and evaluation, the sensitive problems of accountability, the preparation of children for 'life' and the monitoring of innovations.

There has long been a need in this country for a sound, readable and comprehensive text on assessment. David Satterly has at last provided such a book. The subject is not an easy one to put across, especially to busy teachers who need a quick, but valid, introduction. It is written with the less mathematically orientated in mind and his style, I believe, is most appropriate for this purpose.

Assessment is part and parcel of every teacher's day. Teachers who do not evaluate both their own and their pupils' work cannot be doing their jobs properly. Assessment of a wide range of pupil performance is an integral part in monitoring the progress made not only for the benefit of the pupil and teacher, but those outside the classroom such as other teachers, other schools, parents and, with older children, employers and other educational institutions who depend upon reliable knowledge of a pupil's achievement. I am therefore especially grateful that one of our first books in the series deals with assessment.

Newcastle upon Tyne   *Dennis Child*

Acknowledgements

It is impossible to acknowledge all the writers to whom I am indebted for the following pages. However, I am particularly grateful to Robert Ebel, Lee Cronbach, Louis and Marylin Karmel, William Mehrens, Irvin Lehmann, David Payne, Derek Rowntree and Gareth Lewis among others who have written extensively on assessment topics. To Frederic Lord and Melvin Novick whose work on statistical theories in testing is a classic in the field, to Robert Thorndike for his collection of some of the best writing on educational measurement and to numerous other writers whose original contributions to the literature on assessment are to be found in the pages of the relevant journals. A number of publishers have kindly given permission for me to include their material and these are acknowledged at the appropriate points in the text.

I also wish to thank colleagues and students in the Division of Advanced Studies who have helped in too many ways to enumerate. Steve Moulton gave invaluable help with the calculations in chapter 10. I owe a great deal to Beryl Collins, Beryl Wells, Val Maine and Margaret Battson for the careful typing of chapters presented to them in varying degrees of legibility and stages of development. I am grateful, too, to Dennis Child for many helpful comments and suggestions which have always been toward the improvement of the book. My thanks are also due to the editorial staff of Basil Blackwell Publisher for their friendly support and attention to the minutiae. Finally, I wish to thank the Publications Fund of the University of Bristol for a loan towards the costs of typing the manuscript.

1

The Nature of Educational Assessment

Writers of 'academic' books frequently begin by demonstrating their knowledge of the etymology of keywords in their title. For those bereft of a classical education, however, recourse to the dictionary is the only substitute. Nevertheless, the outcome is frequently informative. The word 'assessment' is from the Latin *assidere* to sit beside. Sitting beside children suggests a close relationship and a sharing of experience. It is ironic, therefore (with due allowance for the ways in which the meaning of words changes with time), to find that educational assessment is associated in many people's minds with one of two contrasting interpretations. First there is a hard-nosed objectivity, an obsession with the measurement of performances (many of which are assumed to be relatively trivial) and an increasingly technical vocabulary which defies most teachers save for the determined few with time on their hands. Secondly, and to many others, assessment presents a very different face as the means by which schools and teachers — wittingly or unwittingly — sort out children for occupations of different status and remuneration in a hierarchically ordered society.

Yet the act of assessing others is deeply embedded in the way we come to terms with our environment. We constantly appraise a child's performance, criticize our own (or others') teaching, try to find out the nature of John's reading difficulty or the reason why many are so disruptive, examine a syllabus for its relevance to the lives and prospects of children or search for words to describe a person. In so doing we are, of course, the inheritors of a tradition which influences our judgment as to what is important. In making an assessment, whether informal or formal, we make a great many assumptions about the nature of human ability, its distribution and needs of society and insofar as these often go unexamined and remain accepted by a majority as self-evidently true they constitute an ideology.

We shall look briefly in chapter 2 at some of the contemporary controversies in assessment since all practices have unintended or hidden consequences. Ostensibly, assessment in schools is undertaken largely in the search for relatively unbiased and fair ways of arbitrating intellectual or other merit. In due course, those judged most deserving of the higher positions in the social order are thus identified and the potential of the educational process for ensuring the equal distribution of opportunity realized. Recent sociological analysis has reinterpreted the practices of assessment, however, and argues that they function as 'subtle and complex agencies of social reproduction and control' (Broadfoot, 1979, 85). Briefly, the argument holds that schools socialize children and prepare them to fill particular occupational roles in an hierarchical social order. According to this perspective it is those in elite positions who organize an education which emphasizes teaching, acquisition and assessment of skills representative of their own culture rather than those which are useful in later life. This group not only has the most vested interests in the maintenance of capitalism but so dominates that its viewpoints of the social order have been accepted as commonsense. This idea is expressed through the Marxist concept of hegemony; the ascendancy and domination of the social order by one social class. The consequences for assessment are that the criteria for distinguishing and evaluating individuals native to that class become the dimensions along which all children are to be assessed. This, in its turn, reinforces the elite culture enabling its members to reproduce, in successive generations, their own positions most easily. Nevertheless, the public face of assessment is of a fair and objective process whereby those most able to profit from education are identified. This acts to legitimate both methods and outcomes in the eyes of most participants, dulling the sensibilities even of those whose 'failure' is most obvious and effectively disguising the class bias of the educational system as a whole (Broadfoot, 1979).

Quite obviously many of these issues are highly controversial but their presence early in the book should be borne in mind by all readers who may otherwise identify the writer's position as being firmly entrenched within the ideology the sociological analyses have been designed to explore.

With these warnings in mind it is, nonetheless, difficult to see how any education system in any industrialized society can be other than a very costly enterprise and will, therefore, have to offer an account of itself to those who 'foot the bill'. Indeed, the last few years have seen the establishment by the Department of Education and Science of the Assessment of Performance Unit (APU) (Marjoram, 1977) which several writers have likened to a potential quality control mechanism. This does not involve the direct assessment of the system, but only indirectly through the assessment of the performance of representative samples of children. Whilst being alert to the hidden effects and possible class bias in the system it seems likely that practices of assessment will increase rather than wither away as some may hope. Moreover, even though there have been improvements in the methods for assessing the non-cognitive objectives of teaching (pupil attitudes, aesthetic awareness and appreciation, moral reasoning, for example) there are signs of a concentration on the cognitive aspects even in the work of the APU which was originally set up with far wider terms of reference (see Chapter 10). For this reason, then, the book will concentrate on the assessment of the cognitive characteristics of children whilst maintaining a critical stance with regard to the methods and instruments employed. Not only is it important for teachers to be aware of the strengths and weaknesses in their own practice but also to be able to detect the defects as well as the potential usefulness in the tests devised by others which they may be called upon increasingly to administer and to interpret.

WHAT IS EDUCATIONAL ASSESSMENT?

Educational assessment is an omnibus term which includes all the processes and products which describe the nature and extent of children's learning, its degree of correspondence with the aims and objectives of teaching and its relationship with the environments which are designed to facilitate learning. The overall goal is not to stop at the description (whether quantitative or qualitative) but to provide information to be used in decision making. Some writers on assessment imply that the decisions to be made are those which concern either placement or matching. Typical results of an assessment might be: (a) the matching of a child's characteristics to an educational alternative such as a particular teaching method or materials; (b) a decision to allow or encourage a child to tackle a particular topic having identifiable pre-requisites; (c) a decision to place him or her in a group of similar learners; (d) the selection of one or another educational environment such as type of school or in the case of assessment of a 'young offender', placement in a community home which offers a regime or treatment held to be suitable for young-sters of specified characteristics. Many other examples of assessment for placement could be given. A diagnostic assess-ment often implies the existence of a suitable remedial strategy, and assessment in career guidance — although specially vulnerable to the arguments about certification of pupils for social roles — could be seen as an attempt to match the demands of particular careers (or at least of those who control entry to them) to the features of a child's educational achievement or personal characteristics.

Quite obviously, assessment for placement involves the in-tegration of the information obtained from a variety of tech-niques, instruments and types of judgment. Information may be acquired by formal and systematic methods (such as regular testing) and by impromptu means (such as the judg-ments made by teachers as experience of a child's perfor-mance accumulates in informal classroom observation). The information, though, is always subject to error, especially where teachers' subjective judgements are made and great care must be exercised in interpretation where no corrobora-tive evidence is available. In addition, the information may be required for a number of different purposes and communica-tion to a variety of audiences, and the great variety of tech-niques which have been developed vary in their degree of acceptability to the public at large. External examinations tend to be held in higher esteem than internal examinations, for example, and though mode three in CSE examinations (syllabus and exam internally set and marked) has gained somewhat in respectability it is still treated with suspicion by many, including teachers. Though varied, all these practices have the common feature of data collection and interpretation in order to provide information for making decisions or in an evaluation for the purposes of certification.

It is not at all clear what proportion of a school year is taken up in assessment although it is salutary to remember that every minute spent in formal assessment is time taken from actual teaching. We are not likely to find an answer to this question by work-study methods since assessment may, as we have seen, be barely conscious and certainly hidden from the view of the classroom observer. Additionally, if we were to add the time spent by children in informal self-assessment we might well be surprised at the amount of time it takes. Whilst a good deal of assessment in education is covert there are signs that overt assessment is increasing, not only because more children than before are taking external examinations. Assessment has also become big business. Many quite expensive published tests are available and the cost of administration of O level and CSE examinations alone in 1976 amounted to 13.5 million pounds. From this massive expenditure a visitor from Mars might justifiably deduce the existence of a widely held conviction as to the worthwhile nature of the activity. Whilst making due allowance for naivety in his understanding of earthly economic systems and of human motivation it would be difficult for him not to conclude that assessment must accomplish an indispensable function in the practice of education for it to be so widespread.

The most common arguments for assessment can be classified using three broad categories: effects on teaching, effects on pupils, needs of society.

Effects on Teaching

Arguments put forward in favour of assessment understandably stress the beneficial consequences of the practices adopted. As always, there is 'another side to the coin' which will be examined more fully in chapter 2 but hinted at here.

Teaching and evaluation
Assessment is indispensable for teachers for without it there would be no evaluation of their own effectiveness. Knowledge of the results of pupils' performance provides information which is potentially capable of improving teaching. Where teachers are clear as to the aims and objectives of their instruction and are able to state in advance the criteria by which children may be said to have attained those objectives, assessment is seen not as a time-wasting appendage to classroom practice but as an integral part of planning of effective instruction. Note, however, that the goals of teaching are almost always set by the teacher who is in turn consciously or unconsciously constrained by a view of the function of education which has been transmitted by social processes. Thus there is a danger that other goals may be downgraded especially those in which criteria of attainment cannot easily be set in advance. Nevertheless, whatever is being taught or whatever child-centred activities are being organized, teachers require some sort of information on which to evaluate their own practices whether or not they have to account to some other body for the outcomes which result.

Teaching and setting objectives
Few teachers will be happy to enter a classroom on a purely empirical basis; that is without intention or plan and simply to 'see what happens'. Nevertheless, preliminary objectives may, on evaluation, prove not to have been attained by any pupils. Given this possibility teachers are faced with a dilemma: might those objectives have been attained with more effective teaching or are those objectives unrealistic for the children? There is no easy way of resolving this problem, however. Teaching, like any other human activity is often motivated by a set of ideals and some teachers may constantly strive to enable pupils to reach heights of attainment held by others to be fanciful. Nevertheless, and assuming that the teacher has done all he or she can to teach more effectively towards an objective, there are good grounds in psychological theory

for arguing that unrelieved exposure to failure will be deleterious for *all* pupils. Assessment, then, potentially equips teachers to define and teach for objectives which are suitably poised for the abilities and aptitudes of the pupils in question.

Teaching and diagnosis

Assessment of individual progress will take place continuously and teachers will constantly be appraising their methods in the light of indications received from pupil response. This form of assessment can have constructive or unconstructive consequences. We are all too familiar with the essentially unproductive use of assessment data: it stops at the classification of pupils as 'dull', 'disruptive', 'lazy' and so on. Scarcely less unproductive, although more welcome, are 'bright', 'imaginative' or 'budding genius'. Nonetheless such acts of classification are of little value unless they are followed by an intelligent attempt to modify or to adapt the features of the educational environment to individual characteristics of children. Thus assessment aimed to diagnose does not stop at application of labels. It aims to identify a child's learning needs and to develop a remedial strategy if necessary. By contrast, assessment can equally lead to the recognition that the school is failing to set an appropriate challenge to a pupil whose ability exceeds that of his or her teacher. If one's concept of effective teaching incorporates adaptation to individual children based on their strengths and weaknesses rather than the treatment of the class as unit, some form of assessment is required if this is to be accomplished. Not only is this process one of assessment of the pupil but it also involves assessment of the objectives and strategies of the teacher.

Effects on Pupils

The effects of assessment on the pupil are far more contentious. By and large the chief influences seem to be motivational. If we think of motivation as states of the learner which activate, direct and sustain his or her attention and efforts towards the achievement of goals, assessment can serve three chief functions: goal setting, formative feedback and summative feedback.

Goal setting
Setting goals helps clarify what it is that the learner's efforts are being harnessed to bring about. Goals can be intrinsic (that is, they can be inherent in the competence acquired) or extrinsic (they can indicate the reward to be attained by 'good performance'). We acknowledge, of course, that the rewards can be in the competence but make the distinction to acknowledge that teachers sometimes 'hold out carrots' to spur children on (privileges and prizes for good work) or even punish for poor performance, irrespective of whether the child has decided that the goal of learning is of intrinsic value to his or her own aspirations. Assessment and the knowledge that one is to be assessed at some future date provides one way by which children's attempts to learn can be given focus, for without such points of reference learning can be aimless or even a process of ferreting around to discern just what it is a teacher expects.

Formative feedback
This points to the positive effects of assessment *during* learning, unlike goal setting which is located at its *commencement*. All learners require signs which confirm they are on the right track or provide corrective information if they are not. There is little point in sending a child up a cul-de-sac in problem solving unless the teacher believes that it would be beneficial to do so, either to enhance curiosity or to keep a pupil humble. Positive signs during learning can serve to enhance motivation, negative signs to the need to correct errors or rectify a strategy. Such signs can be externally controlled by teachers or internally derived by the learners themselves. They are obtained largely through informal formative assessment although they may be summative (see below) where a discrete goal must be attained before a second major stage in the development of a skill or competence is attempted.

Summative feedback
This is differentiated from the previous type of feedback in that the assessment is of the end product rather than at an intermediate stage in learning. It can be the stage at which assessment becomes competitive, or at least comparative

between pupils, and it supplies a sort of seal of approval (or disapproval) on the child's efforts. The assessment exerts a potentially powerful effect on the child's self-esteem and growing sense of identity as a learner in a particular subject area.

Teachers recognize the educational value of informal assessment in goal setting and formative feedback yet many are nevertheless aware of the dangers of summative evaluation. This is because of the potentially harmful effects on those whose results are insufficiently encouraging to motivate them to try harder or even sustain their efforts. Moreover summative assessment (as in external or even internal examinations, for example) is typically of cognitive factors and not of the other qualities in which pupils of 'poor academic ability' may excel. Thus for many pupils and the 20% or so of our secondary school population who take no formal examinations at age 16+ the prospect of summative assessment seems unlikely to exert the effect on motivation which might be expected among other pupils. Unfortunately the presence of summative assessment can be so influential and pervasive that even less able pupils have come to expect it, with the result that work which is not to be assessed often receives scant attention. Many would regard as wholly undesirable the state of affairs in which the content of assessment is dictated by the need to identify only those qualities which ensure entry into particular levels of the occupational hierarchy.

The 'Needs of Society'

Writers and people at large differ, often vehemently, on the extent to which education serves or ought to serve as an agent of social change. It is probably true to say, however, that the majority of educational sociologists are of the view that the practices of assessment in education function most effectively as instruments of social control and in perpetuating rather than revolutionizing the existing social order. It is hardly surprising, therefore, to find that the 'needs of society' which assessment is held to serve are threefold: certification of pupils, accountability to those who finance the system and maintenance of standards in teaching and learning.

Certification (sometimes known as 'accreditation')

> Certification [writes Broadfoot] is indeed the epitome
> of the overtly meritocratic basis of our society since in
> theory it allows free competition based on academic
> ability and industry and thus is regarded as the fairest
> basis for the allocation of opportunities for high status
> or remunerative careers. (Broadfoot 1979, 21–2).

This is obviously a simplification but it contains some
truth. We need hardly pause to point out the relatively low
status and low pay of teachers to realize that some are more
fully accredited by academic success than others. At important stages in a child's educational career, in all formal educational systems throughout the world, pupils are afforded the
opportunity to show their achievements in relation to those
of others and certain levels are specified for admission to
institutions of higher education (which have a clear pecking
order easily recognized by the 'man in the street') or to different occupations. Many professions exercise tight control
over entry in this way. Entry is often competitive and the
methods are accepted by many as the fairest that can be
devised. (In weak defence of the British system one could
point out that selection is less draconian here than in certain
other members of the European Economic Community.) Few
can doubt that some occupations demand higher levels of
academic competence than others. But many researchers
have questioned the validity of academic assessment in the
prediction of job performance or success in higher education,
and have pointed out that even objective tests – whose scoring does not depend on a marker's idiosyncracies – are less
than totally reliable and accurate. This issue is discussed more
fully in later chapters but whilst we acknowledge the role of
assessment in the certification of performance to other
teachers, to schools at the next 'level' of education, to the
world of work and to parents, even the best assessments are
rough approximations to the truth and other ways must be
sought if the goal of fairness to all pupils is to be realized.

Accountability and the maintenance of standards
Traditionally schools in this country have done little by way

of formal accountability to justify their expenditure of others' money. But, in practice, what goes on in schools is powerfully constrained by norms and expectancies in the community at large so that practices which depart significantly from mainstream are often viewed with suspicion. Accountability in the United States has been thought of as a negotiated relationship between participants who agree in advance to accept certain levels of support for schools, provided the attainment of specified goals is evaluated in a mutually acceptable way (Alkin, 1970). In this country little or no attempt has been made to negotiate the aims of schools with parents (who, ultimately, as tax payers determine the level of support the education system is to receive) although what actually goes on in schools is monitored by other officials such as local authority or HM inspectors. Only in relatively rare (though possibly increasing) cases are parents actually able to choose schools whose practices conform to their own preferences, however. (Unless of course they are wealthy enough to opt for independent schooling.)

It is not the purpose of this section to examine the principle of accountability nor to identify the problems involved. But in the USA over thirty states have already introduced some form of testing basic skills in all their schools and in this country a step seems to have been taken in this direction by the setting up of the APU (Chapter 10). Other countries, too, have adopted similar attempts to hold schools accountable for the performances of their pupils. Even countries whose educational systems have been revolutionized in comparatively recent years are slowly returning to the implementation of programmes of national testing (Ingenkamp, 1977; Bonavia, 1978). No doubt, nationally standardized testing in British schools would receive the support of large numbers of parents though they seem unlikely to be asked for their opinions by governments which always tend to assume mandates for their policies across the board once they are in office. A later chapter in the book examines the question 'Are standards falling?' in some detail but it is sufficient here to point out that schools cannot account for the performance of pupils without assessment programmes. Just how extensive and systematic these will become will depend upon teacher and pupil reaction to whatever practices the APU may eventually select and whatever is 'politically acceptable' as results begin to come to hand. The debate will be an important one: all participants should be aware of the unintended, hidden and social consequences which extensive assessment will entail.

This section of the chapter can be summed up as follows: assessment in education can be justified by the need to evaluate the effectiveness of teaching, to provide incentive and feedback information to children, to certificate performance, to obtain the data for accountability and to ensure the maintenance of educational standards. In all these uses, however, assessment has certain potentially damaging side effects. Some of these are examined in chapter 2.

A PRELIMINARY CLASSIFICATION OF CLASSROOM ASSESSMENT PRACTICE

The purpose of this section is to provide working definitions of a few central terms to be used throughout the book. A glossary of terms is provided as an appendix so only those necessary to organize the preliminary discussion will be examined here. First, a preliminary and schematic map of the field will be provided (figure 1.1).

Educational assessment takes place in many ways using a variety of instruments designed for the purpose. Many teachers believe, however, that much assessment is antithetical to the education of pupils. There are indeed strong grounds for regretting an ubiquitous pre-disposition to assess children. The argument stems from the belief that they should be afforded maximal opportunity to discover or to experiment — indeed to learn — unencumbered by the constraints imposed by the knowledge that they are being assessed. But even though the requirement to assess and formally to record the results can be minimized, teachers will inevitably form and accumulate impressions from a child's behaviour in a variety of day-to-day circumstances, even when they have not set out to do so. For this reason figure 1.1 incorporates a dimension labelled *impressions versus constructions*.

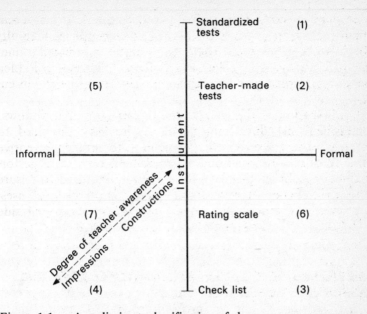

Figure 1.1   A preliminary classification of classroom assessment practices. (1) Standardized testing of ability or attainment; (2) teacher-made tests administered under exam conditions; (3) check list used in assessing practical work under exam conditions; (4) check list used to assess performance during normal class learning activities; (5) assessing performance during pupils' use of text book and work cards; (6) rating scale used under exam conditions; (7) rating scale to assess performance during normal classroom learning activities.

The choice of terms is designed to distinguish an assessment which results from features of a child's performance which — loosely speaking — 'leave their mark on the teacher's mind' yet which lack conscious organization or interpretation until a situation arises in which the teacher is pressed to make a verbal report from those in which the teacher deliberately uses pre-set criteria and where he or she is explicitly aware of what he or she was 'looking for'. Quite obviously the formal record of the former kind of assessment turns it into a 'construction'. Although this dimension may appear to be similar to the distinction usually drawn between *subjective* and *objective* assessment this is not the case. 'Subjective' usually describes those assessments which originate in the mind of the thinker (teacher) and not from an examination of the performance being assessed. Results are, therefore, potentially variable from assessor to assessor. 'Objectivity' of a result (a test score, for example) is not distorted by any personal bias of the assessor and any number of markers are expected to reach agreement by using the same set of clearly defined criteria (as would happen if an objective marking scheme were adopted). This distinction is made again in relation to scoring of essay type tests in chapter 5.

The second dimension in our model is labelled *informal versus formal*. It distinguishes an assessment made during the child's normal learning activities from those made during periods set aside for the purpose. A good deal of the information obtained by teachers and later used in reports and comments is obtained in situations of the former kind. It represents the teachers' interpretation of observations made in the context of everyday classroom activity (working with other children, working alone in problem solving, carrying out a scientific experiment and so on) and most kinds of process assessment as discussed in chapter 3. Formal assessment takes place when settings are organized — critics might say contrived — with the specific aim of evaluating the child's performance. As Rowntree (1977, 119) points out, this difference may in practice correspond with unobtrusive versus obtrusive assessment or even with the covert versus overt distinction. This last named dimension contrasts assessment made without, or with the child's awareness, respectively. Rowntree remarks that teachers may justifiably have ethical twinges about covert assessment especially where downright deception (as has been known in some experiments by social psychologists) is involved. This kind of deception seems highly undesirable in schools, to say the least. But the justification for carrying out informal assessment is that it can obtain information about children's performance in the 'real' context in which it is normally learned and exercised. This can mean that it is more truly representative of the strengths and weaknesses of children in normal activity, especially for those anxiety-prone in test situations.

The question as to whether children ought always to be

aware that they are being assessed is more difficult to answer than whether they should at times be deceived in their own interests. The answer to the latter is an uncompromising 'no', to the former 'maybe' if by assessing without the child's knowledge teachers are enabled to acquire information ultimately helpful to the child which would be less easily obtained if he or she were aware of the assessment taking place. Impression formation (discussed in the previous section) may well have gone on without the awareness by the teacher, of course!

The third dimension of our model is the *instrument* dimension, that is the nature of the tools used to obtain the information. At one extreme (the testing and measuring pole) we have located the formal standardized test of ability or attainment. It is usually a test which has high reliability (chapter 5), makes explicit claims and presents evidence as to its validity (chapter 7), gives norms for interpretation and results in the measurement of the attribute in question, usually on an interval scale (that is where adjacent points on a scale are at equal intervals). Teacher-made tests normally lack some of these properties. Teachers do not commonly estimate reliability and are in no position to carry out validation studies for their tests. The results are probably best thought of as placing children in rank order. This is a 'weaker' form of measurement than interval scales but is itself 'stronger' than rating scales. A rating scale is a method of collecting data using a continuum with points along it, marked by numbers or descriptive phrases, and sometimes by both. Each child is then classified by the number or phrase held to be most applicable to him/her. Although many rating scales are graphic, essentially the same information can be presented in other ways. In general, respondents seem able to cope most easily with a five-point scale.

A fourth type of instrument, which does not involve the use of numbers and cannot, therefore, be thought of as a form of measurement is the check list. Check lists can be used to assess pupils' behaviour in a variety of settings or to record which instructional objectives have been mastered. The usefulness of a check list, however, is proportional to the precision with which the categories can be described. We shall see later that check lists do not preclude a form of scoring which can be achieved if desired by summing the number of items checked. Similarly, check lists overlap in content with criterion-referenced tests (chapter 3).

We have tried to 'locate' many of the methods of educational assessment using three simple dimensions of classification: instruments (ranging from check lists to standardized tests), the degree of formality of the test setting, and a dimension which contrasts teachers' impressions with their structured search for specific kinds of information about performance. These dimensions are not independent, of course. It would be hard to envisage a standardized test being used informally, since, by definition, it is not an assessment made during the child's normal classroom learning activities. In figure 1.1 some of the most common types of assessment are placed according to their position on these dimensions. Chapter 3, however, presents an alternative classification which draws on labels more common in assessment literature.

EVALUATION AND MONITORING

The chapter concludes with a brief examination of the meaning of two other terms frequently encountered in assessment. *Evaluation* refers to the processes by which the worth of something is judged. In assessment terms it is usually applied to the attempts to find out how effectively a teaching programme has achieved its objectives or more especially to its degree of effectiveness in relation to the costs of and effort involved in a curriculum experiment or innovation. It does not apply to the assessment or measurement of children's performances alone, although these may be factors in the overall programme. A curriculum would normally be evaluated in, say, seven essential steps:

(1) specifying goals and objectives;
(2) planning a programme to achieve them;
(3) selecting methods of data collection and developing new ones if necessary;

(4) collection of data, including children's performance if necessary;
(5) processing, summarizing and analysing data;
(6) comparing results of (5) with content of (1);
(7) reporting results.

Notice that in evaluation attention is directed to the effectiveness of the programme.

Monitoring is the name given to a programme of testing designed to check or to keep a continual record of performance over a period of time. It is one of the tasks of the APU (see chapter 10) to carry out periodic checks on performance to record changes in attainment or indirectly to maintain standards.

2

Against Assessment

Theories, assumptions and practices of assessment are deservedly subject to continuous critical scrutiny by professionals and laypeople alike. Indeed, the great debate over reforms in school examinations has been going on for almost a decade with comparatively little concrete result. Although the day-to-day routine of schools prohibits detailed discussion of assessment, many teachers question its necessity whilst others are implacably opposed to all forms of 'labelling'. There are, of course, many problems with educational testing, but although some observers have seen it as indispensable to the maintenance of standards others regard it as tyrannical and antithetical to the process of education itself. As examples of the latter view readers should refer to the widely-quoted writings of Hoffman (1962) and Black (1962) which are extremes of their kind.

The purpose of this chapter is to introduce the reader to some of the most common arguments against assessment and to sketch out the kinds of rejoinder that can be made to them. The issues are varied. Arguments by sociologists have highlighted certain social and political consequences of assessment practices. Ethical objections have also been raised. Other arguments point to the undesirable side-effects of testing on children and teachers and further objections are rooted in an examination of the technical defects of current methods at our disposal. Still more critics have argued the potential danger of forms of assessment which inhibit educational change, control the curriculum and emphasize those objectives of education which are most easily measurable at the expense of equally legitimate (some would say more important) aims of education which are difficult to evaluate, at least in the short term.

Neither the objections nor the replies do full justice to the arguments which are, in any case, likely to be reinterpreted in the light of contemporary social and political circumstances. In indicating the concerns, however, it is hoped to keep teachers aware of the ways in which assessment (which may have become routine and be taken for granted) can have adverse effects on the individual, the institution and on society at large.

ASSESSMENT: A POLITICAL ACTIVITY

An objection often raised is that:

> Assessment is a political activity which preserves the social order in society.

Though teachers are often heard to say that education should be 'kept out of' politics, their actions, particularly when assessing pupils, are inescapably political in the sense that Jencks et al. (1973, 135) have described:

> . . . schools serve primarily as selection and certification agencies, whose job is to measure and label people, and only secondarily as socialization agencies, whose job is to change people. This implies that schools serve primarily to legitimize inequality, not to create it.

According to this argument, which we have already met in chapter 1, assessment is part of the apparatus by which schools perpetuate the existing hierarchical structure of society, for it results in the application of labels which determine children's opportunities in further education and life itself, their social status, privilege and power, and even their 'worth'. A capitalist society such as ours has an authority structure which depends for its continued existence on the identification of an elite to occupy its most influential positions.

It is a convenient assumption for those who would perpetuate this structure that human ability, and the achievement to which it is assumed to give rise, is normally distributed with only a comparative few of sufficiently high potential to profit to any great extent from the opportunities which schools provide. Thus tests which are constructed to produce such a distribution provide a spurious scientific validation that the hierarchical organization of society reflects a law of nature. In concentrating upon the differentiation of individuals, assessments and the schools which perform them make little impact on our society for they fit pupils to existing opportunities. Inevitably, therefore, raising standards of achievement for some pupils can only be accomplished at the expense of others: society has only so much room for success. In short, assessment furthers an unjust process for it is the method of 'sorting children' in ways which serve only to strengthen a bourgeois bureaucratic order.

However, assessment does not act only as an instrument in the reproduction of inequality (which is the opposite of its ostensible function in equalizing opportunity) but that which is assessed is itself biased towards the cultural traditions of the dominant social groups (see next objection). More insidiously, pupils and others come to accept the system of assessment as 'fair' and as a legitimate means by which they are selected to occupy a particular slot in the occupational hierarchy. The result, for many, is a sense of alienation from schooling which increasing attention to examinations at 16+ does little to repair.

Reply

It is obvious that this argument refers to the part played by assessment in the reinforcement of a model of society which is held to be objectionable by the kinds of thought which characterize so much of contemporary sociological writing. Though it cannot be denied that assessment fulfils some of the functions described above it would be an oversimplification to argue that it is a fundamental cause of the value system itself or to suppose that an overnight and permanent union ban on all assessment by teachers would do more than dent the structure!

In addition, this objection refers chiefly to the part played by assessment in the selection of children through norm-referenced testing (i.e. those in which the placement of pupils relative to one another is the principal goal) but with considerably less force to the practices of criterion-referenced assessment (to be described in chapter 3) where no implication of comparison with the performance of other children need be drawn. Thirdly, this objection rests upon the assumption that if schools and teachers were to give up their practices of assessment it would help to pave the way for a better form of order than exists in society at present. Even there, some assessment of competence would presumably be required if only to protect the public from the practice of professions which require special skill and knowledge by those unfitted by lack of training if not by aptitude to perform them. Fourthly, it is difficult to envisage a planned educational programme which has to justify its existence to those who will eventually determine its support without at least some form of assessment, even if this is of the system itself rather than of the individual within it. Many teachers can, and do, refuse to make assessments which, directly or indirectly, compare one child with another. Nevertheless they do appraise their pupils as individuals in informal ways. It could be argued that it is only where the processes of such assessment are open to scrutiny that their excesses and lack of fairness may be identified, for rational discussion of the means as well as the ends of assessment requires that the participants possess the ideas and information for doing so — as well as the conditions under which thought may be exchanged.

To charge schools exclusively with the responsibility for bringing about changes in society at large at the expense of overlooking the paradoxical demand that they maintain and transmit what is held by consensus to be worthwhile is to deny an aspect of reality. It is only in totalitarian states that an educational system is explicitly harnessed to bring about changes required by a single ideology. As the movement towards the accountability of schools gains momentum, practices of assessment will continue only as long as they serve functions required by the majority view, as this is determined by democratic process.

Critics of assessment have not always maintained the distinction between the assessment itself and the uses to which the results are put. The prime purpose of an assessment is to obtain information but one may distinguish those who use it to classify pupils on behalf of others from those who use it to help pupils learn. That the result of an assessment *could* be used to help perpetuate a model of society which a teacher holds to be undesirable is not an argument against the positive use of that same result to inform both teachers' and pupils' efforts to learn. Arguments which help to raise the consciousness of teachers regarding some of the unintended consequences of assessment are a necessary step in the evolution of an improved philosophy and practice of assessment and in a recognition that human ability takes many more forms than those prized most highly by dominant social groups.

ASSESSMENT AND CLASS

The second objection can be stated as:

> Assessment favours children of the middle class, is to the disadvantage of other groups, and is too often interpreted as the result of differences in innate potential.

The processes of education and of assessment are often criticized for being oriented towards the middle class. What teachers assess, whether formally or informally, is the attainment of 'middle class concepts', using 'middle class language' and on the assumption that all children have been exposed to 'middle class experiences'. Tests, in particular, are heavily culture-loaded. Since the development of 'culture-free' or 'culture-fair' tests is a chimera their results are inevitably biased in favour of one rather than another culture or social class group. (Piaget's tests and the inferences he has drawn from them, for example, have often been criticized for his insufficient attention to cultural influences on performance.) As a consequence of this kind of bias, teachers and psychologists will underestimate the capabilities of working class and minority group children. Given circumstances with which such children are familiar, differences in problem solving are no longer apparent. The task of the teacher, therefore, is to devise situations and an assessment idiom which favour those who at present underperform in the middle class milieu.

It would, admittedly, be difficult to construct a test whose results failed to differentiate groups of pupils and yet which was, at the same time, capable of predicting effective functioning within a complex industrial society. Since the ability to learn something new depends upon what pupils already know and what they know is in part a consequence of their previous learning experiences and environment, different types of experience differentially prepare children to profit from teaching. These may be reflected in test scores or other results of assessment; for example, in infant teachers' perception of readiness for school. It seems almost certain that the cultural experiences of some groups in society are more congruous with the assumptions made by schools than others but it is the assumptions of schools rather than those of other cultures which should be changed.

These kinds of criticisms have found American educators more sensitive than their British counterparts. In 1975, for example, the American Psychological Association appointed groups to investigate and clarify the degree of fairness of tests used in education with so-called 'disadvantaged pupils' (Cleary et al., 1975). Cultural bias does undoubtedly exist, and it is doubtful whether it could ever be removed. Too often, however, it can be easily overlooked. The writer recently taught an American student in a group of teachers who were examining the structure and content of an intelligence test used extensively in Britain. The student was defeated by the requirement to supply the 'next but one' in a given series of numbers not through his lack of mathematical competence but because of his unfamiliarity with the phrase itself.

The argument in this second objection applies with greatest force to intelligence testing and the reply which follows will be constructed with special reference to that type of test (including 'verbal reasoning tests').

Reply

The apparent inability of children from minority groups,

especially those of varying ethnic origins, to perform well on tests which assess and predict effectiveness in our culture continues to cause anxiety. This is an extremely complex issue and cannot be dismissed as a mere artefact of an 'unfair' or 'biased' system of assessment but it is worth pointing out that it is only through an assessment that the presence of children unable to make extensive profit from the opportunities currently provided by schools (whatever the reason) can be identified.

Those who are most critical of assessment for its discrimination against certain groups have tended to generalize their conclusions from the effects of intelligence testing on teachers' beliefs about learning potential. Some influential psychologists in Britain (e.g. Eysenck) and the USA (e.g. Jensen) have calculated that the variation in intelligence test scores is predominantly inherited. This has often been mistakenly taken to mean that an individual's intelligence is inherited and subject only to minor changes, and that differences in mean score between certain racial, ethnic and social groups are themselves attributable to biological factors. This view has been savagely attacked and many people believe it should be suppressed. In a counter attack, in 1972, the *American Psychologist* published a strongly worded resolution from fifty scientists in a variety of fields which reasserted, amongst other things, the strength of hereditary influences in human ability (*American Psychologist,* 1972, 660). The issues are obviously 'hot' in both science and politics (Kamin, 1974) and Block and Dworkin (1976) argue that there are few issues in the history of science that present such a complex mingling of conceptual, methodological, psychological, ethical, political and sociological questions.

Several commonly-held views on the relationship of intelligence test scores to school achievement can be identified:

(1) That intelligence and differences in IQ are largely inherited and determine a child's potential for a wide range of learning demands.
(2) That the IQ reflects the result of highly complex interactions between heredity and experience but their relative effects remain unidentified. Nevertheless IQ

scores do predict scholastic differences with some accuracy and the results of the assessment of intelligence are therefore useful to teachers in the placement and selection of pupils for educational alternatives, in the diagnosis of educational disadvantage and in the explanation of differential performance.

(3) That the IQ, within the biological limitations common to all members of the species, reflects chiefly differences in experience: it is therefore largely the result of the environment in which children are conceived, nurtured and reared.

All these views are represented within a typical group of teachers. Whatever the truth of this complex matter, however, certain conclusions, encouraging to teachers, may be drawn. In the first place, even though the results of the IQ assessment do correlate with school achievement, correlations typically range from 0.4 to 0.6. The measurement of correlation will be discussed more fully in chapter 5 but from these figures it can be calculated that only from between 16% and 36% of the differences in achievement in a group of pupils can be predicted from differences in their IQ. Or, to put it another way: between 64% and 84% of differences in achievement are predicted by factors *other than* those measured by intelligence tests.

Secondly, the results of an intelligence test, like all others, are at best only error-ridden approximations to true scores (see chapter 6 on reliability) and like other achievements of children they change in favourable environments. More importantly, if the dependability (the results of two intelligence tests taken close together) and the stability (the agreement between two testings two or three months apart) of IQ are measured for children who have had no marked change in environment, it can be shown that the constancy of the attribute is considerably lower than many studies of intelligence have assumed. Further details of this procedure are described with reference to the work of Cattell (1973) in chapter 6 on test — retest reliability.

Thirdly, any conclusion that potential for learning, insofar as this may be reflected in the IQ, is distributed co-extensively with either social class or ethnic origin depends for its validity on technical arguments and assumptions which are open to a great deal of criticism (Block and Dworkin, 1976). Even so, the cultural bias of tests is not quite so pronounced as is sometimes assumed. For example, the children of high-scoring parents on intelligence tests will, on average, have lower scores than their parents (this is known as 'regression to the mean') but the variation about this mean is almost as large as the variation in scores by children in general (Cleary et al., 1975). This is even more pronounced in scores on achievement tests.

Fourthly, the arguments against the usefulness of intelligence test scores do not apply to criterion-referenced assessment nor to most educational tests, where no implication of the measurement of an innate characteristic is made. This problem will be taken up more fully in the discussion of validity (finding out what tests do actually measure) in chapter 8. It is, of course, quite meaningful to speak of the heritability of any characteristic (that is, the proportion of the variation in individual differences in that trait predictable from genes) but no-one, as Jensen himself has admitted, is in any position to state the causal links which constitute the chain from genes to mental test or achievement test scores (Jensen, 1972, 5) except in the case of relatively rare and pathological conditions such as phenylketonuria or in chromosomal abnormalities (e.g. trisomy in Down's syndrome) which are always accompanied by some deficiency in test scores. It seems safe to say that the heritability of scores in achievement tests is far lower than that claimed for IQ scores.

Cronbach (1975) has described the changes that have taken place in the interpretation of test scores and has demonstrated the relationship between prevailing social conditions and the acceptability of differing emphases. Assessment indicates, not that some children are born inferior, but that the culture exerts a powerful effect — positive or negative — on the performance of children. The tasks which comprise an assessment must reflect the skills and objectives required for effective functioning in our society but the principle of equality of opportunity demands that groups or individuals who have been deprived of the chance to learn fundamental skills and concepts are identified, and remedial action undertaken. Any assessment which is to further this aim must be capable of identifying cultural handicaps. As Wesman (1972) has argued, the remedy is to provide educational opportunity not to do away with the assessment which is the source of the information.

ASSESSMENT: MEASUREMENT OF THE TRIVIAL

The third objection to assessment can be stated as:

> Assessment is limited to relatively trivial educational objectives whilst the most important aims of schooling are inaccessible to testing.

Critics have often seen assessment as a relatively mechanical activity of measurement of the trivial and have pointed out that the achievements of schools and pupils which fall into the affective domain are often overlooked because they are particularly difficult — if not impossible — to assess. The affective domain is a little difficult to define but most educators follow Krathwohl et al. (1964, 8) in their definition as those objectives which 'emphasize a feeling tone, an emotion, or a degree of acceptance or rejection'. The affective aims of teachers are often phrased as a set of abstract virtues which emphasize teaching for attitudes, values, interests and appreciation. It is a perfectly proper aim for a teacher to teach for 'awareness' of literary features, for the 'development of a value system', for 'moral sensitivity' and so on, but rephrasing these aims in terms of observable pupil behaviour trivializes them. Their assessment presents difficulties absent from the assessment of attainment in areas of the curriculum which have a recognizable logical or hierarchical structure or factual basis. Mehrens and Lehmann (1978) suggest that many teachers believe that the attainment of a cognitive objective is accompanied by a corresponding change in the affective domain and that the latter is a by-product of the former. Other people have suggested that teachers lack feelings of personal responsibility or accountability for the general non-cognitive aims of schools. The essence of this third objection, therefore, is that the comparative ease of assessment of the cognitive objectives (those associated with remembering, reproduction of material and with the solution of problems) leads to a lack of attention to the more important objectives which are much more difficult to evaluate.

Reply

Inspection of some attempts to assess affective outcomes reveals some justification for this argument. Those who have tried to establish objective methods for the assessment of affect hold that the first stage is a more careful and detailed specification of objectives in terms of what pupils who exhibit the desired attribute would be able to do by way of demonstration that they had achieved that objective. A typical illustration is provided by Mehrens and Lehmann (1978) who cite as an example of good practice the attempt by Fraenkel (1969) to specify the assessable behaviour which would demonstrate that a learner has 'recognized the dignity and worth of others' as follows:

(1)   waits till others have finished speaking before speaking himself;
(2)   encourages everyone involved in a discussion to offer his opinions;
(3)   revises his own opinions in the light of those of others;
(4)   makes statements in support of others no matter what their social status.

One cannot help but sympathize with Fraenkel who admits that these statements do not totally capture the essence of the more general goal! We also note how all these behaviours could be easily faked. In short, not only is the objective difficult to define in terms which permit its assessment, but it may also be simulated by any learner to a far greater extent than would be possible with any corresponding objective in the cognitive domain. In general, the more abstract the objective the more difficult it will be to assess.

The argument, therefore, has some validity. It is often

difficult to get agreement as to how affective objectives should be phrased but considerable progress has been made in their assessment (see, for example, Payne, 1974). Secondly, if schools and teachers are to be held accountable for their effectiveness in the affective development of pupils what evidence are they to present to justify continued support for their endeavours except by a more determined effort to assess the less tangible than British schools have attempted to date? There is certainly no shortage of types of behaviour that critical outside observers of schools have held to be relevant: truancy, vandalism of school and community property, delinquency, out of school demeanour, reputation of the school and so on. This type of assessment requires a change of focus from the individual pupil to the school as a system. It involves a variety of information acquired by objective testing, as well as informal observation. That it can be integrated into an account of the effectiveness of schools as institutions in the affective domain has recently been demonstrated by Rutter et al. (1979). Although several quite serious difficulties inherent in the methodology have been pointed out by critics, this research suggests that schools can encourage less tangible pupil development and that assessment plays an indispensable part in the demonstration of this claim.

Finally, because some types of aim and objective of teaching are difficult to assess this is irrelevant to the assessment of a great variety and range of cognitive objectives with which this book is principally concerned. Attention to the assessment of attainment in the cognitive domain need not be to the detriment of concern for the affective. Faced with the great demands upon their competence it is understandable to find teachers who emphasize exclusive concern for one or other set of objectives: this remains, nevertheless, a defensive reaction.

ASSESSMENT AND EXPECTANCY

The fourth objection can be stated as:

> The results of assessment have an uncanny knack of being self-fulfilling.

Assessment has an effect on two important expectancies: the teacher's expectancy of pupils and pupils' expectancies of their future performance. To take the latter first. Once an assessment has been made it may be incorporated by pupils into the concepts they are developing of themselves as learners in a particular discipline or area of skill and knowledge. In particular, pupils come to see themselves as — to simplify matters — successes or failures as mathematicians, or whatever. Repeated experience of success or failure (even though the assessment may not actually employ these terms) gradually develops into an expectancy for the results of future attempts to learn. The child who has predominantly 'succeeded', especially if he or she believes this to be the result of ability and effort, anticipates future success; the child who has chiefly failed may, in extreme cases, even withdraw from further attempts to learn.

Assessment can codify and reinforce a pupil's picture of self, but early in his or her development it plays an important part in its formation. From the early days of a child's schooling, teachers are not disinterested observers of all the abilities and performances of pupils but only of selected abilities in contexts defined by teachers. Although human ability expresses itself in a great variety of forms only comparatively few are judged to be sufficiently worthwhile to constitute the school curriculum. Fortunately, though recent attempts to establish the content of a core curriculum have made little or no progress beyond the stage of political rhetoric, there is agreement that this should include the elements of literacy and numeracy. But the children who come fresh to any academic activity at whatever level have little or no idea whether they are any good at it but wait instead for the teacher to assess their attempts to learn or they make their own comparisons with other pupils. Thus assessment which is essentially common to all pupils in a class can lead to levels of expectancy which, in turn, themselves direct future effort, affect performance and powerfully influence the pupil's self-concept of ability. Readers interested in the ways in which children's expectancies of self can be incorporated into personality structure and influence achievement could refer to an article by Bar-Tal (1978).

Teachers also build up expectancies about pupils. These accumulate as a result of informal assessment of pupil and home background and by formal and standardized assessment where used. The teachers' predictions then interact in complex ways with actual classroom behaviour. Difficult and challenging tasks are set for some children, low-level demands for others: there may be prolonged interaction with one child because it is mutually satisfying whilst another is left to get on by himself because little can be expected of him, and so on. The theory holds that children can also detect the more covert ways in which expectation is transmitted. But the overall result of a teacher's assessment can be detrimental for those children who are set low expectations and correspondingly damaging for those, who because of an unreliably optimistic assessment, are set levels they are quite unable to fulfil. The term 'self-fulfilling prophecy' has been coined to describe the state of affairs in which children perform the way we expect them to perform. The mere fact that an assessment has been made is held to be sufficient to influence children's self-concepts, their expectations of their own performance and their motivation. An interesting collection of articles on this topic is presented by Sperry (1972).

Reply

A reply must acknowledge the possibilities outlined by this criticism of assessment. But it has already been said that attempts to predict eventual success in achievement leave a great deal of scope for surprise and teachers must be alert to the many unconscious ways in which their expectancies constrain a child's opportunities to learn. A number of everyday classroom observations indicate these expectations at work. When a child has received a favourable assessment or has made a favourable impression in one context (perhaps because she is assessed as being 'nicely spoken' or 'from a good home') a 'halo effect' can operate. By this is meant that the residual effects of the early assessment can 'spread over' into the later assessment or that the teacher can search for confirmation that the original assessment was correct. No name has been given to its converse but the 'horn effect' seems an apt description in which 'giving a dog a bad assessment' prevents objectivity in later appraisals.

That teachers do indeed have differential expectations arising from earlier assessments has been amply demonstrated by Hargreaves (1967) who also showed that these were clearly perceived by pupils of secondary school age, and by Nash (1972). Attempts to demonstrate the size of the expectancy effect have, however, failed to come up with clear results. One very well known study is apparently thought by many to have provided such a demonstration (Rosenthal and Jacobson, 1968) but its methodology was clumsy and its statistical analysis inept (see, for example, Thorndike, 1968). In spite of the lack of hard experimental data, the intuition of teachers and a wealth of sociological theory (Merton, 1957) points to the possible ways in which the results of assessment can influence the outcome of children's future learning attempts. A clearer realization that no test predicts with other than relatively poor accuracy but that children's performances change in favourable environments, and a movement towards greater use of criterion-referenced assessment (see chapter 3) can help to neutralize the potential effects of the self-fulfilling prophecy.

ASSESSMENT AND SCHOOL CURRICULA

The fifth objection can be stated as:

Published forms of assessment — such as standardized tests — mould school curricula and inhibit new developments.

There are two strands to this objection. In the first place there is the influence on the school curriculum of the adoption of tests which define the objectives of teaching. Secondly, there is the presence of an external assessment programme in which the teacher is not free to decide whether or not pupils take the tests: these are then marked outside the school, and only the overall result is communicated. As an example of the former one could cite the case of teachers who having used only teacher-made tests for some time, wish to see how well their pupils compare with others in different schools. Our teachers choose a standardized test available from a publisher's catalogue but, on inspection, realize that it includes several topics which they have not 'covered'. In order to make time for this teaching, they jettison several topics in the existing syllabus which has been devised on educational principles. In this way the original curriculum designed to meet local needs is shaped by the form of assessment adopted. An obvious example of the second type is an O level syllabus, the 11+ examination or, in the case of schools in the independent system, the Common Entrance Examination. Although the APU (see chapter 10) is at pains to play down possible effects of its testing on the curriculum of very many children each year, some have seen it as inevitable that schools will teach to the content of the tests they come to experience when the work of the unit gets fully underway.

Reply

Domination of the school curriculum by the content of tests reflects their misuse. Where the school decides that the objectives of its curriculum are adequately evaluated by an existing test and this test reflects aims and objectives common to other schools, then the assessment can provide a valuable basis for examinations of the goals of the teaching and a relevant comparison with the achievements of similar children elsewhere. Some critics of the amount of freedom allowed to English schools to determine in detail the aims and objectives of their teaching would, of course, see the control of the curriculum by this use of testing as beneficial.

If teachers develop their assessment skills and use only those tests which are congruent with their own objectives, this fifth objection becomes a minor one. If, however, the content of the assessment — especially where it is determined by and carried out for persons other than the pupils and teacher — is allowed to become the determining criterion, then the assessment tail will be wagging the educational dog to the conceivable detriment of the latter.

The second point implied by this objection is potentially more serious, however. It is acknowledged that teachers have an obligation to cover enough of an external syllabus to ensure a reasonable chance of their pupils' success. This is most certainly a powerful parental expectation of schools, yet concentration on the coverage of content can work against the development of pupils' abilities to learn such that memorization and storage of facts and routine operations for reproduction 'on the day' become the principal teaching goals. Thus learning how to learn, which is an important aspect of the concept of educational processing, often receives scant attention in the pursuit of examination success.

ASSESSMENT AND THE KNACK OF TAKING TESTS

The sixth objection can be stated as:

> Assessment encourages the pupil to develop the styles of thought or intellectual 'tricks' required by tests and, therefore, inhibits the development of other skills.

This argument is usually levelled at those types of assessment which require the respondent to supply or to select the single correct answer to a test item. Such items encourage the production of convergent thinking or, in the case of multiple choice formats, favour certain types of examinees and penalize others for reasons which are unrelated to their knowledge of the material being assessed. Rowley (1974), for example, has shown that candidates who are prepared to take risks score higher than others whose knowledge and ability are equivalent. A related aspect of this objection is that pupils are quick to spot that certain sections of the work which is to be assessed provide the greatest payoff for their efforts and will consequently invest more time and resources in mastering these, whilst ignoring others. Overuse of multiple choice tests discourages the development by the pupil of operations which require the organization of material demanded by essay and open-ended items and leads to a conception of the goal of learning as primarily reproductive memory of material acquired or the production of what Whitehead (1950) has called 'inert ideas'.

Reply

Most of these objections conceive of assessment narrowly and overlook the imaginative instruments for wide-ranging assessment of all types of learning now available (see, for example, Bloom et al., 1971). Secondly, although pupils may acquire the particular knack of being assessed or taking tests, there is no evidence that experience of particular types of test prevents the acquisition of other modes of thought or cramps an individual's style of thinking (Payne, 1974). But because 'test-wiseness' (skill in taking tests *per se*) is learnt, it will be necessary to ensure that all children are given practice in test-taking when (and these occasions need only be rare) norm-referenced assessment for comparative or merit purposes is undertaken. In short, a good deal of action can be taken by the teacher to minimize the force of this objection.

ASSESSMENT AND ROLE-RELATIONSHIP

This seventh objection is stated as:

> Assessment inevitably takes place in a role-relationship. This is antithetical to a truly educational setting where encounters between teachers and pupils are interpersonal.

This objection is implicit in the writings of 'humanistic psychology' (Schmuck and Schmuck, 1974). Any assessment is made *by* someone *about* someone. It is often a spurious attempt by a teacher to distance him or herself from the object of study, the pupil. In so doing the child is placed in a position of inferiority and dependence; he plays, or fails to play, the rules dictated by the teacher. The constructs employed by teachers in making an assessment refer chiefly to the children's level of competence or motivation in relation to subject matter and lead to the application of labels familiar to readers of school reports, for example, 'hard worker', 'conscientious', 'average ability in this subject'. They result from the kind of transactions that Buber (1958) has referred to as 'I — It' transactions; those in which the goal of the teacher is to 'categorize and objectify' aspects of the pupil. By contrast, truly educational transactions occur when 'whole persons encounter one another on an equal basis, each with full respect for the array of qualities to be found in the other' and where each participant in this interaction recognizes, appreciates, respects and values the other as a total being (Schmuck and Schmuck, 1974, 6). These transactions or meetings, called 'I — Thou' transactions, are ruled out by much of the organizational features of schools and are prevented by the type of relationship native to the act of assessment.

Reply

Like the first objection, this involves fundamental criticisms of schooling which, whilst reflected in assessment, are not confined to it. But the objection contains its own reply. I — Thou transactions cannot be pre-meditated; planning an assessment involves attempts to control or manipulate, and requires prior decisions as to who should be assessed, by whom and in what areas of knowledge or competence. As Schmuck and Schmuck (1974, 7) themselves claim 'I — Thou transactions arise as unexpected gifts, the best we can do is to orient ourselves to be receptive to their occurrence'. There seems no reason why, given time, the teacher should be unable to participate in such a transaction when the results of an assessment are discussed with a child. Some teachers have been observed to supply the emotional support and encouragement which are the hallmarks of I — Thou transactions following the admission that they, too, face learning difficulties — even in some of the tasks they have required children to perform! This should not be taken to imply a recommendation for the 'cosy-huddle' model of education (Dearden, 1968) based on sentimentality, but a belief that there is nothing in assessment inherently inimical to the establishment of a teacher—pupil relationship of the type advocated by humanistic psychologists, where pupils have shared with teachers the experiences of learning and in which the assessment of the outcome has been used to promote the competence of the pupil.

ASSESSMENT: AN INVASION OF PRIVACY

This eighth objection can be stated as:

Many types of assessment are an invasion of the privacy of the individual.

There are misuses of the results of educational assessment and tests. In the USA, Messick (1965) has pointed to the sensitivity of this issue but believes that there is inherent danger any time an assessment is made in academic selection or for employment, in diagnosis (especially of personality disorder) and guidance, or in research. So far as the writer is aware no legal action has been taken in respect of this kind of abuse in the UK but Payne (1974, 440–2) presents examples from the United States in which congressional hearings were held into the uses and interpretations of one widely used personality test. Amongst the charges was the claim that personality testing represented a form of 'searching the minds' of employees and applicants, that test records were not kept confidential and that once the assessment had been made it tended to follow people through their careers. Legal hearings were conducted into the discriminatory use of tests: these established that only those assessments which have 'a manifest relationship' to the employment in question should be used. The overall thrust of this argument is that the use of assessment should be pruned to retain only those instruments which result in information directly related to the criterion in question and one should not attempt to derive other kinds of data. In the educational context only those types of data which are of direct relevance to learning or later achievement or job performance would be permitted. Measures of personality, opinion, personal values and attitudes, and indices of family background would be excluded as not directly helpful to the teacher's task of fostering intellectual growth. Under certain circumstances — for example in the kinds of research designed to uncover causal relationships — these latter types of data would be acquired, but subject to strict controls and undertakings on the use and dissemination of the findings.

Reply

The onus is on the test user or the teacher making the assessment to demonstrate that the information gathered will be useful to the child from whom it is obtained. It is probably true that a good deal of the information obtained by teachers serves to reinforce their prejudices or theories of educational progress: there is no reason why any child should be required to state his father's or mother's occupation, for example. The argument does not arise in relation to criterion-referenced assessment (chapter 3) where what is assessed is directly related to the task being learnt. It is valid in the case of the results of intelligence tests if these follow the child throughout his or her school life or if the school is unable to demonstrate their adaptive usefulness in making decisions which benefit the child's education.

Teachers are unlikely to wish to use the results of personality tests: certainly their relationship to school learning is far too tenuous to make the results especially informative. Controls do exist over the use of those types of assessment whose interpretation is particularly difficult. The catalogue of the Test Division of the National Foundation for Educational Research makes clear the restrictions on the availability of these instruments.

Finally, we have already seen the removal from a British publisher's test list of one instrument designed to measure pupil interest on the grounds that it contained a sexist bias through its implicit acceptance of the suitability of different career options for boys and girls. With the increased potential of the computer for detailed record keeping great attention must be maintained to ensure that only the information beneficial to pupils in their efforts to learn is stored if the charge of invasion of privacy or the anticipation of 1984 is to be avoided. Questions of the validity of the results of an assessment are raised in chapter 7.

ASSESSMENT IS UNRELIABLE

The ninth objection may be stated as:

All assessment — especially using tests — is unreliable and predicts imperfectly.

This objection highlights the accepted lack of reliability in test scores and their known inability to afford perfect prediction of a criterion. If one cannot claim the dependability of a score on a given occasion but has, instead, to state an often large margin of error, then the test user is forced to question the cost-effectiveness of the assessment programme. Still further, and in the light of the dangers described by the fourth objection, if these error-ridden scores only marginally improve our predictions over chance prediction this calls into question the advisability of the demand for prediction itself. Instead teachers should adopt a 'teach' rather than 'test' philosophy.

Reply

Decades of work in measurement theory and test construction have sought to reduce the unreliability of tests and to provide better techniques for the estimation of true scores. It is preferable in many cases to use test scores and to quote the best estimate that can be given of the size of the error attached to them than it is to rely on the subjective judgements of teachers which make no pretence at the quantification of error. In the first case the test users do at least know what can and cannot be inferred from the result. Secondly an assessment programme cannot live by tests alone: as Payne (1974, 438) says 'tests can do a very creditable job in combination with other kinds of information'. Thirdly, the less-than-perfect relationship between a test and a criterion which it seeks to predict indicates the difficulty of test validation, and is not a limitation of tests alone but of all kinds of assessment. There is no justification for the continued use of tests or other forms of assessment which are persistently found to lack validity.

A reply to this objection requires some knowledge of the topics of test reliability and validity: these are dealt with in some detail in chapters 6, 7 and 8.

CONCLUSION

Those who have found learning to be a predominantly enjoyable experience have often assumed the value of school learning in its own right. Yet for what is probably the majority of pupils, and for a variety of reasons, learning is not easy and some form of assessment seems to be indispensable in the motivation of many learners especially those at secondary school. Following the raising of the school leaving age there has been an enormous increase in the number of pupils aged 16+ studying for CSE and O level examinations. In 1967, for example, about one-third of the relevant age group were preparing for one or other of these examinations. Today the proportion in some parts of the country is nearer 80%. With such a great concentration on the assessable aspects of schooling the place, extent and methods of assessment in education demand the most critical and continuing appraisal.

Most people would probably comment unfavourably on the stress that accompanies knowledge that they are to be assessed. Certainly some of the most enjoyable experiences of learning are those associated with the intrinsic motivation of self-chosen study. Yet in schools and colleges subjects often lack respectability until they have been assessed in conventional ways. In general, 'non-examination subjects' and 'non-examination children' lack status and reward. For example, teachers of liberal studies in technical colleges and colleges of further education frequently bemoan the low status of their work both within the hierarchy of the institution and in the attention of their students. In polytechnics — especially in faculties of education — teachers of art, physical education and movement studies have rewritten large portions of their syllabus to incorporate material suited to traditional forms of assessment. Students are quick to profit from the dilemma: even in universities (where our most successful learners are, presumably, to be found) it is common to find poor attendance at aspects of the course which are to be left unassessed.

Inevitably an enormous amount of time and effort has been expended in activities associated with assessing children. An industry has developed: hundreds of tests are available to add to the informal assessments which have become a regular feature of classroom practice. In the view of many people, there is far too much assessment. Questioning the practices and pointing out their consequences for pupils, teachers, institutions and society, is, therefore, worthy of disciplined scrutiny and rational discussion. Problems such as those examined in this chapter inevitably raise questions of the significance of education in contemporary society.

Of course, ideologies and the social contexts of the time influence the degree of acceptability of any theory or set of practices. Assessment is no exception to this rule. Readers will not require extensive analysis of the contemporary social and political concerns which have added impetus to the IQ debate. Much earlier, the economic motivation of men to exploit new lands gave added thrust to the development of astronomical and navigational aids to exploration. Many other examples could be given. Sometimes prevailing social influences inhibit or even suppress intellectual enquiry. 'Codex 1181' of 1633 prohibited teaching by Galileo of the Copernican model of the structure of the Universe. One is not, of course, implying that any of the aspects of assessment theory approach, even remotely, the intellectual status of Galileo's ideas nor that assessment theories can only be suppressed by threats of torture! The examples serve to illustrate the principle of the complex interaction of social as well as intellectual components in the determination of the degree of acceptability of practices and fields of study. One example within the sphere of assessment can be given. Intelligence testing in the 1940s and 1950s was widely hailed as the means whereby 'bright' children from working class homes could be identified and selected for 'grammar school education'. This was seen as furthering the basic principles of educational opportunity irrespective of parental income. More recently, a very different interpretation has been adopted. Intelligence tests unfairly discriminate against such pupils: a 'grammar school education' for a few means a 'secondary modern school education' for the majority. The intimate relationship between educational prescription and political alignment is too obvious to require further comment.

The problem of assessment is not only — nor even primarily — one of the development of better techniques. Far more fundamental questions are involved (Rowntree, 1977). Many people have written of their concern for what they see as disturbing trends in modern industrialized society such as ours. Though the discussion is often superficial the worries and anxieties are profound. There is an increasing distrust of 'science', there are suspicions of the widespread use of computerized records and fears that human beings may be 'reduced to numbers' by tests and records. To many people these trends imply a reduction in human freedom. Others fear that too much attention is paid by the education system to only a small portion of the abilities of children — usually their quantitative and verbal skills — with the danger that the complexity of human potential is overlooked.

Several years have passed since the book by Young (1961) warned of the inevitable consequences of a movement towards an obsession with the identification of a meritocracy. Such warnings are necessary if the worst excesses of assessment are to be avoided. Tests and all forms of assessment are tools which can serve the needs of both teachers and pupils, but only if properly used and understood. Although much of this book is concerned with the improvement of assessment, the worst dangers to which the objections in this chapter draw attention can only be avoided by teachers who are aware of the strengths as well as the weaknesses of the various methods, the facts as well as the fallacies of testing. Accordingly, chapter 3 examines some of the options open to teachers so that they may be helped to develop their own informed perspective on what is likely to remain an important part of educational practice. Understanding the options is a necessary preliminary to setting up assessment programmes both within the individual classroom and the education system.

3

Choosing the Mode of Assessment

An attempt is made in this chapter to indicate some of the options open to teachers on how to assess. It is a difficult task to choose which of several apparently conflicting modes of assessment best reflect the educational intentions of teachers and schools or which combination best serves the evaluation of the attainment of educational objectives. The term 'mode of assessment' concerns the way the practices are carried out, not the actual instruments employed. As we saw in the previous chapter, substantive objections to the effects of assessment have been advanced. But the increasing emphasis on the 'accountability' of schools seems likely to require at least as much attention as at present if we are to justify our activities.

The accountability bandwagon has been somewhat slower moving in Britain than in the United States. As with many slogans, its meaning is not particularly clear. A reading of the literature on the topic, however, suggests that its effect on teachers is to place upon them an increasing obligation to account to 'the public' (who ultimately determine their support) for a number of different aspects of the work of schools. These obligations seem, principally, to be threefold:

(1) to provide information on the nature and relative importance of educational goals;
(2) to evaluate the extent to which these goals have been achieved and at what cost to 'the taxpayer';
(3) to accept a share of the responsibility for results which are judged to be inadequate: this responsibility to be shared jointly by schools, teachers and those employed at national and local levels in the planning and administration of education.

Some of these statements are extraordinarily vague and it would be a task for a philosopher to disentangle the points of substance from among the rhetoric. Browder (1971) for example, has dismissed much of the discussion as boiling down to the two major considerations: who gets hung up when things go wrong and who does the hanging? Formally, however, teachers' responsibility in relation to assessment may be thought of as involving:

(1)   the ability to offer a reasoned account, to all interested parties, of the practices they adopt;

(2)   an examination of the assumptions made about the purposes of testing, the distribution of human ability and the relationship of school life to life after school;

(3)   a justification for the use made of the results of assessment and, in particular, where it is claimed that any result should be withheld;

(4)   a demonstration that the practices are fair, do not infringe the rights of the individual and that they aid the children in the realization of their potential;

(5)   the demonstration of a professional competence in the principles and practices of assessment.

These are obviously pretty tall orders. Yet the curricula for teachers in training pay only a very small amount of attention to the development of (5), for example, and interviews at 'parents' evenings' provide precious little opportunity for discussion of items (1) to (4). In spite of generations of 'democracy' it is arguable just how well informed 'the public' actually is as to what goes on in its institutions. Governments claim that the release of certain kinds of information is not in the public interest; hospital doctors argue that patients should seldom be given full details of what is wrong with their intestines and those responsible for the security of nuclear power stations may withhold information as to the exact extent and risk of the accidental but hazardous radiation leaks from the plant. We have no space to examine the justification for secrecy or prevarication in the above examples, nor to study the reasons why holders of high office in the US are publicly 'grilled' about their expenditure in open hearings whilst our leaders are allowed — except at election time — to escape with hand-picked questions framed by highly paid 'personalities' more interested in 'good television' than in the truth. The point of this polemic is not to argue the case, strong though it is, for open government but to underline the assertion that teachers have considerable responsibility to account for their assessment practices and that to do so effectively demands a rationale for the type adopted and an evaluation of its effectiveness in relation to the educational purposes it is designed to fulfil, or is capable of fulfilling.

We are, of course, talking about the assessments which a teacher intentionally adopts, for informal assessment, by contrast, is often a semi-conscious but inevitable activity of everyday life. Rowntree (1977) — whose book is to be thoroughly recommended as an honest and readable account of many of the dilemmas and complexities in the assessment of students — has provided some interesting examples of the assessments we make in human relationships. Here we seek quite naturally to understand ourselves and others. We might interpret this activity as a manifestation of a basic need to come to know and to understand our social world so that we may adapt to it. Indeed, the adjustments we make in our behaviour are often the response to our assessment of the effects we have upon others. And although it is true that while we assess our children they are assessing us, it is also true that the consequences are one-sided because of our unequal share of power. Their assessment of us affects their attitudes to learning and leads to the formation of their views about us as worthy (or unworthy!) of their respect or even (most awe-inspiringly of all) as model for themselves to aspire to. But it is our assessment of them which shapes their educational opportunities, which carries weight with future employers and which influences the behaviour of admissions tutors at Oxbridge colleges and elsewhere.

If, then, teachers have this power, they have important responsibilities to exercise it in the interests of those they seek to serve. This involves, amongst other things, a formal choice among the alternatives available and the ability to justify this decision to all participants who as Rowntree

(1977, 118) has said, 'rapidly become aware of it (assessment) recognize it as a necessary and continuous component of their situation and make decisions as to the role they will play in it'.

We shall argue in the pages which follow that there are two dominant approaches to the assessment and testing of children and several ways of going about each. We shall begin by spending some space on a fundamental distinction between two types of practice which, though they overlap to a quite considerable extent, reflect different emphases in the measurement of performance and fulfil different assessment goals. These two approaches have come to be known as 'norm-referenced' and 'criterion-referenced' assessment and each is associated with a somewhat different type of measurement. Teachers have been carrying out both types of assessment for generations but it is only comparatively recently that a formal distinction has been drawn between them and only in the last ten years that criterion-referenced assessment has become of much interest to psychometricians – those concerned with the measurement of individual differences.

The differences between norm- and criterion-referenced testing lie in the respective purposes, the types of score they derive and their interpretation, and the philosophies of education which they embody.

NORM-REFERENCED ASSESSMENT

When a school or teacher reports a child's progress or receives an external evaluation of a pupil's performance in the cognitive domain (as in the case of an internal or external exam result) a norm-referenced approach is adopted. We shall consider more fully in chapter 12 the teacher's responsibility to communicate an interpretation of the results of an assessment but for present purposes it is sufficient to identify – without evaluating them – some of the most common techniques. In many schools, grades (which may be numerical or literal) are reported and these are often accompanied by labels or short verbal descriptions: these labels or descriptions evaluate the children's performance in relation to the group to which they belong. Typically a grade 'A' might be described as 'outstanding', 'C' as 'average', and so on. Thus the norm is the group and the assessment refers to it. Take, as another example, the report: 'John's reading age is 8 years and 9 months'. Just as in our first example, the score acquires meaning, not as a measure of the amount of anything, but only with reference to the scores of a much larger group, from which the average has been calculated. To take one final example, suppose a class of pupils takes one of the tests developed by the National Foundation for Educational Research (say the Basic Mathematics Test C, age range 9.07 to 10.10 years, designed to assess the child's attainment in area, graphs, symmetry and knowledge of sets, decimals and fractions). From the test the teacher obtains the 'raw score' (the number 'right'), refers this to a table of 'standardized scores' given in the manual for the child's age and finds the standardized score to be 115 (see chapter 5). This is interpreted to mean that, in a very large group of children of that age the obtained raw score will separate the 16% highest scores from the remaining 84%. (See figure 5.8 which translates standardized scores into percentages.) As before, the score can be interpreted only in relation to a large number of scores obtained by other children who constitute the norm.

From these examples we can abstract one common feature: a score or grade which has meaning only insofar as it is compared with others which make up a group. The basic purpose of norm-referenced testing, therefore, is to discriminate among individuals. In the generalizable sense, a norm-referenced measurement has the following logical form:

Individual i exhibits more (or less) of characteristic x than the mean amount of x in group y (the population).

Notice the importance of the reference point: 'mean amount of x in group y'. Parents who receive a school report which states that 'John is slightly above average in French for the group' with no indication of the composition of the group and its average performance are told very little indeed about their son's achievement.

To summarize, norm-referenced testing:

(1) is carried out for the purposes of comparison and discrimination between individuals;
(2) aims at high variability among scores to maximize this discrimination;
(3) interprets scores in relation to those of a number (preferably large) of other individuals (norm groups);
(4) is indispensable on the relatively rare occasions in education where fixed quota selection decisions have to be taken, for example, when selecting from a larger pool of children for the distribution of limited resources as in the competition for places.

CRITERION-REFERENCED TESTS AND MASTERY LEARNING

Criterion-referenced tests have been developed in response to some of the limitations of norm-referenced testing, both practical and philosophical. Many teachers believe that drawing comparisons between individuals and providing scores which describe the child's standing in a group serve chiefly to foster a spirit of competition which is inimical to the maintenance of a climate for learning in which children are able to develop at their own pace. Certainly a score which describes only the standing of a child relative to a group is uninformative about the actual achievements made and tells the teacher only which pupils have made greatest, average, or least attainment. Because of this, attempts have been made to develop tests and other instruments which describe the achievements of children compared with established standards. Moreover certain approaches to learning — for example, in programmed learning or computer-assisted instruction — have emphasized individual differences in rate of learning and have proposed that time taken to learn to a given standard is the most important and educationally relevant dimension on which children differ. Some researchers who have developed individualized systems for learning have claimed that an education which is truly oriented towards individual differences is one in which most children could master almost all the basic objectives in schooling if given time to do so. Norm-referenced tests are obviously unable to provide much of the necessary information for a teacher who wants to give children as much time as is practicable to master a given objective, to monitor children's achievements while they are learning a sequence of clearly defined goals and to provide other interested parties with as precise a description as possible of the actual features of a child's achievement. In short, objectors to exclusive reliance on norm-referenced testing have argued that knowledge of a child's standing relative to the achievements of others is of trivial interest compared with knowledge of the extent to which a learner's attainment approaches a given standard or performance. Any instrument which provides this latter type of information is known as 'criterion-referenced'.

To propose a simple example: a teacher has drawn up a list of objectives in elementary arithmetic. Four objectives in the sequence are as follows:

(1)   add two, two-digit numbers without carrying
(2)   add two, three-digit numbers without carrying
(3)   add two, two-digit numbers involving carrying
(4)   add two, three-digit numbers involving carrying

A number of items is drawn up for each objective: two per objective are given as examples, but a minimum of ten per objective would probably be required to establish mastery of the objective.

	Items		
Objective	(a)	(b)	
(1)	15 + 24	33 + 15	+ 8 others
(2)	206 +153	623 +312	+ 8 others
(3)	38 + 46	17 + 68	+ 8 others
(4)	397 +844	178 +669	+ 8 others

Items for each objective are homogeneous, that is they are, on the face of it, of equal difficulty, and the objectives are organized hierarchically, that is later objectives build upon the knowledge and skills required by earlier objectives. These items are criterion-referenced when a criterion level of performance ('C') is specified. A frequently adopted criterion for these kinds of objectives would be a score of at least 80% correct. Children who scored, eight, nine or ten of the items for a given objective would be described as masters of that objective. Thus a child who has mastered objective (3) will be able to perform the operation of addition using two-digit numbers plus carrying with at least 80% accuracy — an unambiguous description of what he or she is able to do. The boy or girl who gets seven or fewer items correct per objective is deemed to require further teaching or practice in the attainment of this objective. Thus only two 'states' are assessed: 'mastery' and 'non-mastery' of the objective. Given that these objectives are quickly mastered by most children a criterion of 90% accuracy might well be reasonable. (Problems of setting standards are more fully discussed in chapter 9.)

Opponents of criterion-referenced testing have pointed out some of its limitations. It is appropriate chiefly in the evaluation of learning where objectives can be clearly stated, where criterion performances can be established and where objectives are organized hierarchically. In our example, objective (1), too, has its pre-requisites although these are not specifically stated. They require that the child discriminate the signs which indicate the basic arithmetical operations, recognition of numerals and so on. Some subjects, for example in basic mathematics or reading, have such a structure which can be presented in logical sequence and it is for this reason that most of the published criterion-referenced tests to date are in areas of elementary skill. In English literature, however, to cite one contrasting example, it is not at all apparent just what is the logical structure of the subject. A second objection concerns the arbitrary definition of 'mastery'. In our previous example a criterion score of 80% was specified to discriminate the two states but there may be other instances in which the teacher would set an even more stringent criterion. In other cases, where some learning of a later objective does not appear to depend upon complete mastery of one logically earlier in the sequence, somewhat lower demands might be set. In addition, whilst we can draw up logical sequences in the presentation of objectives, educational psychology has not yet reached a stage of theoretical or empirical precision which enables it to define just how much of a 'lower' objective need be mastered for attainment of one at a 'higher' level. Moreover, specifying a sequence in which all children should learn is to overlook the possibility that there are often many routes to attainment of the same objective, particularly where the material to be learned becomes increasingly abstract and where intellectual abilities and skills such as analysis and synthesis are required.

A third criticism of mastery learning is that it proposes a 'closed' or convergent model of teaching and learning: it implies a structured approach which all must follow and seems to remove the possibility of excitement and discovery. Those in favour of mastery learning argue that although criterion-referenced assessment may have its simplest application in learning basic skills, most subject matter in school can be thought of as organized hierarchically if only teachers were more systematic in their analysis of the tasks and demands they set children (Ausubel et al., 1978).

A further argument against the mastery model points to the absurdity which would result if it were blindly applied. If time spent to mastery of a criterion is of paramount importance then one could easily envisage some children taking years to reach a level of mastery attained by others within weeks! Quite probably this is already the case, but rigid adherence to the approach could lock slower learners into an inexorable and morale-sapping ritual, and bore the most able. Although mastery testing is indispensable in formal systems of individually prescribed learning (such as is practised in 'individually guided education' (IGE) developed for schools by psychologists and teachers at the University of Wisconsin) Glaser (1968) has demonstrated that if the slowest 5% of learners in schools are omitted from consideration, the ratio of time spent by slower to faster learners is of the order six to one. If this is the case, teachers who favour mastery learning are faced with the tricky decision as to just how long they should require a learner to persist towards the attainment of a particularly obdurate objective. This would be easier to determine if we really were in a position to establish exactly what are the basic academic skills indispensable for a child's future survival. These are probably fewer than most teachers care to admit. Whatever they are, they seem likely to change with time. Many teachers already believe that the widespread availability of electronic calculators renders the learning of a good deal of basic arithmetic technologically — if not culturally — redundant! The suggestion by Gronlund (1971) that schools distinguish objectives which are minimum essentials from those which encourage maximum development and reserve the use of the mastery learning approach for the former begs the question. Recent discussion in Britain of the content of the 'core curriculum' seems to have made little or no progress: the emphasis in the USA on the teaching of the elements of 'functional literacy and numeracy' has run into similar problems in identifying the functional 'elements'.

Perhaps the most fundamental objection to criterion-referenced testing and mastery learning concerns their psychological parentage. The use of educational objectives which are stated in terms of a pupil's observable behaviour can be traced to the principles of behaviourist psychology and represents a conscious extension of those precepts into educational practice. In behaviourism, learning is studied only at its observable level and all other terminology or interpretations in terms of hidden entities or mental processes is denied. Early behaviourism was influenced by a philosophical movement known as positivism which dismissed as meaningless all statements which were not empirically verifiable. Accordingly the cardinal educational principle derived from this set of beliefs was that the only meaningful goals of learning and teaching were those which are objectively measurable as observable outcomes. Other aims are dismissed as little more than pious hopes.

One notable exponent of a behaviourist standpoint on teaching was Skinner. According to his view, learners respond to stimuli from their environments and acquire behaviour as a consequence of the events which follow — that is by reinforcement. The technology of teaching is seen as the definition of goals, the search for appropriate reinforcers that will produce the desired behaviour and, finally, careful measurement of the reinforcer's effects. Not all users of behavioural objectives subscribe to the behaviourist traditions, however, and many are simply borrowing from it what seems to them to be a useful device to help precise specification of objectives in areas which are too often confused by the use of vague and lofty prescriptions. Nevertheless, blind application of the principles of behaviourism (and of its offshoot the objectives approach) could easily end in an overemphasis by schools on training programmes to elicit from learners narrowly defined and 'correct' responses to specific stimuli. There are very many elements of understanding and of attitude which are legitimate goals of teaching which simply do not submit to behaviourist analysis and objective assessment.

Some technical problems of criterion-referenced tests have not yet been overcome. No agreement has yet been reached as to the most appropriate method for establishing the reliability and validity: these difficulties are dealt with in some detail in chapters 6, 7 and 8. Nevertheless criterion-referenced tests form a valuable addition to teachers' techniques of assessment. They provide information which complements that available from norm-referenced tests and enable the teacher to communicate far more precisely what children can actually *do* than is permitted by norm-referenced assessment. The two types of test are not mutually exclusive, however. A criterion-referenced test can easily be used to make norm-referenced statements about pupils: it may even describe in greater detail the actual structure of the differences which lie behind the discriminations made by norm-referenced tests. Because they include too few homogeneous items to establish mastery of an objective, norm-referenced tests are seldom used in a criterion-referenced way but a single test score on either test could be given either type of interpretation. We can say that 'Mary got 80% of the items correct in a test on the solution of two linear equations with two unknowns' (criterion-referenced) and, equally, that 'Mary did better than 85% of her class' in the same test (norm-referenced). Each has its uses, but the distinction between the two types of assessment becomes even more blurred when one realizes that the standards which form the criterion may well be levels of performance established by other children elsewhere!

The implication of this previous paragraph is that norm- and criterion-referenced tests do not represent discrete and mutually exclusive methods of assessment, but, that they reflect different emphases, interpretations and purposes of the teacher. Table 3.1 attempts to summarize these differences.

Table 3.1 — A comparison of norm-referenced (NR) and criterion-referenced (CR) assessment.

Difference	Emphasis of NR assessment	Emphasis of CR assessment
(1) Purpose	To make comparisons between pupils and to relate these to the average performances by large numbers of similar children	To evaluate the achievements of pupils relative to an established criterion of performance
(2) Interpretation score	If standardized the score indicates the position of a child's score in a large normally distributed group of scores (see page 164). If unstandardized, the score shows the child's relative standing in the group to which he/she belongs (e.g. the class or year group)	Indicates the level of a child's mastery of a given objective. It does not refer to a distribution of scores by other pupils

Table 3.1 *continued*

Difference	Emphasis of NR assessment	Emphasis of CR assessment
(3) Diagnostic value	In the identification of relative performance to see *who needs* remedial work or special education	In the identification of actual strengths and weaknesses in performance to see *what kind* of remedial action is necessary
(4) Variation in scores	Needs to be relatively high to discriminate effectively between pupils	Usually relatively low. Could be a useful test even if no differences between pupils are observed, e.g. when all achieve the criterion
(5) Reliability: 'How effectively does the test measure whatever it is it measures?' (see chapters 6 and 7)	Estimated using test — retest, parallel form or homogeneity methods	Estimated by the consistency with which the set of items for an objective classifies pupils as 'masters' or 'non-masters'
(6) Validity: 'What exactly *does* this test measure?' (see chapter 8)	Examined by reference to an external criterion (a present or future performance) and by studying its relationship to other tests, which claim to measure the 'same' attribute	Examined chiefly by comparing the actual content of each item with the statement of the objective
(7) Types of item in test	Usually a large number of different items designed to sample a *range* of skills and concepts	Each *objective* has a number of very similar items designed to test a narrowly defined skill or concept

Table 3.1 *continued*

Difference	Emphasis of NR assessment	Emphasis of CR assessment
(8) Selection of items to make up test	Item difficulty is an important criterion. Those answered correctly by about 50% of children who take it are chosen since these 'spread out' the final totals most effectively	Items tend to be easier and the spread of correct responses is relatively small
(9) Applicability to school 'subject'	Can describe relative standing of pupils in any subject for which information from group performance is available	Useful only in those subjects where precise objectives can be stated
(10) Role in education	In selection, grading, competition and career guidance. In comparing schools and the *relative* performance of children. (These last named are probably of greater interest to researchers than to teachers)	In evaluating the absolute success of instruction. In decisions as to the speed at which children are to be allowed to progress through a fixed sequence of instruction. In individualized instruction and the assessment of readiness
(11) Logical inference	'Child i exhibits an amount of x which is greater than or less than the mean amount of x in population y.'	'Child i exhibits an amount of x which is greater than or equal to c.' (c = Criterion score)

MODES OF ASSESSMENT

Rowntree (1977, 119) has collected the labels for eight modes of assessment prevalent in education. For convenience he has presented them as a set of polar opposites but they are best regarded as dimensions by which the emphasis of current practices may be described. They are:

formal	versus	informal
formative	versus	summative
continuous	versus	terminal (or final)
course work	versus	examination
process	versus	product
internal	versus	external
convergent	versus	divergent
idiographic	versus	nomothetic

(As Rowntree wryly comments: 'People in education contrive many more ways of finding out about students than they would dream of using on their family and friends.')

It is obvious that no one dimension represents mutually exclusive alternatives. Most schools employ a mixture of formal and informal methods, of continuous and terminal modes and many examination systems use both course work and final examination, with different weightings, in arriving at a classification, e.g. of a university degree. Few guidelines can be given as to the degree of emphasis which teachers could place on these types. What is important, however, is that teachers should be informed of the choices available to them. Schools, departments within schools and teachers as individuals will decide on the programme best suited to their purposes. Only by knowing the relative strengths and weaknesses of the approaches can an informed choice be made.

We shall adopt Rowntree's useful classification and deal briefly with those of the above dimensions most frequently encountered in practice. The discussion departs from that provided by Rowntree (1977, 119–62) but interested readers may like to read his accounts for purposes of comparison.

Formative versus Summative Evaluation

This is a favourite distinction among American educators. The terms are used in a variety of ways but, so far as the writer can tell, choice of the word 'evaluation' rather than of 'assessment' is to indicate its application to a judgment of the effectiveness of an educational programme or curriculum rather than the performances of children. Some assessment of one of the outcomes of major interest – pupil learning – would, of course, be part of the evaluation programme but many other facets would be considered (see Anderson et al., 1975). The basic distinction may be stated as follows. Formative evaluation focuses on the programme whilst it is in operation. In particular it provides information to help all those responsible for the development of materials used (books, worksheets, other resources for learning) and in the recording of all the unintended consequences (more often undesirable than desirable!) for the attitudes and motivation of pupils. Summative evaluation is concerned with evaluating the overall effectiveness of a curriculum or programme once it has been completed and especially whether the goals and objectives have been attained. Whereas formative evaluation is carried out principally by and for those responsible for the development of the programme or course of study, summative evaluation is more detached and is preferably carried out by someone not personally involved in its development. Quite obviously the results of summative evaluation may well have implications for future formative work.

Here again we see one of the cardinal principles of assessment: the method to be adopted depends on the purposes for which the work is carried out. Applying the formative– summative distinction to the assessment of individuals we could say that formative aspects are present whenever the results of an assessment – however formal or informal – are communicated to learners and these have feedback consequences for their efforts. Feedback can be corrective (showing how and where a learner 'went wrong' and how to improve) or confirmatory (a demonstration that what the learner has acquired in skills and concepts is suitable for the tasks which lie ahead). Assessment of a child's learning or performance is summative when information is not made available for feedback purposes, not necessarily because it is obtained for other parties but perhaps because it comes too late in a learner's career. Much of the day-to-day assessment of pupils is formative: helpful written and oral comments on children's work accomplish this function.

Continuous versus Terminal (or Final) Assessment

This is not so much a method as an indication of when and how often assessments are made. Continuous assessment was introduced partly because of complaints that it was unfair and unnecessarily stressful to learners to know that they were being examined on only a single occasion or over a short period of time where luck with the questions played a particularly significant part in their chances of success (Miller, 1976).

If assessors do take into account a child's performance over a longer period of time and in a variety of situations, it should be possible to obtain a more representative view of his or her capabilities than in the artificial context of the examination room. (Assessment as part of mastery learning is continuous in this sense.) Amongst other advantages claimed for continuous assessment are that it encourages steady application throughout the course, does not unduly penalize learners for one or two poor pieces of work and encourages more closely the development of a variety of problem solving skills which are inhibited by the need to develop examination 'tricks'.

In practice, continuous assessment has also been found to have its share of disadvantages. It has been reported (Rowntree, 1977) that only work which is to be assessed receives the attention of learners (at least in an examination you do not know what is going to come up). Also, it is often difficult to establish just what is and what is not the learner's own personal contribution (tutors known to the writer often find themselves spending considerable amounts of time investigating plagiarism) and anxious students have experienced only slightly less stress but over much longer periods of time than with terminal or final assessments. One thing seems clear. All assessment practice is potentially capable of raising levels of anxiety. This, according to one psychological theory, is not necessarily a bad thing but it depends upon the level of difficulty of the task being assessed for the learner (Child, 1977, 54). Where teachers are using an assessment to help pupils learn and not making decisions or norm-referenced judgments about them for other people's purposes, it can be minimized. In this case it seems important that the learner is helped to understand the purpose and be convinced that no other (ulterior) motive is in mind.

There seems little justification for a practice which may be more widespread in institutions of higher education than is sometimes thought, that is, making an assessment in order to determine a grade or mark which is then withheld from the student. If the grades are so unreliable that it would be dangerous for a student to know of them, then what is the point of applying them? If assessors lack confidence in their judgments to the point at which they cannot defend their assessments to students, then this problem must be faced not displaced onto the unfortunate learner.

Some institutions have decided to grade their students using a weighted combination of both continuous assessment and final examination grades but the weightings often appear to be largely arbitrary. Some have abolished examinations altogether: others have graded all pieces of work but have allowed students to submit only their best pieces of work for final assessment. Nevertheless it should be possible in schools to reduce the number of occasions on which it is necessary to supply anything resembling a terminal or final grade. One cannot for long remain a starry-eyed idealist about this, however. Although it may be highly desirable to emphasize the school's educative function and to de-emphasize its selecting and sorting functions, these apparently irreconcilable demands seem likely to constitute a tension on schools, teachers and pupils for very many years to come. Nevertheless, in reaching an overall grade for any pupil the teacher can profitably consider which of continuous or final assessment most adequately permits the development of skills and concepts which forms the educational objectives guiding the teaching. Teachers who have considered this point often conclude that both are required, but to varying degrees.

Course Work versus Examinations

Although continuous assessment is more likely to be of course work it could incorporate the results of tests and even of examinations. Likewise, final assessment could consist of a summation of course work grades. Examination grades tend to enjoy greater respectability in the eyes of the public than course work grades: the latter can too easily be contaminated by favouritism and cheating and be achieved in a variety of conditions which render the principle of comparability inoperative. But whilst the external conditions of an examination (time limit, invigilation, unavailability of sources of reference and so on) remain the same for all examinees and the actual contents of the paper are the same for all, most examination papers allow choice from a larger set of questions or problems, such that the assumption that a common basis for comparison has been obtained can be illusory. As Rowntree has said, if a student is required to choose four topics out of ten, 210 different choices are available. (One examination paper known to the author requires the respondent to answer three from 24 questions. This allows for no fewer than 2024 possible combinations of questions chosen!) Moreover, examination questions are frequently set with only the haziest concept of difficulty in mind so the notion that 'all have sat the same paper' is true only in a limited sense where so much choice is available.

There are other difficulties inherent in the assumptions drawn from examination results. For example, the marks of examiners often differ quite widely in some subjects (see the section on the reliability of essay marks in chapter 7), the conditions under which the candidates have to answer bear little or no resemblance to any conditions under which people usually work in later life and are, therefore, of poor predictive validity (see chapter 8) and the results frequently testify to the luck or skill with which the candidate (or his teacher) have 'spotted the questions', or effectively revised.

Since all teachers will almost certainly have sat an examination paper at some time in their lives they will know from personal experience some of the deficiencies of assessing in this way. Little justification seems possible for premature examination (that is before the relatively later stages in a child's school career). If it is chosen as an appropriate method of obtaining information about children's performance then the teacher can consider how to ameliorate some of its worst features. Some institutions have experimented with so-called 'pre-set' examinations in which candidates receive the paper several days in advance but answer it 'under examination conditions'. The author has acted as external examiner to one such procedure. There some students have commented that the method places even greater demands upon them to write 'good answers' and removes from them the grounds for face-saving excuses when they fail to do so!

Quite clearly, arguments can be advanced for and against both methods of assessment. Teachers must decide where to place the emphasis in the light of evidence they acquire from use of both methods; in particular how far they encourage the attainment of objectives and motivate pupils.

Process versus Product Assessment

Teachers are most accustomed to the assessments of product, most frequently those by children using pencil or pen on paper or their equivalent. Quite obviously this kind of outcome is of great importance: the essay, the technical drawing, the painting, the 'page of sums' and so on. The demonstration of the pupils' ability to make something is an important educational objective, in art, craft, home economics, physics, chemistry, biology: right across the curriculum in fact. In those subjects where products are not the goal, assessment tends to be avoided: in contemporary religious education where the ability to discuss and to appreciate the point of view of others is encouraged; in sex education (where products would be viewed with mixed feelings!) and in all those situations where civilized conduct is implicitly and explicitly encouraged.

Process and product are intimately related — there would be no product without processes. Although it is easier to assess a product than the processes which went into it, we often assess both in the former. Our evidence of life in past civilizations is from their artefacts and written records; we infer process from products where direct observation of process is not possible. We reproduce Seurat's technique of painting by studying his pictures, we study a child's method of problem solving from the 'working' on his paper, we infer the difficulties faced in reading by a girl's stumbling attempts and errors and we assess the strength and movement of Egyptian peasants before Christ by an examination of the force required to turn the handle of an Archimedean screw. But these are retrospective assessments — they were not observed while they were being executed.

Although assessment of product is easier to carry out than assessment of process, studies of the concepts used by teachers in their appraisal of children show that they do indeed, use many which refer to process. Amongst the most common are the processes of class participation and the children's approach to tasks (Wood and Napthali, 1975). The comments made about students in colleges of education often reveal that a final grade has been reached on teaching practice which includes assessment of relationships with children, with other staff and so on, as well as of the products produced by the children in their class — not to mention the ubiquitous 'TP file'. It is almost too obvious to point out that much of the assessment of a person's job performance is process-oriented, especially where this does not end in a tangible product. Nevertheless, the formal assessment of process has got off to a relatively slow start in British education where comparatively little value is attached to any process until it has been verbalized or otherwise made available as its product for sustained and critical appraisal — not without good reason, of course!

One of the reasons for the emphasis on product is the sheer difficulty of assessing process except in a very trivial sense (for example, studies of pupil—teacher interaction, Flanders, 1970). If we were interested in the processes by which children attempt to solve problems — as distinct from whether they are 'correct' or not — one way of doing this might appear to be through the method of introspection: that is by asking children to verbalize their behaviour whilst performing it, or immediately afterwards ('retrospection'). The problems here are both practical and logical. In the first place, numerous psychological studies have shown the human inability to perform two intellectual operations at one and the same time (two components of skill can be integrated but what appears to be 'doing two things at once' is often accomplished by a process which involves rapid switching of attention, as in landing an aircraft). We cannot logically require a child both to solve a problem and at the same time to observe him or herself solving it — *and* report on it! Practically, the method of introspection is seldom particularly informative with children especially where the intellectual demands are complex. Indeed, the results of introspective reports by even the world's greatest thinkers have often thrown little light on the process involved (see for example, Wertheimer's work with Einstein; Wertheimer, 1945). Readers who might envy the accomplishments of 'lightning calculators' and who would like to emulate them will receive very little guidance as to how to begin by a study of introspective reports during quick-fire arithmetical manipulation (see, for example, Hunter's account of Aitkin; Hunter, 1962). In the first place, then, there is the sheer difficulty of 'getting at' the process in a good deal of human cognitive activity. Computers may stimulate human thought and provide valuable insights into effective problem solving strategies but these models do not provide help in the assessment of processes in children. In any case, models are formal structures and much of the process of everyday thought is intuitive. We proceed by a mixture of formal thinking, setting up hypotheses as to how we might proceed, using 'hunches' or by 'taking a chance'. Some solutions are even achieved by happy accident. The processes of intuition are, by definition, those of which the learner can offer no explicit account: he is unaware of the steps in the process by which a conclusion was reached.

In spite of these problems we pay lip service to the role of the teacher in understanding and adapting to the cognitive style of the learner (that is to the learner's preferred and consistent ways of thinking), in the development of the pupil's capacity for problem solving, to help pupils co-operate with others and to 'relate' to other people, amongst a host of other objectives which emphasize process. We may even succeed in some of these aims without knowing precisely how we have managed it. (We may begin to see some of the reasons why behaviourism concentrated its attention on the observable and denied all reference to processes hidden from view.)

The nub of the difficulty then is that where process assessment is possible it demands direct observation of the processes of interest whilst they are taking place (Green, 1970). Some assessments are explicitly directed at process (the 'oral' in a modern language is one obvious example). In some cases the product may provide a clue to process, but in others it is more than likely that a similar product can be achieved by markedly different processes. If one is simply interested in the children's ability to solve linear equations correctly (i.e. product) many teachers might consider it irrelevant whether they solved it by the method of substitution, by addition, by the equating or by the determinant method. But where the objective of the teaching *is* the development of process an attempt should be made to assess it.

No 'ground rules' for the assessment of process can be given. But if the teacher decides to attempt the task a number of possibilities suggest themselves. Although this chapter is concerned with the ways of carrying out assessments rather than with the instruments for doing so, the idea of process assessment is probably a little unfamiliar. In order to clarify some of the ideas one or two of the main types of instrument are briefly described here.

By the use of rating scales
These can be numerical, graphic or of the check list type. An example is shown in table 3.2.

By the use of an interaction schedule
This means a prior decision as to what is going to be observed, a list of categories and a matrix.

Example: for observing the relationships between children during a group activity.
(a) *Statements.* These include 'affective' (statements which

Table 3.2 — Example of a rating scale

Examples A	To assess a pupil's participation in discussion (numerical)
Question	To what extent does a pupil participate in discussion?
Respond	Ring appropriate number

(1)	(2)	(3)	(4)	(5)
Unsatis-factory	Below average	Average	Above average	Out-standing

Examples B	To assess a pupil's level of concentration in laboratory work (graphical)
Question	How much concentration does a pupil display in class?
Respond	Mark an 'X' at the appropriate place on the continuum

(1)	(2)	(3)	(4)	(5)
Very easily distracted		Averagely attentive		Shows great con-centration

Examples C	To assess basic study habits by children during individual work (*check list*)
Question	Which of the following does the child display when working individually?
Respond	Circle the number in front of each statement which applies to the child

(1)	(2)	(3)	(4) —	(5)
Has short attention span and weak powers of concen-tration	Seeks frequent help from teacher	Lacks confidence to get on by him or herself		
			etc.	etc.

encourage, discourage, blame, etc.), 'procedural' (statements about how to do the task, what should be done next, etc.), 'substantive' (resolving conclusions, evaluating the product, etc.).

(b) *Interchanges.* Those which involve a unit which consists of a question, a formal response and an evaluation of the response.

Table 3.3 — Observation schedule for the assessment of process during group activity

		Children		
		1	2	3
(a) Statements	(1) Affective			
	(2) Procedural			
	(3) Substantive			
(b) Interchanges				

(This is a much simplified version of OSCAR (observation schedule and record) developed by Medley, Schluck and Ames (1968). It is used for illustrative purposes only.) Table 3.3 gives an idea of what such a schedule might look like. Tally marks can then be entered as the observations are made. A similar interaction schedule has been developed by Flanders for the study of teacher—pupil interaction (Flanders, 1970).

By the use of self-reporting devices, anecdotal records, etc.
Rating scales could be completed by pupils instead of by teachers. Teachers can prepare anecdotal records of incidents and record their comments. Over time both these techniques can provide a record of the longitudinal development of any pupil.

By simulation methods
Where performance in a task is to be assessed and provided the teacher can simulate that task in a realistic way, observation schedules can be applied to the performance of pupils during their carrying out the exercise. These seem more appropriate for the older pupils and fall into one of three categories:

(1) *In-basket exercises.* In these the pupil is presented with data, such as letters, reports, memoranda and so on and

asked to reach decisions to a specified problem, e.g. the pupil is presented with documents relating to the conduct of a youth club member and is asked to decide on a course of action.

(2) *Situation tests.* Pupils play the roles in a lifelike context, e.g. an immigrant pupil new to a British school meets classmates and teacher.

(3) *Problem solving games.* Groups are given tasks to perform against a criterion, e.g. a time limit or to build a structure which supports weight across a 'stream'.

This section has served as no more than a brief introduction to the assessment of process. In choosing between process and product assessment, teachers will obviously be guided by which is the more appropriate for assessing the objective in mind. This decision having been reached, one may fairly safely conclude that product assessment is the only viable choice if the processes remain unobservable (despite the ingenuity of the teacher), if methods for describing and measuring products are already available and where the product itself provides evidence of the processes of interest.

This chapter concludes with a brief commentary on some of the remaining modes of assessment identified by Rowntree.

Internal versus External Assessment

To a very large extent teachers are unable to decide this question but are more likely to have a practice thrust upon them. Current practices in British educational institutions are very variable. GCE syllabuses are almost entirely externally set and papers externally marked; CSE syllabuses can be either external or internal but papers are internally marked in the first instance; university syllabuses are set internally and papers marked internally but with external examiners who see a small sample of the work. Unlike universities, schools are not yet sufficiently 'respectable' to be trusted both to teach and examine.

In favour of internal assessment is the argument that the teacher knows the pupil 'better' than an outsider (this could work both ways). Without some sort of external 'check', however, charges of favouritism and antagonism are difficult to refute. The big argument in favour of external assessment is that it forces a comparison of local and national standards and provides a check on the complacency which may result if teachers remain in ignorance of levels of achievement by similar children elsewhere. The danger of external assessment comes when teachers passively allow the objectives of others to become their own. On the other hand, floundering teachers may be helped by this.

Thus external assessment can take two forms. In the strong sense it applies to the assessment of children's achievements in tests externally set and externally examined. In the weak sense it points to the possibility of teachers accepting the tests set or published externally (and the objectives which they imply) but marking them internally in accordance with the test's specification. Where the goals of teaching form a core of widely accepted objectives, an external test is likely to have wide application across regions and schools within regions (a diagnostic reading test, for example). Where teachers have adopted structured sequences of instruction or have developed their own objectives which effect local needs or a new curriculum, teacher-made instruments are more likely to form the appropriate way of carrying out internal assessment.

CHOOSING AMONGST THE ALTERNATIVES

The purpose of this chapter has been to inform teachers of some of the options in assessment open to them. Faced with the bewildering array of modes (let alone instruments!) available, how is the choice to be made? No rules, obviously, but a few guidelines may be advanced. Remember we are talking about the main modes described in the chapter. The strengths and weaknesses of the available instruments are discussed elsewhere. Obviously a given instrument (such as a test, rating scale or check list) whether objective or subjective, could be used in more than one mode. For example a standardized test could be used in either continuous or final assessment. By contrast some tests are more closely associated with one mode of assessment than with what appears to be its opposite in Rowntree's list (p. 24). An obvious example is a test to assess mastery of a given object which is likely to find its principal use in criterion-referenced assessment although it may also be used to discriminate among individuals — this, however, would be more probably for secondary purposes only.

The assumption is made that by this time the teacher will have his or her ideas of the relative merits (and the unintended side-effects) of the types discussed through personal experience and reading chapters 2 and 3. In making decisions it is recommended that teachers apply the following principles:

(1) *Identify the constraints.* For example, school custom may well require that a termly or yearly rank order be drawn up for children in the class or year group. Here a norm-referenced statement is required. Is this purpose best served by setting the same test to all pupils or can this aim be achieved by a summative report based on the cumulative records of the results of criterion-referenced assessment? If the latter is true, then no *extra* testing is required over and above that which informs the day-to-day decisions of teachers as to those children who are ready to move further in the instructional sequence. If there is an 'exam timetable' then there's probably little or no room for manoeuvre! Other constraints obviously include whether or not you have to 'prepare' children for an external examination.

(2) Be clear on the objectives and 'spirit' of your teaching and choose a method of assessment which encourages (or, at least, is not antagonistic to) the exercise of the skills and concepts you have been trying to teach. This is probably the most important choice point once you have established what you are free or not free to do. Many examples could be given. If your aim is to encourage children to *learn* how to organize their own ideas and to express them effectively, then essays as part of continuous assessment are indicated. If the aim is to encourage the development of problem solving skills then process assessment is required (for example, in

'Nuffield Science'). If major attention is paid to build up children's background of knowledge, this would best be accomplished by formal objective tests rather than by *ad hoc* informal testing. The 'golden rule' is: see what method is congruent with your educational aims — the aims come first.

(3) Be clear on the kinds of information you wish to acquire from the assessment and the kinds of inference you wish to draw. For example, if you wish to study the results of different methods of presenting the same objective with a view to improving upon your teaching you will need to adopt formative methods. If a teacher wants to study the progress of one or two 'special' children in his or her class, an assessment which is informal and continuous (looking for change) seems best suited to this end. By contrast, if your aim is to advise a pupil on his or her suitability for a particular choice of subject or career, cumulative records may be backed up by an aptitude test which is norm-referenced. If you wish to predict a pupil's chances of high performance in a future criterion you might try a norm-referenced and external test known to have high validity for this purpose. The general advice is: make sure you get what you want from the assessment — if you do not know what you want, you deserve what you get!

(4) From your knowledge of the characteristics and personalities of pupils in your class consider whether certain types of assessment might not be suitable for them. A pupil known to have a history of failure can probably be more appropriately assessed using a criterion-referenced test where each criterion is suitably poised for his/her level of competence. Norm-referenced testing is only likely to reinforce the sense of failure so it could be avoided where possible. With children who become highly anxious in formal assessments, try informal and continuous assessment in preference to final testing.

The converse of this principle also applies. When pupils or classes have been poorly motivated under continuous assessment try a termly or final exam. Require the pupil who is complacent (but without justification) to take a norm-referenced test with age norms. (Teachers who might object that this principle implies a method of assessment *per child* should consider the assumptions inherent in the practice where all children take the same test.)

(5) Examine available published methods of assessment to see if one is available that fulfils your objectives. Assessment takes time — the teacher's and the pupils'. Teachers' time is spent in devising the assessment (possibly in constructing the instrument) and in 'marking'. If a test already exists that meets your objectives then external assessment (in its weaker sense, p. 69) may be appropriate. If a need exists to diagnose children's learning difficulties in basic subjects a test in print will probably meet this need. But if no test exists (e.g. to examine exactly why so many children cannot 'do' logarithms) then develop your own criterion-referenced tests and study the mistakes, not the correct answers.

(6) Decide who is going to use the results of the assessment. Teachers will know the meaning of the various types of assessment. Parents, employers, children may not understand. Unless teachers wish to emulate doctors in the assumption that it is 'not good for patients (pupils) to know what is wrong with them' choose a method of assessment which enables the results to be communicated simply but accurately in a form which helps in the education of the child. Informal assessment is often the most useful type of assessment in the day-to-day interaction of pupils with teachers. Standardized test scores may be most appropriate where the child's standing in a large peer group needs to be described.

4

Construction and Use of Teacher-made Tests

WHY TEACHER-MADE TESTS?

The most recent edition of a well known publisher's catalogue presents a variety of tests for use on different occasions. It shows that attainment and ability tests are easily available for use by qualified teachers and that many have the most impressive properties. All have very high reliability (see chapter 6), and validity (chapter 8) an attractive format, and some have been standardized using very large samples of children (one as large as 20 000). Teachers have taken an active part in the construction of some of the tests: those in Worcestershire, Middlesex and Surrey appear to have been particularly involved and other tests acknowledge the advice of (unlocated) panels of teachers. Nor need teachers doubt their conscientious attention to real educational needs: one test is comprised of topics 'considered essential for pupils beginning secondary school'; in another, items have been selected 'after extensive pre-testing and rigorous analysis'. One series (in Basic Mathematics) has taken ten years to complete and is appropriate for 'a wide age range from first year juniors to middle adolescence'. There are, of course, anomalies. One test still in use was only provisionally standardized almost 25 years ago. In another the provisional norms appear to be restricted to rural and urban children in east England whilst two further tests are unavailable to teachers in Bournemouth (at the request of the Chief Education Officer).

Quite obviously these tests have been constructed with the aid of resources far beyond those available to classroom teachers. But with so many commercially produced tests available why is it necessary for teachers to construct their own tests? It is no criticism of published tests nor of the service offered by those agencies responsible for their distribution to note that commercial tests are expensive and limited chiefly to the assessment of basic skills in reading, English and mathematics. Nor is it derogatory to point out that there is an inevitable time lag between an innovation in the curriculum and the appearance of a published test which reflects that content. And whilst it may be true that the subject matter of 'English' (grammatical usage, punctuation and to a lesser extent vocabulary and written expression) changes sufficiently slowly to justify the use of a test published in 1955, the material which constitutes the curriculum in science, geography or other social sciences is subject to considerable modification and incorporation in response to growth in knowledge and changes in educational aims and objectives. These are some of the most obvious limitations of the best published tests, but teacher-made tests do, also, offer other considerable advantages if properly constructed.

The strengths of teacher-made tests are as follows:

(1) They provide a closer fit between test and course content, except perhaps in basic subjects where courses are common to most schools for children of corresponding age.

(2) Tests which match the educational objectives of teachers can provide more day-to-day, formative evaluation of pupils and their progress. Tests which correspond with units of a course provide a check of the effectiveness of teaching and learning.

(3) Teacher-made tests can provide a more extensive sampling of specific areas of learning. Commercially produced tests normally sample a wide range of knowledge, skills and concepts.

(4) Teacher-made tests can consist of a small number of relevant items and provide immediate feedback in the form of knowledge of results to both pupil and teacher.

(5) Teacher-made tests provide information regarding a pupil's attainment relative to specific objectives which then provide a basis for report to parents concerning his/her educational progress.

Item Banking

As we shall see later in this chapter, the writing of items and compilation of tests can be more difficult than might appear at first sight. For this reason the ideas of 'item banking' are of potential value. Item banking combines the advantages of teacher-made tests — in particular the 'tailoring' of a test to the content and emphasis of the teaching — with the benefits of the best technology of item development. The idea is to establish a bank of items of various specified levels of difficulty in several areas of the school curriculum, from which tests tailored to meet teachers' needs may be compiled. The bank would not only be open to individual schools or authorities but could also be used to gain an idea of 'national standards' insofar as pupils all over the country could be asked to respond to calibrated items, for example, as part of the work of the APU. More about the uses of item banking is discussed in chapter 10 but readers may care to speculate why the ideas, cogently argued ten years ago by Wood and Skurnik (1969), have had comparatively little practical effect on the construction of teacher-made tests so far.

CONSTRUCTING TEACHER-MADE TESTS

It is not expected that teachers will have a great deal of time available in which to build tests but it is certainly not recommended that they 'knock something out' two or three days before tests are to be used! Of course, published tests can and do suffer from a variety of deficiencies in spite of the concentration of time, skill and attention paid to them by professional test constructors. Indeed, many of the side-effects of a test, or the ambiguities or special difficulties presented by an item, may not come to light until after several years of usage. Examples can be given where items have proved more difficult to particularly able pupils than to pupils of average ability because the former have perceived problems hidden from even the authors of the items! Nevertheless, and without pursuing a counsel of perfection, a systematic approach to the construction of a test or instrument — which still allows considerable scope for the creativity and ingenuity of teachers — can be recommended. An attempt has been made to provide such a framework in the pages which follow. As with all learning, the skills of testing would be acquired gradually, but it repays time and effort if teachers accumulate their own files of good items with experience and application. There are very many books on the subject, progressively concerned with suggestions for the improvement of the technical efficiency of the assessment. Books have been written on single aspects of testing (e.g. the construction of multiple choice instruments; the statistics of item analysis; methods of ensuring a higher degree of examiner's consistency when making essay or other open-ended tests). The recommendations offered here do not assume that teachers have little else to do than to construct tests! They propose a minimum set of activities which, if followed, provide a working basis for the construction of instruments more likely to meet educational criteria than tests constructed hastily the night before they are required by a head of department or head teacher, or as yet another annoying appendage to the teacher's main task. In addition, as teachers become more practised, these skills are capable of transfer to the many *ad hoc* occasions on which informal assessment is made in the classroom.

What and How to Test: Sorting Out your Objectives

The simple answer to the question: 'What to assess?' is of course, 'the objectives of the course of teaching and learning'. We identify a teacher's objectives when we pose the question: 'What are you trying to achieve and what kinds of changes do you hope to make to your pupils' capabilities?' But we do not always receive very precise answers, as we have already discussed in chapter 2. For this reason, definition of objectives in behavioural terms is often held to be a fundamental stage in both teaching and testing. Now the language of behavioural objectives is somewhat limited in its expressive potential but it is often useful in the statement of the ends we hope to achieve where these are the actual 'new' or extensions to pupils' accomplishments in the cognitive domain.

One influential source of ideas for educational objectives is the *Taxonomy of Educational Objectives (for the cognitive domain)* by Bloom et al. (1956). Although many who have used it find it unnecessarily restricting and think that the advance specification of objectives inhibits spontaneity in learning (as, indeed, anything can if followed slavishly), others have found it a useful means of correcting an overemphasis on a narrow range of outcomes, in particular the ubiquitous demand for recall and memory for knowledge that makes up so much of traditional examination.

The classification is into six major categories. Metfessel et al. (1969) have proposed a number of verbs which specify the kinds of activities native to each level of the classification. These verbs are representative, but since too much time can easily be spent in trying to show their unique suitability for the heading under which each has been placed, they are quoted here only as one possible guide to the amplification of the category (see table 4.1).

There is no room here to provide a complete breakdown

Table 4.1 — Taxonomy of educational objectives

Levels in the taxonomy	Verbs to define the relevant activity
1.00 Knowledge	to recall, reorganize, explain, define, identify
2.00 Comprehension	as *translation* to change, give in own words, rephrase, illustrate, translate
	as *interpretation* to illustrate, represent, reorder
	as *extrapolation* to conclude, deduce, estimate, generalize, infer, predict
3.00 Application	to apply, calculate, classify, develop, organize, transfer
4.00 Analysis	to distinguish, detect, classify, categorize
5.00 Synthesis	to unite, tell, relate, produce, derive, organize, formulate
6.00 Evaluation	to argue, judge, compare, contrast, appraise

of the classification, but each major category is itself divided into sections. Thus, for knowledge (from Bloom et al., 1956):

1.00   Knowledge
        . . . involves the recall of specifics and universals, the recall of methods and processes, or the recall of a pattern, structure or setting
1.10   Knowledge of specifics
1.11   Knowledge of terminology
1.12   Knowledge of specific facts
1.20   Knowledge of ways and means of dealing with specifics
1.21   Knowledge of conventions
1.22   Knowledge of trends and sequences
1.23   Knowledge of classifications and categories
1.24   Knowledge of criteria
1.25   Knowledge of methodology
1.30   Knowledge of the universals and abstractions in a field
1.31   Knowledge of principles and generalizations
1.32   Knowledge of theories and structure

It is not suggested that teachers will find it particularly rewarding to classify minutely all their objectives in teaching for knowledge using the above scheme. But an awareness of the qualitative differences in the objectives at the six main levels enables teachers to analyse the very different types of outcome they are seeking to achieve. And if teachers do not know what they are trying to achieve (and many, privately, express this doubt) it is difficult to see how they can plan learning experiences intelligently. A clear concept of the objective is an indispensable focus for determining the content and form of the teaching and learning experiences as well as an indication of what can, and what cannot, be assessed.

Many writers have urged the desirability of writing objectives only by using verbs which match the various levels in Bloom's taxonomy. But others have argued that it is often very difficult to write a 'pure' objective (that is one which belongs exclusively to only one level in the classification) and have suggested that so long as ambiguity is excluded and the objective is phrased in terms of desired learning outcomes this is sufficient for most teachers' practical purposes. Moreover, a great deal of time and effort has already been expended to determine whether or not the levels in the taxonomy correspond with separable psychological processes. It is clear, however, that it would be a mistake to confuse a formal analysis of educational outcomes with a psychological theory of human ability.

As a rule-of-thumb it is helpful for teachers to be as analytic as possible in the identification of what it is they want children to be able to do (as process or as product) as a result of teaching: this will then constitute the teaching objectives. The question: 'Can they do these things?' then makes up the assessment objective. The question of the context in which the learning is demonstrated remains to be decided of course, and it is here that knowledge of Bloom's taxonomy proves useful. If the teacher wishes to assess knowledge or comprehension (levels 1 and 2) the context of the assessment can correspond very closely with that in which the *original* learning was presented. If, however, the teacher wishes to assess the extent to which pupils can transfer what they have learned to a *new* situation, then an item which tests application (level 3) should be prepared. Since the total context in which something is originally learned provides valuable clues to recall (psychologists have called this tendency 'episodic memory') teaching for levels 1 and 2 is likely to prove 'easier' than for level 3 — at least in the short term.

Examples of rule-of-thumb objectives (see preceding paragraph) are given by the following.

Can my pupils:
(1) Add two-, three- and four-digit numbers with decimals?
(2) Label the chambers and blood vessels into and out of the heart?
(3) Draw and label a diagram to show total internal reflection in a 60° prism?
(4) Summarize the chief features in the character of Lady Macbeth?
(5) Recall Boyle's law?
(6) Recall the features of 'chernozems' and 'podsols'?

(7)   Construct and use a simple clinometer?
(8)   Give the perfect tense of the following French irregular verbs: *aller, être?*
(9)   Remember the main incidents in the campaigns of Boadicea?

and so on.

Readers may object that this advice is scarcely innovative and point out that even a year's work would soon accumulate a vast number of objectives. This latter point is undoubtedly true. Nevertheless, we can make a distinction between 'core' and other objectives, the former being those which the teacher holds to be indispensable or of central importance when learning a particular topic or subject. We are not arguing that teachers everywhere will agree as to the constituents of that core although there will be a good deal of common ground in basic subjects, but rather that the teacher implicitly in the way he or she teaches will emphasize those that 'matter' in a variety of ways. The exercise might work the other way: the process of seeing these objectives on paper can well lead one to reallocate a rank order of importance by 'downgrading' some, 'upgrading' others and discarding those found by formative evaluation to be unrealistic. One point cannot be overemphasized: verbs which are open to a wide variety of meanings are avoided where possible. Although the verb 'to know' plays an important part in teachers' discussions about their aims, it is not sufficiently precise to serve as a specific objective. A simple illustration will do here. Suppose a teacher believes that children ought to learn about the EEC and decides that at least children should know where Strasbourg is. 'Knowing where Strasbourg is' could be manifest in a variety of highly dissimilar ways: by *recalling* that Strasbourg is in France: by *naming* a dot on a map as Strasbourg; by *locating* and *naming* a dot on a map; by stating its position in latitutde and longitude, miles from London, and so on. One can easily see that very different teaching would be required to achieve these objectives and different kinds of 'knowledge' would be involved. Indeed, some of these would not be classified as 'knowledge' by Bloom's taxonomy.

As might be expected, reliance on behavioural objectives is

open to serious criticism. Some of these were described in chapter 2, in the third objection. A good summary of the pros and cons of this approach has been provided by Payne (1974, 41–2) which readers should consult. The chief dangers of slavish adherence to the objectives approach seem to be:

(1)   the trivialization of the goals of education and the possible danger of under emphasizing the most important;
(2)   the process can become mechanical; and
(3)   the pre-specification of objectives can conceivably prevent the teacher from capitalizing on the unexpected opportunities which occur in classrooms.

Preparing the Specification Table (sometimes called the 'Test Blueprint')

Having determined the objectives of teaching (and, presumably, taught for their attainment) or having identified the outcomes judged to be educationally worthwhile which were attained but not planned in advance, the next task is to prepare a table which shows the way in which the test or instrument is to reflect that content. This is an important aspect of a test's content validity (see chapter 8). By and large it is unfair to pupils to incorporate material not covered by the teaching or other learning activities into a test: such a test would be constitutionally incapable of use in the formative evaluation of teaching effectiveness. The table can be constructed *before* teaching has begun as part of course preparation but left incomplete to enable the unexpected but worthwhile to be incorporated.

Most published specification tables have employed a version of Bloom's taxonomy by which to classify the abilities or performance involved in the objectives (vertical dimension) and their conceptions of the structure of the 'subjects' to classify the contents (horizontal dimension). There is clearly no *one* way in which to classify the material: a suitable method is to study the syllabus with an eye to the process–product distinction and to make some differentiation between levels of outcome ranging from recall of essentials ('knowledge' in the taxonomy) to problem solving, if appropriate. A useful example has been provided by Child (1978, 324) taken from the Nuffield Chemistry Project. In keeping with the process-oriented objectives of the project, the content was classified as 'activities' required in study of: (a) composition and change in materials; (b) practical techniques; (c) patterns in the behaviour of materials; (d) essential measurement; and (e) concepts. This represented the broad headings under which the various parts of the syllabus could be grouped. Four levels of Bloom's taxonomy were used and the final form of the grid was as shown in table 4.2.

From the totals (which appear in the margins) we can see that greater importance has been attached to comprehension than to the other abilities involved and that measurement (d) was rated almost four times as important as the practical techniques involved (b). Obviously, no rules for determining the weights can be given (indeed they are omitted from this version of the table): they may be arbitrary but will almost certainly express the explicit or implicit value attached to the cells by the teacher. For example, as measurement is the most important activity (d) one might expect a distribution of marks to be awarded for the knowledge level (1) as follows:

Knowledge of composition of changes in materials	5
Knowledge of practical techniques	2
Knowledge of behaviour of materials	4
Knowledge of essential measurement	6
Knowledge of concepts	4
Total	21

If the test designers decided to set one multiple choice question for each point, then the number of items is determined by the emphasis to be placed on the different aspects of knowledge. If weights are applied *initially*, that is before teaching begins, they will certainly be tentative. When teaching begins one may find an inordinate amount of time being

Table 4.2 — Specification table: Nuffield Chemistry Project

		Activity/content					
		(a)	(b)	(c)	(d)	(e)	Total (%)
Knowledge	1						21
Comprehension	2						42
Application	3						18
Analysis/evaluation	4						19
Total (%)		24	9	16	32	19	100

spent on the teaching of one aspect of a syllabus, when the table is drawn up an overemphasis of a narrow aspect of the syllabus may be identified: in both cases the specification table is a potential corrective. Construction of the specification table implicit in teacher-made tests often reveals an imbalance: too much emphasis on the recall of isolated factual material or the reproduction of computational skills learned by rote is often seen as a fundamental defect. If a final examination is prepared in this way pupils could be given the specification table to guide them in their revision. If the distribution of weights is justifiable on educational grounds then there seems no fundamental objection to pupils distributing their revision time and efforts accordingly. But if the test is designed to sample (and therefore estimate) the pupils knowledge of the *entire* course this would clearly be a mistake. Generalizations to a child's competence in the domain of learning being tested cannot be obtained if the children are encouraged to learn only a small part of that domain.

Possibly the chief difference between a specification table for norm-referenced and criterion-referenced tests is that the former will express a much broader range of objectives than the latter: in certain cases, a specification table for a criterion-referenced test will consist of a single cell (i.e. one level of ability x one content). Other examples of specification tables may be inspected in Gronlund (1971) and Mehrens and Lehmann (1978).

Table 4.3 — Types of teacher-made test

Objective tests	Other name

(1) Recall or completion type
    (a) single word, symbol, formula, etc.
    (b) multiple words or phrases
	Supply type

(2) Alternative response type
    (a) true/false; yes/no
    (b) multiple choice
	Selection type

(3) Matching type	Selection type
(4) Context dependent or unit type	Either supply or selection

Essay tests	
(1) Restricted response (paragraph length)	Supply type
(2) Extended or discussion response	Supply type
(3) Oral	Supply type

Deciding upon the Type of Test Item

Having made a decision as to the objectives to be assessed, and the items which embody the levels of ability and contexts in which they are to be examined, the next decision concerns the type of test to be constructed. Broadly speaking teacher-made tests fall into two categories: the objective test or the essay type. Objective types are those in which criteria for the correctness of an answer are set up in advance of the pupil's responses and in which the scores are affected — if at all — in only very minor ways by the subjective judgments or opinions of the markers. One useful classification of teacher-made tests is modified from Lien (1976) and is shown in table 4.3.

Each of these tests has a typical type of *item* associated with it and many variants.

A number of permutations of types of items could be made to make up a total test although it is probably better, if different types are to be used, to keep items of a similar type to the same part of a test. (It is very confusing for children to have to switch types rapidly since each type has a different kind of instruction to respondents.)

In the sections which follow a few examples of each type will first be given; these will be followed by a discussion of their advantages and limitations and a few tips on how to distinguish 'good' from 'poor' items will be offered.

TYPE A1: SIMPLE RECALL/COMPLETION TYPE

Examples:

Question Type

- (1)   What is the name of the capital city of France?
- (2)   Who is the present British prime minister?
- (3)   What is the formula for the 'refractive index'?

Completion Type

- (5)   The chemical formula for sulphuric acid is . . .
- (6)   Solve $5x + 4 = 24$; $x = . . .$
- (7)   Draw the ordnance survey map sign for a church with a tower

Advantages
These items are limited to those cases in which a single correct answer can be given. They are useful in mathematics and the sciences not only to test knowledge of specific facts but also where computation is required. Although teachers are likely to use these predominantly as tests of knowledge of bits of information, their format is not limited to these occasions. Reference to Bloom, Hastings and Madaus (1971) reveals several examples where this type has been used to test comprehension and application. For example, the item:

- (8)   A car accelerating from 48 to 80 km/h in four seconds has an average acceleration of . . . km/h per second requires knowledge of the relevant formula, the ability to substitute the values into the formula and to work out the value for *a*, the acceleration. In this case the item would not be very useful in the diagnosis of errors. If three separate stages in answering the item are required the teacher will not know which one or combination of these has 'broken down' if an incorrect answer is selected.

In general type A1 is a fairly easy item to construct in order to test for the knowledge of technical terms, the symbols used in a discipline and definitions. The chief limitations of such items are that, if relied on exclusively to assess how much has been learned, they can encourage the child to depend on the rote learning of highly specific and unrelated facts. A second disadvantage is that they are restricted chiefly to the 'lower' levels in Bloom's taxonomy and place a premium on the child's ability to recall. Mehrens and Lehmann (1978) are of the opinion that the testing of synthesis and interpretation are extremely difficult subjects for this type of item, for example. Thirdly, the ease and speed with which these items seem to be constructed can often lull the teacher into believing that 'any fool can write them'. One common mistake is to fail to notice that an apparently objective item can be answered in a number of ways, thus setting the respondent an ambiguous problem and the marker a subjective decision (which defeats the object of the exercise!).

For example:

(9)   Where are the athletics in the 1980 Olympic Games to be held?
(10) A circle has a diameter of five inches; what is its area?
(11) Columbus discovered America in . . .

are all indefinite: item (9) because 'Russia', 'the USSR' or 'Moscow' are all applicable, item (10) because the degree of accuracy required is not specified and item (11) because the sentence can be completed in a number of perfectly correct ways ('a boat which sailed from Europe'; 'the fifteenth century') are just two of many responses which present the marker with a subjective decision on whether or not the answers are to be allowed). These items could be improved as follows:

(9)   In what city are the athletics in the Olympic Games of 1980 to be held?
(10) A circle has a diameter of five inches. Its area, correct to two decimal places, is ... square inches
(11) In what year did Columbus discover America?

Hints on writing recall/completion items
In general, then, the rules for writing (and not writing!) items of type A1 are:

(a) Require short, definite answers in response to complete sentences.
(b) Specify the degree of accuracy required in computational items.
(c) If the item is of the completion type make sure the blanks occur at or near the end of the sentence to ensure that the readers have not forgotten the requirements by the end of the sentence. (This is particularly important when testing young children whose retention span is small and who find it difficult to comprehend 'backwards'.)
(d) Try and *avoid* items that can be answered by general ability rather than by the knowledge being tested.
(e) Specify the terms in which the answer is to be given (for example in item (9) above, 'in what city' is much better than 'where').
(f) Do not write a completion type which is long and includes many blanks. Items with a large number of gaps are often ambiguous and set the child the task of guessing what was in the item-writer's mind.

An extreme example:

(12) If ... solution is ... using ... electrodes ... is deposited at ...

And while on the subject of blanks, keep them all the same length and do not vary them with the number of letters in the missing word.

(g) Avoid giving external clues to the answer, e.g. of a grammatical kind, which may lead the children to the correct answer independently of their knowledge.

TYPE A2: ALTERNATIVE RESPONSE TYPES

True/False Type

In these, children are presented with a proposition that is either true or false and are asked to underline which answer they consider correct.

Examples:

(1) True   False   In the play, Hamlet is killed by his wife

(2) True   False   In a truly normal distribution, the median, mode and mean coincide

Sometimes, especially in the assessment of attitudes, opinions and beliefs, a yes/no format is adopted:

(3) Yes   No   I prefer reading a good book to attending a good party

(4) Yes   No   Capital punishment should be restored for all murders

A further variant is known as the cluster type. In it there is a statement (or 'stem') followed by more than one item requiring a response:

(5) The arithmetic mean is

True   False   (a)   the value about which the sum of the deviations is zero

True   False   (b)   another word for median

True   False   (c)   less affected by extreme scores than is the median

The disadvantages of true/false items are probably more apparent than their advantages. The probability of obtaining a correct answer by guessing is high, the items are restricted in use to those propositions which are unequivocally true or false, tests containing only few items are very poor at discriminating among children and the tendency to respond 'true' when in doubt (known as 'acquiescence') confounds the interpretation of the score.

The advantages of true/false items are that they can be scored very quickly indeed, they permit coverage of a large area of content in a relatively short time and, contrary to the misconception of some teachers, can be extended to test comprehension and understanding if constructed with ingenuity. For example:

(6) True   False   Given that an electric kettle is rated '2 kW, 240 V' and when filled with cold water takes five minutes to boil, the average weekly cost of boiling the kettle six times each day is 21 pence if 1 kW costs three pence.

Hints on writing true/false items
(a) Avoid any source of ambiguity or imprecision. Examples of words or phrases which signal this difficulty are 'most important', 'never', 'largely', 'always', 'essential', 'only'. If children are 'test-wise' they will have learned that certain words of this type (known as 'specific determiners') are more likely to signal that the proposition is false than that it is true. Conversely, any proposition which contains words like 'may', 'might', 'can', 'sometimes' is more likely to be true than false.
(b) Avoid the use of negative statements. Try answering this one:

    True   False   It is not true that Baldwin was Prime Minister in 1920

(c) Avoid using words which are open to more than a single

interpretation: use quantitative rather than qualitative terms where possible. For example:

> True   False   Many people voted Liberal in the 1979 General Election

presents a problem because 'many' is open to different interpretations.

(d) Only use this type of item for propositions which are unequivocally true or false.

(e) Balance the number of true and false statements in the test but keep the length of statements roughly equal. (Extra long statements, such as those containing subordinate clauses or qualification often indicate that the item-writer has taken special care to construct a true statement.)

(f) Avoid lifting statements verbatim from text books: the children may have memorized passages.

TYPE A2: MULTIPLE CHOICE TYPE

Teachers will be very familiar with this type of item, but it is difficult to construct effectively. The basic structure is in two parts: a 'stem', which states the problem and a set of possible answers or 'options' one of which (the 'key') is correct and the others of which are incorrect (the 'distracters'). There are many variations on this format. Stems can be direct questions or incomplete statements: only one, or several options can be correct; with stems which are difficult to prepare the candidate may be required to select the 'best' answer. The concern of this section is to describe those which the teacher can construct with little difficulty rather than to demonstrate the extent of the ingenuity exhibited by professional item-writers. Whole books and lengthy chapters have been written on this topic and the interested reader is referred to the thorough descriptions provided by Gerberich (1956) and by Wesman (1971, chapter 4). The chief varieties are now given.

Single Correct Answer Type

(1) Who invented the sewing machine?
    (a) Singer   (d) Fulton
    (b) Howe   (e) White
    (c) Whitney

(2) If 36% of the variance in test X can be predicted from test Y, what is the value of the correlation coefficient?
    (a) 0.36   (d) 0.70
    (b) 0.50   (e) 0.80
    (c) 0.60

'Best Answer' Type

Whereas the previous examples have a single correct answer, teachers may wish to extend the multiple choice format to examine the children's knowledge in an area where several versions of 'fact' have been proposed. This type of item bristles with problems: the item-writer has the responsibility of providing the evidence that experts agree on the 'best' answer or to inform the respondent of the source or authority for the best answer. The respondent must, of course, be directed to select the 'best' response from among the options.

(3) What was the basic purpose in setting up the National Health Service?
    (a) To supply cheap medical care to the community
    (b) To keep an election promise made by politicians
    (c) To remove the privileges of those who could pay for private care
    (d) To make medical care available to all regardless of income
    (e) To improve the health of underprivileged sections of the community

Incomplete Stem Type

(4) The correlation coefficient between test X and test

Y is 0.71. The amount of variance in Y which is predictable from X is

(a) 3%   (c) 50%
(b) 7%   (d) 70%

Multiple Response Type

If several correct answers to a question exist it is sometimes a stringent test of the child's knowledge to include two or more correct answers among the options. (The teacher would obviously have to prepare an instruction that the child is allowed to pick one or more than one of the options.)

(5) What factor or factors are chiefly responsible for the clotting of the blood?
(a) Contact of blood with injured tissue
(b) Oxidation of haemoglobin
(c) Contact of blood with a foreign surface
(d) Presence of unaltered prothrombin

Where questions are set which have several equally acceptable answers as in the above example, writers have sometimes prepared a negative version of the multiple response type. The respondent is instructed to mark the option which does *not* correctly answer the question.

(6) Which of these statements is *not* true of a virus?
(a) It can live only in plant and animal cells
(b) It can reproduce itself
(c) It is composed of large living cells
(d) It can cause disease

(the above two examples are taken from Wesman, 1971).

Incomplete Alternatives Type

This type can be used where a unique but simple answer exists to a problem and where the teacher wishes to make the respondent a little more active than in other types. It is particularly useful for arithmetical problems.

(7) If you calculate the square root of 27, what num-
     ber should appear as the second decimal place?
     (a) four   (d) eight
     (b) five   (e) nine
     (c) seven

Substitution Type

This type has been extensively used to assess children's
ability to detect errors of style or syntax in well-written
prose. A short extract from a written passage is presented but
with alterations to include errors (e.g. of punctuation, grammar, spelling). These are underlined and identified with a
number. For each number the child is required to select the
phrase (either the original or an alternative) which provides
the best expression. Unfortunately they often have a somewhat contrived appearance.

(8) 'Star Trek' is a fantastic story about the future.
     The aim of the crew of the star ship 'Enterprise' is
     to boldly go[1] where no man has been before. The
     crew consists[2] of a motley array of men and
     women of many nationalities, but each one seems
     to spend most of their[3] time sitting[4] at a com-
     puter terminal.
     Item
     (1) (a) to boldly travel   (3) (a) their
          (b) boldly to go   (b) his
          (c) to boldly go   (c) his or her
     (2) (a) consist   (4) (a) sat
          (b) consists   (b) in front of
          (c) comprises   (c) sitting

As can be seen from this example it can be difficult to
choose plausible alternatives and items of this type are probably most easily constructed by the pedantic!
   There are many more types but this has dealt with those
most frequently encountered. Each type presents its own
source of difficulty but certain 'rules for writing' are generalizable.

Tips on preparation of multiple choice items

(a) Ensure that the *instructions* to the children are clear. For example, a set of single correct answer items could be introduced as follows:
'Each of the questions below is followed by several answers marked (a), (b), (c), (d) and (e). From these, you are to choose the *one* answer which is correct. Mark your answer by underlining the letter alongside the one you choose'. (This would be followed by an example showing how it is to be done. If separate answer sheets are to be provided the children could be asked to respond by placing the letter of the chosen answer in a space provided.)

(b) Stems which present a direct question are easiest to write.

(c) Keep the stem short and the options of roughly the same length as one another in a single item. If this is not done and one option is longer or shorter than the others the child may suspect that it is the correct answer. In general, avoid making the correct option systematically different from the distracters.

(d) Make all options equally plausible. This is sometimes quite difficult. As an example of alternatives which are not equally plausible consider the completion item:

   (9)   The logarithm of 27.56 is
      (a) 1.4702   (c) 1.3712
      (b) 1.4507   (d) 1.4402

This item was set presumably to test the child's ability to read the body of the logarithm table and to interpolate using the table of differences. Options (a), (b) and (c) are, therefore, quite implausible since none occurs in the required line of the table.

(e) Make sure that all options are mutually exclusive unless you have deliberately written an item of the multiple response type. Payne (1974, 113) has provided a good example of an item which 'fails' on this tip.

  (10)   If a test has a reliability of 0.78 what percentage

of an observed score is attributable to errors of measurement?

(a) over 5%   (c) over 20%
(b) over 10%   (d) over 30%

The precise answer is 22% and the closest option (c), but (a) and (b) are also correct.

(f) Do not overwork the option 'none of the above'. It suggests that you have run out of plausible alternatives but the biggest objection is that a child may get the answer correct (when 'none of the above' *is* the correct answer) for the wrong reasons. For example

(11) What is the area of a circle whose radius is 5.2 inches? Give your answer to two decimal places (take pi = 3.14).
(a) 83.09 square inches
(b) 84.95 square inches
(c) 84.98 square inches
(d) 85.91 square inches
(e) none of the above

Any child who got an answer not found among (a) to (d) inclusive would choose (e), the correct answer. But this would not necessarily mean that he or she had calculated the answer correctly as 84.91 square inches. 'None of the above' can be used if the correct answer *is* one of the other options provided.

(g) In the incomplete stem type make sure that the alternatives are grammatically consistent with the stem and parallel with each other. The oldest mistake with this type of item is to give a grammatical clue to the correct item, most commonly the use of the article, 'an', which applies to only one alternative.

(h) Eliminate the use of the same wording in stem and option. If there is a common term in stem and one option this provides a clue to the correct answer.

(i) Place the correct option at random throughout the tests. In other words, do not place more of the correct options in any one position than in any other. This can be accomplished by shuffling cards.

(j) Use four or five options. The problem here is one of compromise between what is practicable and what ensures greatest reliability. Theoretically, the larger the number of *plausible* alternatives the lower the probability of obtaining the correct answer by chance. But really plausible alternatives are quite often difficult to prepare and take up time and space. By convention, then, four or five options are usually adopted.

These tips by no means exhaust all the advice that could be given on the writing of items, but if followed they should help the teacher avoid some of the most common errors in the preparation of this type of item. The purpose in setting high standards of item preparation is not, of course, to improve the technical properties of the test for the sake of it. It is to reduce as far as possible the sources and magnitude of the error variance in the test as a whole. Chapter 6 explains the importance of the concept of error variance and shows how it may be calculated.

One of the most useful ways of spotting deficient items is by consultation with the children who have taken the tests. They are often capable of picking up many of the often unforeseeable problems in items. Gradually the teacher can build a bank of items classified by content and by ability required or tested in their solution. Good items can be retained, poor items discarded or rewritten.

HOW TO DEAL WITH GUESSING

One of the most hackneyed but fundamental criticisms of the types of item we have been considering is that children can gain marks by guessing even when they are ignorant of the answers to the tests or quite unprepared to take them. Guessing cannot entirely be eliminated even from essay type tests but the chances of gaining marks by guesswork are much higher in multiple choice items. Suppose there are just two options to a question, as in the true/false items. By chance alone one might expect a child to get half marks (that is even if he or she 'knows nothing' of the content being sampled). Similarly in a test composed of items each having four options, a chance mark of 25% would be expected.

Faced with this problem a number of solutions have been proposed:

(a)   the use of instructions designed to discourage or equalize the effects of guessing;
(b)   the use of 'correction formulae' which are designed to penalize guessing;
(c)   the use of weights to modify the scores in the light of the degree of confidence expressed by respondents when choosing options.

Methods (a) and (b) are those most commonly encountered. But there are problems with both methods. Some writers have favoured the use of instructions which tell children only to respond to those items where they are certain of their answers. This seems to run counter to our common experience that the knowledge we possess is held with very varying degrees of 'certainty' which is, itself, in any case, open to a number of interpretations. Given that the personalities of children are very different this instruction could serve to reward the disobedient! Some writers have agreed that the best way to proceed is to instruct the children not to guess and to tell them that they will be penalized if they do so. Another view is that children should be told to attempt all items but without threat that a penalty for guessing will be exacted; the formula for the correction for guessing is, then, applied as part of the scoring procedure. Probably the most commonly used formula is:

$$S = R - \frac{W}{n - 1} \qquad [4.1]$$

where

   S = corrected score
   R = number correct
   W = number incorrect (not counting omitted items)
   n = number of options per item

The rationale for this formula is simple (too simple!). If there are n choices per item the chance of a correct guess is $1/n$, and of an incorrect guess $n-1/n$. Thus for every $n-1$ incorrect guesses we expect one guess to turn out correct. Thorndike (1971, 59–61) gives a full account of the difficulties in dealing with guessing. The obvious problem with the 'correction formula' is that its assumption is wrong: 'guessing' is not a chance phenomenon any more than 'knowledge' is an all or none affair. Although this problem has been extensively studied, no final answer has been reached. It has been reported that the 'correction formula' reduces reliability (see chapter 6) but increases validity (see chapter 8). Other statisticians have suggested that instructions not to guess have made a slight increase in the test's power to predict a criterion. It is known that, if everyone guesses (as would, perhaps, be the case if the test were grossly unfair to all respondents) the size of errors of measurement (see chapter 6) shoots up. On the other hand, if all pupils have the time to answer all items and, indeed, do so, there is a perfect correlation between corrected and uncorrected scores, i.e. the rank order of scores will not change (Tinkelman, 1971).

The suggestion that teachers require each child to indicate (on say a four–five point scale) the degree of confidence with which an option has been chosen, followed by the practice of weighting the option accordingly (that is, of giving greater credit when a correct answer has been chosen and rated five for 'absolutely confident' than when it is chosen but only with rank two – 'not at all confident') seems not to have been widely practised. This method is deficient in that it offers no particular hope of a common basis for comparison between the respondent who is a 'natural gambler' and one who is shy, timid and self-deprecatory.

Sound advice on dealing with this problem has been provided by Cronbach (1961). This is to provide the respondents with encouragement to answer as best they can with a cautionary note that blind guessing can lower as well as raise scores. However, guessing is likely to operate extensively only where something is to be gained by 'chancing one's arm'. If the multiple choice test is used in criterion-referenced assessment and pupils understand that it is part of the process by which they are to decide whether or not to continue to the next most advanced topic, one might expect them to be as interested as is the teacher in a reasonable assessment of their readiness and to admit their ignorance if remedial help is available. Perhaps guessing is less prevalent in a relaxed atmosphere of assessment free from competitiveness.

TYPE A3: MATCHING TYPE

This is a further variety of multiple choice item but one which conserves space. The child taking the test is presented with two tests. The instructions require the child to make the correct link between an entry in list A with one in list B and indicate this link in the blank space.
    For example:

(12)   Painters and painting
        Famous painters are listed in list A and paintings in list B. Place the letter corresponding to the painting in the space next to the artist who painted it.

List A	List B
(1) Paul Cézanne	(a) Bal Champêtre
(2) Auguste Renoir	(b) Young woman powdering herself
(3) Georges Seurat	(c) Rocks — Forest of Fontainebleau
(4) Antoine Watteau	(d) The Fiddler
	(e) La Première Sortie
	(f) The Supper at Emmaus

Mehrens and Lehmann (1978) have described this type of item as most suitable for the 'who', 'what', 'when', 'where', types of learning and for any others which involve simple relationships. Many examples will come to mind. They require relatively little reading time and providing the matching

requirements within an item deal with a single area of knowledge (painting and painters in the above example) they can
sample quite a large content. The type is less well suited to
the assessment of the abilities higher than 'knowledge' in
Bloom's taxonomy and is quite difficult to construct (the
reader should try to spot the deficiencies in our example).

There are many variants of this type: in fact Gerberich
(1956) lists no fewer than 38 versions! They can be used to
test comprehension or knowledge of cause—effect relationship. Child (1977, 325—6) provides one such example drawn
from the Nuffield Chemistry Project:

> (13)   Directions: the group of questions below consists
> of five lettered headings followed by a list of
> numbered phrases. For each numbered phrase
> select the one heading which is most closely rela-
> ted to it. Each heading may be used once, more
> than once, or not at all.
>
> Classify the following changes into one of the
> categories (a)—(e):
> (a) radioactive decay   (d) cracking
> (b) catalysis   (e) oxidation
> (c) hydrolysis
> (1) the conversion of heat alone of an organic
>   liquid consisting of one compound only, into
>   a mixture of components which are gaseous at
>   room temperature
> (2) the production of thermal energy from the
>   fossil fuels
> (3) changes in the nuclei of atoms

Experiences with these items has shown that, despite their
advantages in efficiency in use of time and space, they are
particularly open to irrelevant cues and the task of producing
plausible alternatives is often very difficult. If you do decide
to use them the following points should be observed:
(a) Write responses which are related (our examples were all
      paintings or physical/chemical processes) but mutually
      exclusive.

(b) Keep the number of stimuli small (say four or five but let the number of responses be larger, by about two or three). Long lists are more difficult to construct homogeneously and will involve the child in a much larger number of comparisons between stimuli and response. If the number of stimuli equals the number of responses a child may get a correct answer simply by the process of elimination. The practice (adopted in the Nuffield example) of requiring the child to respond 'once, more than once, or not at all' may help to minimize guessing.

(c) Write the directions for matching and responding clearly. (The Nuffield Chemistry item as presented here tells the respondent to classify and select, but not where/how to do so.)

(d) Present the responses in some sort of logical order (in the painters' list the artists are presented in alphabetical order of surname). This has been shown to help the respondent scan the lists quickly.

TYPE A4: CONTEXT DEPENDENT TYPE

So far we have concentrated on the production of items in which every one is independent of every other, in the sense that each contains all the information the child is offered. Occasions arise, however, especially where the teacher is assessing comprehension rather than knowledge, in which it is convenient to provide respondents with a stimulus about which a number of questions is posed. These fall into two main types: the *pictorial type* or the *reading type*. Space will permit only a single example but the reader is referred to many examples present in standard texts.

Pictorial Type

These are most frequently used to present stimulus material in the form of graphs, tabulated data, maps or scientific and mechanical diagrams.

Example (nine—ten year olds):

(14) The graph below shows the number of bicycles sold by one shop in one week last year. Study the graph then answer the questions which follow.

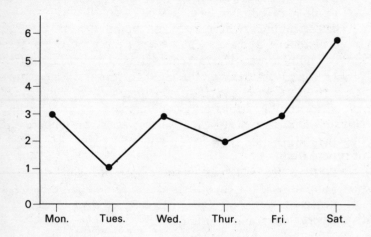

(1) On which day were fewest bicycles sold?
    (a) Monday   (c) Thursday
    (b) Tuesday   (d) Friday
(2) How *many more* bicycles were sold on the 'best' day than on the 'next best' day?
    (a) four   (c) three
    (b) two   (d) five
(3) How many bicycles were sold altogether on the *two* 'poorest' days?
    (a) one   (c) two
    (b) four   (d) three

If you decide to use the pictorial form the following points should be borne in mind:

(a) Choose pictures/graphs because they are appropriate to what you wish to measure, not just because they are novel or interesting.
(b) Use pictorial material which is clear and uncluttered with detail unless you *wish* to test for perceptual analysis.

(c) Adhere to the principles of multiple choice construction as have already been described.
(d) Make the instructions to children very clear. You are assessing the ability of children to deal with the information in the picture not their comprehension of the instructions.

Reading Type

Typically, this type consists of a piece of writing (usually of good quality though one can often detect material written especially for the purpose) followed by multiple choice questions requiring comprehension and application of the material. The special difficulties with this type of test include the time taken to select passages and to construct interesting questions (especially plausible options, where interpretation is being assessed); the low reliability relative to the time taken to enable children to respond, and their inappropriateness for a wide range of ability in view of the demands placed upon reading skill.

If teachers do intend to try this type of item:

(a) Choose material which is worth interpreting.
(b) Rewrite or edit it to incorporate the interpretations desired. Include several distinct ideas that lend themselves to questions clearly differing in content.
(c) Make sure the resulting material is within the reading ability of the children for whom it is intended.
(d) Base the items on the material in the passage: do not write items which depend on background or general knowledge.

THE ANALYSIS OF OBJECTIVE TEST ITEMS

We shall defer for a while consideration of the type of test beloved by British teachers — the essay type — to study the methods by which items may be examined. No matter how carefully the items have been constructed some will turn out to be 'better' than others — but 'better', of course, needs to be defined. 'Item analysis' refers to all the techniques available for the examination of the responses of groups of children to each item. The section will concentrate on those methods within the competence of classroom teachers: in a later chapter the Rasch technique, which forms the principal method of item analysis adopted by the APU but which demands large samples of children and computer facilities, will also be described.

A very large number of techniques of item analysis is available at varying levels of sophistication. Since rather stringent criteria of item preparation have been advocated which will take time to master, it is recommended that teachers do carry out item analysis in order to retain, for repeated use where appropriate, those which have the most satisfactory properties. For purposes of simplification, we shall restrict the discussion at this point to the analysis of items which are to form part of tests designed to discriminate among pupils; that is, of norm-referenced tests. We shall assume that individual teachers will be too busy to conduct extensive 'try-outs' of items although this will be possible if teachers join working parties – such as those set up by the Schools Council – or collaborate in the development of new curricula as in the Nuffield projects. In practice, the actual assessment is likely to constitute the try-outs of the items. But other informal opportunities may be devised, perhaps with small groups of pupils as part of their normal lessons or in another school where the items are appropriate to the teaching objectives.

The aims of the try-out are as follows:

(a)   To identify items with such weak construction that they should be discarded on the grounds of their ambiguity, misleading instructions, undue complexity or lack of plausibility in the distracters, if used.

(b)   To determine the degree of difficulty of each item. Items which are 'too difficult' or 'too easy' are of little or no use in norm-referenced assessment.

(c)   To examine the plausibility of the distracters.

(d)   To determine the effectiveness of the item in discriminating pupils who are 'high' or 'low' in the ability or achievement being tested.

(e) To gain information on the number of items to make up the test and to determine the time limit for the final test.

(f) To examine the relationships among the items chosen in order to eliminate redundancy of information if the test is to be used for norm-referenced assessment (i.e. to see the extent to which items are measuring the same or different attributes of the group of respondents).

Aim (f) demands rather complex statistical treatment and will be dealt with in chapter 5. The 'bare bones' of the processes by which aims (a) to (d) may be realized are now considered. We divide the processes into steps.

Step 1: Conditions for the Try-out

Ideally the items should be tried out on a sample of children comparable with the group for which they are intended. It would be quite easy to do this if, say, an entire age group in a single school had followed a course of study. In practice, however, no more than two classes (say 60 pupils) may have followed a similar course of study; in this case the group may be smaller than desirable[1]. If a group of teachers were to pilot items on, say, a year group in a comprehensive or middle school, a short cut may be adopted. In this case the items could be divided at random into subsets containing equal numbers of items. Each subset would constitute a 'mini-test'. The year group would then be divided at random into test groups and a 'mini-test' allocated at random to each test group. In this way attainment of a large number of objectives can be studied and the behaviour of a large number of items examined without the need for any child to take all items. This economic method is known as multiple *'matrix*

---

[1] Very-large-scale try-outs of items will obviously be beyond the scope of practising teachers but they can be accomplished by professional test constructors wishing to standardize tests and establish norms of wide applicability, or by the APU. In these cases independent sampling of individual pupils within randomly selected schools is the method adopted.

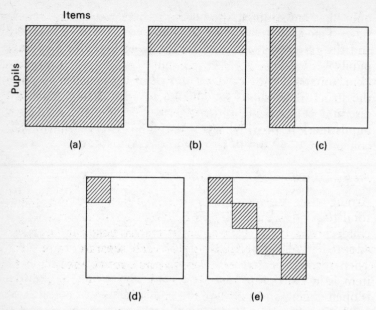

Figure 4.1   Types of sampling: (a) population type; (b) pupil sample type; (c) item sample type; (d) matrix sample type; (e) multiple matrix sample type.

sampling' but the random requirement and at least 20 children per subgroup must be adhered to if the results are not to be misleading. Teachers may obtain information about the performances of pupils and the characteristics of items using a number of basic types of sampling. These are, respectively: (a) using the population; (b) using a pupil sample; (c) using an item sample; (d) using matrix sampling; and (e) using multiple matrix sampling. These are illustrated in figure 4.1.

Strictly speaking type (a) is not a form of sampling since all items are administered to all pupils. In (b) all items are taken by a random sample of pupils whereas in (c) a random sample of items is administered to all pupils. In type (d) only a sample of items is taken by a sample of pupils whereas in type (e) subsets of items are administered to subsets of pupils. Type (e) is the most economic in gaining estimates of performances of the largest number of pupils.

Assuming the teacher has constructed the items with care,

only few ambiguities should go undetected at the try-out stage. One way to gain relevant information of the try-out and the assessment on one and the same occasion is to invite pupils — especially those in secondary schools — to mark an item 'unfair' if they detect a source of difficulty inherent in the structure of the item. The teacher can then guarantee to discount performance on that particular item if a number of pupils mark it, provided a reason can be given by the children concerned.

Step 2: Finding Item Difficulties

Arrange the answer papers in rank order from the highest total to the lowest. This will be done for the entire group of children who took the test but if matrix sampling has been adopted it will be carried out for each separate 'mini-test'. Then record the number choosing the correct answer if the item is in multiple choice format or supplying it if the item is open ended, and calculate the difficulty index.

This and subsequent steps are illustrated using a small sample of data acquired from a mathematics test taken by all pupils on entry to a large comprehensive school. In order to simplify the arithmetic involved, the papers of 120 children were extracted at random for item analysis. The test consisted of 64 items but the chief points can be made with reference to only a few of these.

To calculate the difficulty index
The following numbers of correct responses to the first five items were obtained:

	1	2	3	4	5
Correct response	68	69	59	56	46

Difficulty index $= \dfrac{R}{T}$

where
R = number of correct responses
T = total number of children

Hence the corresponding difficulty indexes[2] are

	1	2	3	4	5
Index	0.57	0.58	0.49	0.47	0.40

Some people refer to this as the *facility index*. We can obtain a simple alternative 'difficulty index' which actually does indicate how difficult each item is using

$$\text{Difficulty index} = 1 - \frac{R}{T}$$

Thus the corresponding values for this index would be

	1	2	3	4	5
Index	0.43	0.42	0.51	0.53	0.60

Item number 28 in the test proved particularly difficult. Only 13 got it right. Corresponding indices for this item therefore are 0.11 and 0.89 respectively. It does not matter which index you use, but be sure you get hold of its *meaning*!

The use one makes of these values depends on the purpose for which the items were used. If the teacher wants to compile a test of items which maximally discriminates among the children in terms of total test scores then items with value for the index of between 0.40 and 0.60 are best for this purpose (actually at 0.50, but for practical classroom purposes the above range is suitable). If one uses each item primarily as a test of an objective, as in criterion-referenced tests, then no particular value can be specified. But assuming item 28 (and any others with very low values for the difficulty index) is not technically deficient (badly worded, ambiguous) it clearly indicates a state of non-mastery by almost all respondents. What view do we take of items with facility values

---

[2] Although this is called the 'difficulty index' it actually indicates how *easy* the item was, because the higher the index the *more* children get it right.

greater than 0.90? Apart from the fact that it is a very easy item and not likely to help discriminate between levels of achievement, its incorporation into a test may be justified on the grounds that it helps anxious pupils to settle into the test-taking routine. By and large, however, and as a compromise, most tests useful in assessing achievement will consist of items whose difficulty values lie within the range of 0.30 and 0.70.

Step 3: Checking Plausibility and Discrimination Values

For each item in the multiple choice or matching type, examine the behaviour of the correct answer and its distracters. This is done by dividing the total sample into levels of achievement on total scores. If the teacher has only about 30 or 40 pupils available, two levels ('upper' and 'lower') each with half the number of pupils will be suitable.

In an example of 120 pupils division into fifths seems a reasonable decision. Item 32 in the mathematics test will be used to illustrate the procedure.

> (32) A litre of paint will cover approximately 50 square feet. How many litres of paint will you need to buy to paint the walls of a room 12 ft long, 10 ft wide and 8 ft high?
> (a) 2   (d) 10
> (b) 6   (e) 20
> (c) 8

Table 4.4 shows the distribution of responses to item 32. Of the total group of 120, 69 pupils got the answer right (keyed (c)). Thus the item has a difficulty index of 0.58, and is well within the range specified in step 2 as desirable. Distracters (b) and (d) seem to have proved fairly attractive but the response rate to distracter (a) shows that pupils regarded it as an implausible one probably because it is so disparate from the others. Distracter (e), also, showed a large discrepancy, probably for the same reason but in the opposite direction. The way in which the correct answer (c) worked (the number correct decreases with decreasing overall ability)

Table 4.4 — Distribution of responses to item 32

Option	(a)	(b)	(c)	(d)	(e)	Omitted	Pupils not read item	Total
Range of pupils on *total* scores								
Top fifth		1	21	2	—	—	—	24
Next highest fifth		1	18	3	2	—	—	24
Middle fifth		2	14	6	1	1	—	24
Next lowest fifth		5	10	7	—	2	—	24
Bottom fifth	1	9	6	2	1	2	3	24
Total	1	18	69	20	4	5	3	120

is satisfactory and only few children omitted the item altogether. the overall conclusion from the analysis is that item 32 is some use but needs to be improved by the provision of more plausible alternatives than options (a) and (e).

To reiterate: the number of divisions into which the range of total scores can be grouped depends on the size of the group. Less than 20 children per division is probably not adequate. Division into top and bottom halves is often quite appropriate. If the teacher were to find items having an inverse relationship to overall score (i.e. being answered correctly more often by pupils 'low' than by those 'high' in ability) this item should be treated with caution and scrutinized for a possible explanation.

Step 4: Calculating the Discrimination Index

For each item, compute the discrimination index. This is a simple technique to examine how well the items discriminate between 'high' and 'low' scores overall. Where large numbers of children are available most authorities recommend a comparison between top and bottom 27% of scores (Henrysson, 1971). Using the data of table 4.4 we find that of the top 32 pupils (approximately 27% of 120) 26 got the item correct and of the bottom 32, eight were correct. So 26 out of 32

(0.8125) and eight out of 32 (0.25) in top and bottom groups of scores were successful

$$\begin{aligned} \text{Discrimination index} &= p_1 - p_2 \\ &= 0.8125 - 0.25 \\ &= 0.56 \end{aligned}$$

where
p_1 = proportion in top 27% responding correctly
p_2 = proportion in bottom 27% responding correctly

Obviously the higher the value for the discrimination index the more effectively performance on the item reflects performance overall. If the discrimination index is near zero the item, whatever else it may be doing (like encouraging the poorest pupils), is redundant in terms of differentiating levels of ability or achievement in the test as a whole.

Step 5: Deciding on the Length and Time Limit of the Test

This is not strictly an aspect of item analysis but the results of item analysis play a part in these decisions. In tests which are criterion-referenced, knowledge of the difficulty of an item is not very helpful. As a rule-of-thumb for criterion-referenced tests, each objective tested required about eight to ten similar items. In norm-referenced testing the inclusion of a few very easy items at the beginning is recommended: all pupils who are required to take a test should be given a reasonable opportunity to get at least some right because the use of tests to destroy any semblance of self-esteem is strongly deprecated. Similarly, the practice of including a few really difficult items is also recommended. This is to challenge the most able pupils and to offer some basis for discrimination at the top end of the ability range. The majority of the items (say 80%) should, however, be of average difficulty (those in the range 0.30–0.70 as already indicated).

Deciding on the length of the test is a matter of the teacher's judgment but some pretty obvious considerations apply: the purpose of the test, the age and ability of the pupils and the level of reliability required are probably the most important.

If the test is used to assess a term's work or year's work it will need to be longer than for a short unit of work or a small number of objectives. If the purpose of the test is principally diagnostic, more items per objective will be necessary.

Quite obviously, young children read and write more slowly than older children. Similarly, brighter children think, read and write more quickly than less able children. With objective tests, having four or five options in multiple choice form, 45 item tests can be taken in about one hour. Children aged over 11 years should certainly be capable of an hour of testing. For pupils in the early years of junior schooling 30 minutes is probably sufficiently long. You can obtain your own estimates by supplying each child with three coloured pencils, giving the test and asking them to mark in one colour the point reached after 20 minutes, in another the point at 30 minutes and in the third at 45 minutes, to get some idea of what is a reasonable expectation of the speed of responding by motivated children.

Reliability is a big concept and is fully examined in chapters 6 and 7. There you will see that, all other things being equal, the longer the test the more reliable it seems to be. No one can state what a reliability *ought* to be. Reliability is usually expressed as a coefficient and most published tests in the cognitive domain have values of around 0.95 (a value of 1.0 would indicate that *no* measurement error is present). Teacher-made tests can approach this value but as the amount of error increases as the coefficient falls, a target reliability of 0.85 seems not an unreasonable one to aim for in teacher-made tests.

Teachers will be guided by experience in these important aspects of testing. If the test is seen to provide valuable information teachers will feel justified in spending time on it. If testing is haphazard and does not form part of a coherent programme of assessment more than a few minutes on tests may justifiably be begrudged. So far as a time limit for a test is concerned, if teachers are in doubt it seems preferable to be generous and to allow as many to complete as is organizationally feasible.

ALTERNATIVE METHODS OF ITEM ANALYSIS

What have been suggested so far are extremely simple but quite valuable methods of item analysis. For a variety of reasons, measurement theorists have been dissatisfied with these methods, however, and have developed more rigorous statistical techniques. If teachers opt for the simpler techniques they will, by now, have decided which items to retain, which to modify and which should be discarded. Items which fall into the last category because of the difficulty of finding plausible options but which nevertheless appear to be appropriate for a given objective can sometimes be salvaged for presentation in a true/false format. Gradually files of items of known difficulty can be built which, in the long run, greatly economize on time and effort in the preparation of future tests. Notice, however, a rather stringent limitation in what has been done so far: item difficulties are sample dependent. It is certain that the values will vary from sample to sample. Our item number 32 in this chapter would obtain a proportion of near zero if administered to an average group of seven year olds and near 1.0 if taken by A level students of mathematics (one or two might make careless errors). This, of course, is an extreme example since if items are written to satisfy the criteria of the teaching objective they would not be applicable to the learning by pupils ranging from seven to 18 years of age. Nevertheless, the point still holds with reference to different ability groups within an age band. If the items are for use with a representative 'all-ability group' (as would be the case with the mathematics test taken by all entrants to a comprehensive school or by all on transfer from junior to middle school) and the teacher can be sure he or she is using them on a similar group each year, item difficulty values would be expected to remain relatively stable provided similar teaching programmes have been followed. The Rasch technique (described in chapter 10) is designed to overcome the sampling dependency of the difficulty indices, however. Although problems with that technique remain, its use by the APU is likely to increase its importance to the work of classroom teachers.

CONSTRUCTING THE ESSAY TYPE

This is probably the most extensively used type of item in Britain outside mathematics and the physical sciences. Although it is not much loved by measurement theorists, who have demonstrated its deficiencies over many years, it remains a standard device for the assessment of achievement over a wide range of the curriculum. Many who hold the objective test in the deepest suspicion have continued to set essays, and generations of learners at all levels have been invited to 'write brief notes', 'to explain', 'to discuss', 'to describe', 'to compare and contrast', and so on, on a wide variety of topics.

As a working definition the essay may be thought of as a test item which requires the respondent to compose a response in sentence form, and in which the productions cannot be regarded as correct or incorrect but, rather, vary in a number of respects in quality or merit which experts in the subject can recognize and evaluate.

At a superficial level essay tests are the easiest possible to prepare: it takes only a few minutes to permutate the standard introductory phrases and a variety of topics. Yet this ease is deceptive. Not only is it difficult to decide what essays actually do assess, but, more importantly, it is difficult to know just what inferences about ability can be drawn from them. Allied to this is the subjective nature of essay marking and the frequently low agreement between markers acting independently. All this has been known for decades, so unless the persistence of essays is attributable to the sheer inertia in assessment practice there must be reasons for their longevity.

Amongst the advantages claimed for essay tests is that they uniquely assess the cluster of intellectual components required to marshal facts and present an argument; secondly, they are a versatile means whereby tests may be quickly compiled by most teachers whereas objective tests, by contrast, are popularly thought to demand mastery of a skilled technology; thirdly, the almost unquestioned assumption that the production of language and the verbalization of thought is the most scholarly of all activities, lends support to their continued use; and finally, unlike objective tests which have an undesirable effect on teaching and learning, essays are thought to encourage learners to develop study habits which will stand them in good stead in higher education.

Types B1 and B2

Very many types of essay items come under our working definition but an arbitrary classification as *restricted* (B1) or *extended* (B2) type will be sufficient for classroom purposes. In the *extended* type no limits are placed upon the respondent in regard to the type of organization to be adopted, the material adjudged to be relevant or the points to be discussed; a maximum length can, however, be specified. Typical examples might be:

(1) Compare and contrast objective with essay type tests.
(2) Describe the factors responsible for the distribution of population in India.
(3) Which inventions of the twentieth century do you consider have been most important in the well-being of people in Britain?

In both of these, children have to decide which aspects of their knowledge are relevant to the answer and which are most important; to retrieve this knowledge, organize it and present an argument or opinions in a logical manner as well as using syntax and spelling of a sufficiently high standard not to put the marker off! Many intellectual skills are involved: understanding, recall, application, synthesis, judgment, writing skills and so on, and no two productions will embody these in similar proportions.

In the restricted type, a deliberate constraint is imposed on the answer required. Example (1) in the extended version could be rewritten thus:

(4) Discuss the advantages and disadvantages of objective and essay type tests with respect to: (a) reliability; (b) validity; and (c) usefulness in evaluating teaching objectives.

In its restricted form, the specific areas of the required answer are indicated by the use of organizational headings, whilst sufficient scope for respondents to organize and express their ideas within them is retained. One advantage of the restricted form is that it increases reliability in marking and helps the less able learner: one major disadvantage is that it reduces the opportunity to assess the ability of the respondent to recall and synthesize and to impose an overall organization which is logical and progressive.

Careful construction of essay tests enables the teacher to retain some of their advantages but at the same time to elicit certain comparatively clearly defined mental processes. As examples (in no particular order and with no particular age range in mind):

(a) Understanding cause and effect

Give three reasons why more cars are sold in Britain than in Iceland.

(b) Summarizing

Summarize in 100 words or less the story of Beowulf.

(c) Decision for or against

Should the death penalty be restored for terrorist murders? Defend your answer.

(d) Application of rules or principles

Where would you weigh more, on the moon or on Mars? Explain your answer.

(e) Analysis

Why is there so much violence on football terraces?

(f) Formulating questions

Two children stole a packet of biscuits from a supermarket. What questions should the teacher ask before deciding whether to punish them?

(g) Criticism of the adequacy or relevance of a statement

Criticize or defend the statement: 'The central conflict in *Far from the Madding Crowd* is between Boldwood and Troy'.

(h) Giving examples or illustrating principles

Name three examples of the use of the lever in your home.

(i) Making comparisons

Compare trawling and drifting as methods of catching fish.

(j) Explanation

Macbeth says 'Life's but a walking shadow, a poor player,
That struts and frets his hour upon the stage'.
Explain the meaning of this statement.

Items of this kind can provide quite a stringent test of a variety of teaching objectives. Care needs to be given to the key words which indicate specifically the process required. There are, however, many pitfalls in setting and marking essay type tests. Before looking at these the claims and counter-claims for their usefulness are summarized in table 4.5.

Some General Considerations in Presenting Essay Test Items

(1) Be fair to your pupils. Children cannot write many essays in a fixed period of time. Whereas one or two badly constructed objective test items may not have

Table 4.5 — Arguments for and against the use of essay tests

Pro-essay	Anti-essay
(1) Ease of construction. Item for item, it takes much less time to prepare an extended or restricted response test than a corresponding objective test	(1) In the time available for testing, only a small part of the content of a course can be assessed by essays
(2) It has great potential for assessing the writer's ability to organize, integrate and synthesize his/her knowledge	(2) It has very low reliability (i.e. agreement amongst markers). The mark given depends too much on who reads it
(3) It encourages a range of approaches to learning, in particular 'good study habits'	(3) It presents the respondent with ambiguous options on how to respond. It involves the child in guessing what the teacher is 'looking for'
(4) It fosters the development of substantive (i.e. 'in own words') rather than rote learning	(4) An inordinate amount of time is needed to read and mark essays. The task cannot be made automatic and requires the availability of another expert if the degree of agreement is to be measured
(5) It provides great scope for exercise of the candidate's creativity	(5) Marking is too contaminated by extraneous features of a child's response: handwriting, spelling, etc.
	(6) Except in short and restricted form, the essay is not a suitable item for younger children still mastering the mechanics of writing a connected piece of prose

very serious consequences, a badly thought out essay title can be damaging.

(2)   Write the question in such a way that it indicates the level of response you are looking for. Titles that are wide open are inappropriate especially for children in primary and middle schools. Try to ensure that the title makes clear what you are looking for in the answer, or provide a structure (headings) to aid organization.

(3)   With children in primary and middle schools it is preferable to use a number of questions which require short answers rather than a few which involve long answers.

(4)   Avoid questions of the 'who' or 'what' variety: these can usually be dealt with more effectively by the objective item.

(5)   Remember that some of the advantages claimed for the essay test are less applicable for the level of maturity expected in children of primary and middle school age ranges than for older pupils. Adapt the length of the response to what may reasonably be expected of pupils of the age range being assessed. There are considerable limitations in the younger child's ability to conceptualize and organize information in free response and whilst children learn to write by writing, do not expect too much.

(6)   If the essay item is being used in norm-referenced testing do not provide optional questions. No comparisons of achievement are possible if children in a class tackle heterogeneous items of differing levels of difficulty.

(7)   Do allow time for pupils to write their answers. There is little justification for measuring handwriting speed under the guise of an essay test.

Marking Essay Tests

Generally speaking, teachers in primary and in the first years of middle schools are likely to use essay tests in assessment which are of the restricted, short answer (up to 100 words) type. Only in comprehensive schools will long answers be expected and even here (except in the 'essay question' in English language) examinations such as CSE require them comparatively infrequently. For these reasons we shall concentrate on marking the short answer type but the principles are capable of extension to longer answers of the extended variety.

We shall assume that the questions set match the teaching objectives and are prepared with the preceding points in mind. Given that all reasonable care has been taken in these important aspects two approaches to marking may be considered: these are the analytical and impressionistic (sometimes called 'global') methods.

The analytical method

This consists of the production of a check list of points considered essential to a good answer to the question. Deciding in advance which points to look for and the number of marks to be allocated to each point permits easier and fairer comparability between papers, helps consistency between markers and provides a ready-made set of points by which to help the child understand the reason for the mark given (and how he or she could have improved the answer). This last point is particularly important where the assessment is seen as part of a continuing process of formative or criterion-referenced assessment. No guidelines can be given as to an appropriate differential marking scheme since the importance of the points will depend upon the objective of the teaching. Although teachers may object that preparation of a scoring key takes more time than they can afford, it is often a way of coming to recognize the difficulties faced by pupils in answering the questions and, if the testing is competitive, it provides a basis for a demonstration that fair comparisons have been made. It should not be too onerous for use with the short answer restricted type, however. Teachers can in fact adopt a sort of 'halfway house' between analytic and impressionistic marking. The scoring key need not refer to actual points of content (as would be the case in fully analytic assessment) but to certain headings rather than making an overall global judgment as in impressionistic marking. One such sample example is given in table 4.5.

Table 4.6 — An example of a scoring key based on Diederich's scale for grading English composition in Jewett and Bisch (1965).

---

1 = inferior; 2 = below average; 3 = average; 4 = above average;
5 = superior

(a) Quality and development of ideas   1 2 3 4 5
     Organization and relevance   1 2 3 4 5 _____ x 5
                                          subtotal

(b) Style, individuality   1 2 3 4 5
     Wording and phrasing   1 2 3 4 5 _____ x 3
                                          subtotal

(c) Grammar, sentence construction   1 2 3 4 5
     Punctuation   1 2 3 4 5
     Spelling   1 2 3 4 5
     Legibility   1 2 3 4 5 _____ x 1
                                          subtotal   Total (%) =

The impressionistic method

This applies where teachers wish, for whatever reason, to award a grade or mark for the essay as a whole. This method is usually defended on the grounds that teachers' reading time is limited and that the purpose of the assessment is not norm-referenced. The number of points on the scale is often quite arbitrary: some may have only two points, the five-point scale is very common and, where marks are given, a maximum of ten is frequently adopted.

Many teachers will claim that a grading is of no interest to them or to their children. But, even here, verbal comments of a summary kind are often given — or even just a tick! (We are not defending these practices: one teacher said 'at least a tick shows the child you've looked at it'). Where the marking or acknowledgement of the essay is only of this kind, the purpose in setting the essay is presumably to provide a stimulus for the child to write something. It may be that the teacher employs an implicitly analytical scheme by which to identify the strengths and weaknesses of a pupil's answer but that its purpose is purely diagnostic or to inform the direction and content of future teaching and learning activities.

If impressionistic marking is to be used in norm-referenced assessment a minimal requirement is to establish some sort of standard of comparison. Let us suppose that the marking is to a five-point scale of quality, such as

5 = superior
4 = above average
3 = average
2 = below average
1 = inferior

(the actual choice of label is unimportant for our purposes). A rather tedious method of standard setting is to prepare model answers to represent each grade. (It is not a bad thing to make teachers answer their own questions!) A less onerous method is to select from the actual answers papers to represent each grade. In public examinations experienced markers are asked independently to select answers which exemplify the grade and other examiners meet to be trained in application of the system. Rapid reading is then undertaken to place each paper in the relevant pile. In order to determine a measure of inter-judge consistency or concordance (see chapter 7 on essay reliability) a second reading should be undertaken by a further independent reader. Any discrepancy of more than one point is then resolved in consultation with a senior examiner. Admittedly little of this is likely to take place in schools, but a single teacher with, say, 30 answers could assign papers to piles on first reading and then carry out a self-imposed check to determine the level of 'self-consistency' (chapter 7). It is fairer to children to provide them with the average grades given by more than one marker (or of the teacher's two grades if they differ) and for teachers to grade only one question at a time for all papers (i.e. read all answers to question one first, then two, and so on) otherwise you switch from standard to standard and cannot hold them properly in mind).

Type B3: The Oral Test

Oral examinations are seldom held but informal assessment of oral output is one of the major sources of teachers' inferences about children. As has been argued in chapter 3 assessment of one person by another is an inevitable part of social processes, and teachers receive numerous and accumulating impressions of children from their informal observations of children's oral production. Formal use of oral tests is found most frequently in universities, in secondary school examinations of a foreign language, in assessments by educational psychologists and, of course, in oral reading tests in primary schools. This last named is excluded from this discussion because whilst other varieties of the oral test are a kind of 'unwritten essay' reading from print cannot be thus regarded. Yet, potentially, the oral is of great use with children who for various reasons are unable to take written tests; if conducted with skill it can reassure the anxious child and can exhibit a flexibility for eliciting a variety of responses in interaction with pupils not permitted by static written tests.

In this section the concern is simply to draw the attention of teachers to the advantages and limitations in the use of oral information. Probably the chief limitations are: it is time-consuming, transient (unless recorded), limited in its sampling width, especially vulnerable to halo effect (chapter 3) and low in reliability. Chief amongst its advantages are its flexibility in enabling the teacher to assess a level of knowledge and understanding especially where the pupil has writing difficulties, the way it permits a free response by pupils and it can institute a very stringent test of a child's ability to reason in a specified context (most of Piaget's information on children's thinking came from the use of oral tests).

To some extent study of the presentation of oral tests is the study of the art of questioning. Very often the child gives an incorrect response not from lack of knowledge but because wording is not clear or because of misinterpretation of what was asked for, or what was only partially heard. To spell out the implications of these difficulties for the assessment of a child's oral response to questions would require a book in itself. All teachers will have been aware of the dangers in the impulsive assessment of a child's oral work, although use of questioning over a period of time will inevitably lead to their developing generalized assessments of this ('takes little or no part in oral work'; 'quick and eager to answer'; 'always ready with an intelligent answer' are typical of this type of description made). If teachers wish to incorporate an assessment of oral work, it is advisable that this be done systematically if any comparisons are to be made between children. *Ad hoc* assessment is far too easily influenced by halo effect resulting from speech style, dialect or accent to form the basis of the study of children's capabilities. Whilst it is always dangerous to infer lack of knowledge from the absence of response to a question in whatever medium it has been posed, different factors inhibit the exploration of a child's knowledge through oral questioning (especially in the presence of other children) from those involved in testing in the written medium.

Some of the principles of good oral assessment are similar to those proposed for the setting of objective items. High on the list is the need to set questions which are not too long nor involve subordinate clauses, especially with younger children whose span of apprehension and attention is limited. Similarly, teachers should make clear that a question is to be posed either by an introductory phrase (such as 'I'm going to ask you some questions; listen carefully') or by the use of familiar interrogatives. It is also advisable to state the terms in which the answer is required ('Where is Paris?' is much less satisfactory than 'In what country is Paris situated?') and the context which makes the question meaningful if this is not obvious from the question itself.

Inevitably, slipshod questioning will occur. The important point is that it should not be allowed to occur if the teacher wishes to draw inferences about ability from the answers received. Quite recently the writer observed a lesson in a school in the centre of a large industrial city where all the children were second generation immigrants. A discussion on safety in the home was taking place with infant pupils aged five to six years. By and large, the children were inattentive when suddenly the question: 'What must we remember to take out at night Mohammed?' was posed. Mohammed was not the only participant to find the point of the teacher's question somewhat elusive!

Item Analysis of Essay Tests

Most of the methods of item analysis described in earlier

sections of this chapter are inappropriate for essay type tests. The essay 'item', by its nature, assesses a very large number of intellectual skills. It is obviously possible, if analytic marking is adopted, to break down the knowledge components and theoretically possible to evaluate the extent to which alternative organizational headings elicit or fail to elicit the required factual knowledge. Where a correct answer is supplied as one of four or five options as in an objective test and the item is refined as a result of item analysis, failure to respond correctly can be attributed with a high degree of confidence to a property of the respondent. But failure to supply the information required by the marking scheme used in analytic assessment of an essay can never be thus attributed: it is always possible that it is the item which is at fault. The fact that one cannot determine in advance the responses to essay items is one of their most attractive features: interesting answers are often produced to items which are not worthy of them!

Unfortunately, even in higher education, students respond to essay titles by writing all they can think of about the key concepts *in* the question but at the same time overlooking — possibly deliberately — the relational terms or key verbs in the title which specify the demands made upon them by the teacher who set the question. (One would not normally expect qualitatively different responses from a group of teachers in training to essays which begin 'discuss', 'evaluate', 'examine', despite the clear differences in meaning between these three terms, for example).

The analysis of essay items, therefore, is best undertaken as follows:

(1) Record your impressions of the answers to given essay questions, in particular the features of the responses which match the demands of the analytic marking scheme (these will be 'good' items) and where the responses 'do not answer the question' or omit the fundamental components of a model answer (these might well be 'poor' items).

(2) Note the frequency with which different items/titles are chosen if optional. Where items are consistently ignored,

try to determine whether this is because they do not match the course content or whether they contain features which are perceived by the respondents as conferring particular complexity. This will be done in consultation with the students themselves.

(3) Try out substantially the same item but with alternative organizational headings. See which is associated with the most satisfactory answers. Compare responses to an item when presented in its extended form with those to its restricted form. (The restricted form of items, is, however, almost always to be recommended for use with children up to, say, fifth form level, except, of course, in English language.)

(4) Examine your own literary style to eliminate ambiguities and excess verbiage from titles. This, of course, is mainly an aspect of preparation, but study of the responses to items often indicates the presence of ambiguities unidentified at the preparation stage.

The chapter up to this point has been concerned with the following aspects of teacher-made test construction and use:

(1) Identifying the potential strengths of teacher-made tests.
(2) Matching items to the objectives of teaching.
(3) Preparing the specification table, or test blueprint.
(4) Deciding upon the type of test item.
(5) The preparation of various types of objective test item: a comparison of their advantages and disadvantages, with examples.
(6) Methods of item analysis and improvement.
(7) Preparing and marking essay type tests. Advantages and disadvantages of essay tests.
(8) Analysing the results of essay type tests.

ASSEMBLING THE TEST

During the course of this discussion we have seen that different types of item tend to be suited to the assessment of different types of intellectual objective. There is no one-to-one correspondence here: the multiple choice test is potentially versatile and can be used to assess objectives at all levels of Bloom's taxonomy, for example. But the essay type of test does call for the integration of a number of intellectual skills in a way that no other type of item can. We have seen, however, that this advantage can be achieved only at the expense of lowered objectivity and reliability. One question that arises, therefore, is how does one assemble an instrument for the assessment of a fairly lengthy course of study which has sought to enable learners to acquire a variety of knowledge, skills and concepts across a relatively large content area? We have seen how a specification table aids the construction of a test to assess comparatively 'compact' sets of teaching objectives but, as such, it leaves open the question of the type of item best suited to the assessment of each objective. There will, of course, be many constraints on the final form of a test and it is all too easy to throw together a variety of items which, though good in themselves, do not constitute an appropriate mixture overall by which to assess children's abilities in subject areas.

To specify what the overall test instrument *should* look like would be to run the risk of violating one of the cardinal principles of assessment: teacher control of the objectives, emphasis and evaluation of the teaching. A few writers have, however, tried to set up guidelines to help the assembly and arrangement of tests. Gronlund (1971) has suggested that the test will be arranged in such a way that items progress from lower level intellectual abilities (recall of knowledge) to the most complex that can reasonably be expected from knowledge of the teaching that has taken place and level of ability of the group for which the test is intended. Thus tests might begin with simple recall as measured by the completion or true/false type of item, progress through short answer or multiple choice items to the essay type of item. Keeping items of similar type together will make it easier for the examinee to understand and comply with the instructions without switching from one type to another and, of course, make the test easier to mark. It also helps if the actual items within types are as homogeneous as possible in respect of the teaching objectives. (In multiple choice items those that deal with say, knowledge of terminology should be kept together and those that deal with knowledge of principles should be separated from those which deal with comprehension, and so on). This will aid the teacher considerably in his or her analysis of results and in the identification of those objectives which have been most successfully mastered, least successfully, and so on. If items have been the subject of a try-out and difficulty values are known it seems desirable for them to be arranged in order of difficulty.

Many other technical recommendations on the layout of tests could, of course, be made. Thorndike (1971) provides a useful, comprehensive and comparatively brief source of information of value to teachers in these aspects. The chapter will conclude, however, with brief reference to the psychological rather than the technical aspects of test taking and administration.

PSYCHOLOGICAL ASPECTS OF 'BEING ASSESSED'

In chapter 6, some of the most prevalent sources of variation in test performance will be described. Those sources which interfere with the measurement of the characteristic in question are known as sources of error variance. Error is inherent in every score and assessment but the purpose in testing is to try to reduce as far as possible the influence of factors other than those embedded in the knowledge and intellectual skills the test is ostensibly measuring, so that any differences between children which result can be attributed with reasonable confidence to real difference in the human characteristic being assessed. One assumption which is commonly made is that the child being tested is doing the best he or she can do at that time. The importance of motivation to a child's test score has been repeatedly demonstrated by controlled studies (for example, by Flanagan, 1955, and McClelland, 1966) and by common sense. It is true that children differ in the extent to which they 'lay blame' on external or internal factors for their own performances. Children who attribute their successes and failures to the amount of their effort are sometimes described as 'internals'; children who see success because the task is 'easy' and failure when it is 'difficult' are correspondingly described as 'externals' (Bar-Tal, 1978). But all learners are aware that sometimes they 'try hard', at other times they do not. Lack of effort in test taking has various origins: in some cases it may reflect lack of interest in the test because it is not expected that the results can be put to positive advantage. Equally, lack of effort may be a consequence of a defensive attitude on the part of the child in the face of anticipated failure (Goldman, 1971). No matter how able, a child who has no motivation to perform is not going to obtain a high score on the test. Thus we distinguish the motivation to acquire the knowledge and skills which are being assessed by the test from the motivation to exhibit that knowledge in the test itself.

We have already implied that motivation to take the test is greater where the child sees the payoff in taking it (the payoff can take many forms, of course). But motivation is also more likely where the child sees the point of what he or she is being asked to do. Donaldson (1978) has quite convincingly demonstrated that very young children can think about problems which make sense to them but are defeated by problems involving similar logic where the task presented is arbitrary or is set in an abstract context. The implications for pupils who are 'culturally disadvantaged' or who are naive in test-taking skills are clear. We take it for granted that children will understand the point of the 'testing game' we are asking them to play but it seems very unlikely that young children especially will understand the unspoken customs (particularly where the tester is an outsider chiefly interested in obtaining data for his research project!).

To sum up, we can go some way towards minimizing the error due to motivational differences amongst pupils if we ensure that they understand the point of the assessment and the benefits which may result from accurate assessment. Secondly we can see to it that children who are not 'test-wise' are instructed in the principles and procedures of test taking. This is particularly important in norm-referenced assessment: in criterion-referenced assessment the test is continuous with the learning. Thirdly, testing may be more acceptable, particularly to older learners, where their part in helping them to learn is explained and where the entire procedure and content of the tests is fair. In carrying out standardized testing it is important to adhere to the manual's instructions, but the motivational levels of pupils in normal classroom testing are influenced to a far greater extent by a classroom climate and teacher—pupil relationships which are psychologically supportive of the individual.

Closely allied to the motivational aspects of testing is the topic of anxiety. There are two chief views of this ubiquitous phenomenon. Some psychologists believe that anxiety is a pre-disposition or state of the individual looking, as it were, for an object or outcome to which to attach itself. Others have seen anxiety as a learned response to a threatening stimulus. The actual role of anxiety in human performance seems to vary with the individual and with the degree of complexity of the task he or she is asked to attempt (Gaudry and Spielberger, 1974) but the experience of anxiety in taking a test or when the pupil knows an assessment is taking place is probably universal. Psychologists have concluded that whilst a certain amount of anxiety enhances the general alertness of many pupils, test anxiety tends to depress test performance. Others, of course, are 'intellectually frozen' by it! (Karmel and Karmel, 1978). Some writers have claimed social class differences in the extent and productive use of anxiety, however, but there is no universally effective practice of ensuring optimal anxiety in test taking. It would be futile to try to remove it altogether. Everyone experiences anxiety in taking tests especially if the results are to have long-term implications for the type of secondary school to be attended, if vocational opportunity is at stake or where the label 'fail' is to be applied. Regular formative classroom assessment of learning is generally free from the worst excesses of those practices and teachers will normally seek to inform pupils of the purposes of testing and the uses to be made of the results in as relaxed a manner as possible. The teacher who is aware of the limitations of the inferences which can be drawn from any assessment will probably emphasize its formative aspects and reduce to a minimum the occasions on which judgments which appear to be final are made.

It is not unknown for teachers themselves to feel threatened by tests and this anxiety can easily be communicated to the pupils. This is likely to be more prevalent in external assessment or in programmes which attempt to evaluate teacher effectiveness. Knowledge of the effects of anxiety on individual pupils is just one of the factors to be taken into account in trying to reach a just appraisal of a child's work.

5

The Statistical Description and Interpretation of Test Scores

In an idealistic educational system, free from competition and comparison, most assessment would probably be of the criterion-referenced type. The purpose of the criterion-referenced mode of assessment, it will be remembered, is twofold:

(1) the objective description of the strengths and weaknesses of a child's performance in relation to a specified standard (this is sometimes known as 'telling what the child can actually do'); and
(2) (where what is being learned can be thought of as organized hierarchically or sequentially) the level of mastery attained of a given objective.

Few problems arise in the description and interpretation of criterion-referenced scores. If an objective has been described as in the case of the addition of numbers or the solution of linear equations in chapter 3, and a level of mastery set at 90% (nine out of ten items testing each objective correctly answered) then that is what mastery means, by definition. But few, if any, schools have given up the more traditional forms of assessment, and other interpretations of the scores obtained are required. Questions typically posed about the interpretation of scores include: 'What is the average score?'; 'How did the children taught mathematics in set A compare with those in set B?'; 'How much overlap is there between the scores in the two groups?'; 'You say Mary is outstanding in biology, but how much better is she than the average for her class?'; 'I see John has a standardized score on the English test of 132. What does that really mean?'

In order to answer questions such as these or to give a really informative answer to the parents' anxious query 'How is she getting on?' some understanding of the statistical methods basic to educational measurement is required. There are already very many excellent books available and one is inclined, pessimistically, to believe that if readers cannot achieve a basic competence from the mass of material now available one further chapter is likely to be of no significance. Yet it is hoped that readers will appreciate that good reasons exist for attempting to master the elementary ideas contained in this chapter and be encouraged by the fact that the arithmetic required is well within the competence of many of the pupils who are being assessed! Moreover, many of the cheap electronic calculators now available will perform some of the basic operations to be described here and greatly reduce the drudgery of number crunching.

LEVELS OF MEASUREMENT

It is undoubtedly the case that naive beliefs held by teachers about measurement have helped to inhibit a high level of professional expertise in assessment methods and to maintain current primitive standards of interpretation of test scores even in some schools which pride themselves on their 'academic excellence'. (Such schools are, of course, usually referring to the achievements of pupils rather than of themselves.) Quite obviously, measurement of children's ability and achievement differs in several fundamental respects from measurement of their physical attributes, say their height or weight. In the first place, when we measure height we do so by employing a series of real numbers having order, an origin (nought) and a fixed distance between adjacent numerals. Because we have a zero point which actually indicates the absence of height we are able to carry out certain algebraic operations on the numerals: for example, we can say that John who is five feet ten inches tall is twice as tall as his young brother who is two feet eleven inches; and that Mary, who is five feet two inches tall is that much taller than Susan (five feet nought inches) as is Susan than Helen (four feet ten inches). But the first type of statement cannot be made about mathematics scores. Even if Nigel *scored* nought on a test it would make no sense to say that he had *no* mathematics ability or that he knew *no* mathematics. (Teachers may often be heard to say this kind of thing but since one could easily put into the test items which all children could answer, the scale of ability in mathematics has no true zero point.) Scales which have a zero point, then, are often called *ratio scales* of measurement but we do not have any such scales for educational data.

For practical purposes, educators often assume that their scales of measurement have some of the properties of ratio scales, but not the zero point. To revert to our hypothetical mathematics test: John scored 50 marks, Peter 40 but Norman only 20 marks out of a total of 75. This is usually interpreted to mean that the difference between Peter's score and Norman's score is twice as great as that between John's score and Peter's score. This interpretation is based on the assumption that intervals along the scale are fixed: for this reason the scale is called the *interval type*. Quite a lot of assessment data is of this type.

Quite often, in education, the numerical data which are obtained by assessment do not imply fixed intervals along a scale. We could use our mathematics test to put children in rank order. Although the original scores were on an interval scale the distances between abilities in adjacent ranks are not. Indeed, in a class list, for example, the top two may be close together in raw scores and get many more marks than the third, but the mere statement of the ranks ('first', 'second', 'third') would disguise this fact. Because this type of measurement scale has order but lacks properties of distance and of a zero point it is known as an *ordinal* scale of measurement.

Some writers have argued that there is an even simpler scale of measurement than this. It is known as the *nominal* scale and really only consists of the assignment of numbers in order to differentiate whole categories of objects or events. Thus one might, for purposes of data analysis, use 'one' to represent the girls, 'nought' to stand for the boys in a class. In this case 'one' does not mean 'more than nought': we have neither the concept of order, nor of distance and no zero point. If we adopt Stevens's (1946) definition of measurement as assigning numerals according to rules, this would presumably qualify as measurement but we have no further use for nominal measurement in this chapter.

What is the relevance of this distinction between levels of measurement for teachers? In the first place it is an important aspect of the meaning (interpretation) of data. For example, the statement 'John scored 50 in a mathematics test' cannot be fully interpreted because the scale is an interval one and has no zero point. Secondly, different types of score allow different kinds of arithmetical and statistical operations to be carried out on them. We can never interpret scores to mean that one child has half, twice or three times as much ability in the subject as another child, for the same reason (no zero point). Thus, if scores are of the ordinal or interval type they cannot be interpreted as if they were on ratio scales and they require different kinds of processing if they are to be made meaningful.

In the examples which follow we shall assume the data obtained in education to be interval type unless otherwise stated. Actually it is not all that easy to decide which type of score we have. Take grades, for example. We can say that grade B is higher (more of the attribute used to grade the child) than grade C which in turn is higher than grade D, without being contentious (i.e. we can claim ordinal properties for the scale). But can we claim that the interval between adjacent grades remains the same? Almost certainly not. Yet grades are often treated as if they were on an interval scale and extensively used in averaging and so on, especially in the USA.

SUMMARIZING THE DATA

Because interval and ordinal scores have no zero point, we often need to interpret them in terms of the distribution of scores to which they belong. Tabulating the distribution in one way or another is a first step in summarizing the data. Table 5.1 represents the scores obtained in a geography test taken by 32 children aged 12–13 years. They appear in

Table 5.1 — Scores of 32 pupils on geography test (maximum mark = 50).

Pupil	Score	Pupil	Score	Pupil	Score	Pupil	Score
Paul A	25	Charles E	40	Nigel L	29	Anne S	35
William B	36	Richard E	26	Geoffrey L	43	John S	34
Jean B	33	Robert F	21	Sandra M	36	Susan S	31
Mary C	24	Dean G	22	Elizabeth M	38	Sarah T	30
Peter C	32	Margaret H	38	James N	28	Clive T	42
Sylvia D	41	William H	23	Dennis O	39	Anthony W	34
Ken D	33	Norman K	35	Joan P	37	Marlene W	27
Jim D	37	Peter K	27	John R	37	Jane W	39

alphabetical order just as they were recorded in the teacher's mark book.

The purpose of statistical treatment is to describe scores like these and to bring out their meaning by relating any one score to certain important characteristics of the scores of the entire group. One simple way to begin is by putting the scores in rank order. It is then easy to tell at a glance who has achieved the highest score and who the lowest score, how far apart these are (the 'range'), how often a particular score occurs (the 'frequency') and so on. Ranking is usually done from highest to lowest score using a table such as table 5.2. A slight reduction in the space taken up can be achieved as in the third and fourth columns of the table where each score and its frequency (the number of times it occurs in the group) is tabulated.

Notice that several ranks are 'tied'. Two children scored 39, for example: where this happens it is usual to assign the average of the ranks to each score. Thus, three children scored 37 and as there are eight scores higher than 37 these are assigned the average of ranks nine, ten and 11. Quite a lot of ties have occurred, but this often happens with real data.

Several simple things can be done with these data to bring out their meaning.

Finding the Inclusive Range of the Scores

The highest score obtained in the geography test was 43 and

Table 5.2 — Geography scores in table 5.1 in rank order with frequencies.

Score order	Rank	Raw score	frequency (f)
43	1	43	1
42	2	42	1
41	3	41	1
40	4	40	1
39 39	5.5	39	2
		38	2
38 38	7.5	37	3
		36	2
37 37 37	10	35	2
		34	2
		33	2
36 36	11.5	32	1
		31	1
35 35	14.5	30	1
		29	1
34 34	16.5	28	1
		27	2
33 33	18.5	26	1
		25	1
32	20	24	1
31	21	23	1
30	22	22	1
29	23	21	1
28	24		
27 27	25.5		n = 32
26	27		
25	28		
24	29		
23	30		
22	31		
21	32		

the lowest 21. In statistics we think of each score not as a point on a scale but as occupying the mid-point of an interval on it. For example, 43 covers the interval from 42.5 to 43.5, 21 from 20.5 to 21.5, and so on. The reason for this will become clear later. *The inclusive range* is therefore found as follows:

$$\text{(highest score - lowest score)} + 1 \qquad [5.1]$$

In our example the inclusive range using formula [5.1] is:

$$(43 - 21) + 1 = 23$$

Some writers report the *range* of scores. The range of scores in table 5.2 is simply 22 (i.e. highest - lowest). (Notice that for some types of scores, the interval would not be equal to the score ± 0.5. For example, if we asked people to report their age *last birthday* all people who report themselves as, say 35 years old would lie within the interval '35 years old today to 36 years old tomorrow'. Here the interval would be 35.00 to 35.99 years. If, however, we asked them their age to the *nearest birthday* the interval would be 34.5 to 35.5 with a mid-point of 35.)

Constructing a Frequency Polygon

This is a simple form of graph. A figure is drawn in which the mid-point of each score interval has been placed along the horizontal ('x') axis and the frequency up the vertical ('y') axis. For our example, to simplify, the scores have been grouped into *class intervals* of two. Class intervals, frequencies and frequency polygon are shown in table 5.3 and figure 5.1.

The same data could just as easily be depicted using the *histogram,* familiar to most pupils in primary schools but not shown here. Where large numbers of scores are obtained covering a much larger range, class intervals may have to be as large as, say five.

Using Quantiles

This is a very useful method of describing scores and of giving meaning to the score of any pupil. *Quantiles* is the name of a group of examples of which the *percentile* is the most familiar and the only type to be calculated here. A quantile is the point on the scale which divides the scores in a distribution into a number of equal groups. For example, if the entire

Table 5.3 — Class intervals and frequencies of 32 scores used to
construct the frequency polygon of figure 5.1

Score	20–21	22–23	24–25	26–27	28–29	30–31
Frequency	1	2	2	3	2	2

Score	32–33	34–35	36–37	38–39	40–41	42–43
Frequency	3	4	5	4	2	2

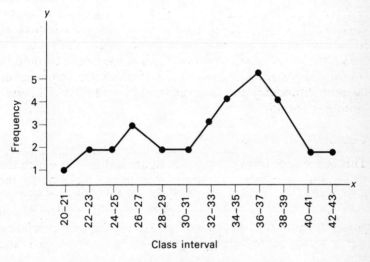

Figure 5.1   Frequency polygon of 32 scores in table 5.1.

range of scores is divided into four quarters then this can be
accomplished by three points on the scale called *quartiles*
(Q_1, Q_2 and Q_3). When the entire group is divided into 100
sets of scores this is done using 99 points known as *percen-
tiles* (P_1, P_2, . . . , P_{99}). Similarly, *deciles* (D_1, D_2, . . . , D_9)
divide the scores into ten groups. Data in table 5.3 are used
below to show how percentiles are determined.

Determining percentiles
Scores must be arranged from highest to lowest, frequencies
plotted and the cumulative frequency determined as in table
5.4. The cumulative frequency is simply the number of scores

Table 5.4 — How to determine percentiles in the frequency distribution.

Score	Frequency	Cumulative frequency
42–43	2	32
40–41	2	30
38–39	4	28
36–37	5	24
34–35	4	19
32–33	3	15
30–31	2	12
28–29	2	10
26–27	3	8
24–25	2	5
22–23	2	3
20–21	1	1
	$n = 32$	

at or below the score. For example, the number of scores in or below interval 24–25 is five. We shall illustrate by finding the 75th percentile (P_{75}).

The summary of steps to calculate P_{75} is as follows:

(1)   Find $0.75n = 24$

(2)   Find lower limit of score class containing 24th score:

$$L = 35.5 \text{ (i.e. } 36.0 - 0.5)$$

(3)   Subtract the cumulative frequency up to L from 24:

$$24 - 19 = 5$$

(4)   Divide results of (3) by the value for f in the interval containing the 24th score and multiply by the width (2):

$$5/5 = 1, 1 \times 2 = 2$$

(5)   Add result of (4) to L:

$$P_{75} = 35.5 + 2.0$$
$$= 37.5$$

This result could have been obtained by inspection since 25% of scores (eight out of 32) are either in or greater than the interval whose mid-point is 38.5. The method is generalizable to the determination of all percentiles, however, and to the calculation of other quantiles simply by placing the required coefficient of n in step (1).

The advantages of quantiles are that they provide a useful summary of data which is easily obtained and understood by children and parents alike. Simply reporting the inclusive range of scores and providing certain percentile values enables the reader to build up a picture of the data quickly and easily with a little practice. Moreover, as we shall see later, these values can easily be related to other measures which summarize distributions, provided certain assumptions are made about the shape of the distribution of scores.

Constructing a Smooth Curve or Ogive

The word 'ogive' (pronounced 'ojive') is an architectural term which describes the shape of an arch. It has wide use in the representation of scores and it can also be used in their standardization. Table 5.5 and figure 5.2 show the construc-

Table 5.5 – Construction of an ogive for data of table 5.4.

Score	Cumulative frequency	Rounded cumulative percentage
42–43	32	100
40–41	30	94
38–39	28	88
36–37	24	75
34–35	19	59
32–33	15	47
30–31	12	38
28–29	10	31
26–27	8	25
24–25	5	16
22–23	3	9
20–21	1	3

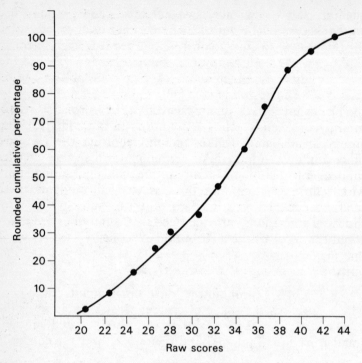

Figure 5.2   Ogive constructed from data of table 5.5.

tion of an ogive. As ours is a small group of only 32 scores, it is best to smooth the curve out a little by omitting some of the points on each side of the line so that the curve provides the best possible fit to the trend.

The first two columns in the table are taken from table 5.4. The third column — the rounded cumulative percentage — is found by expressing the cumulative frequency as a percentage of 32. For example, class interval 32–33 has an entry for the cumulative frequency of 15. Thus,

$$\frac{15}{32} \times 100 = 46.88 = 47\% \text{ approximately}$$

The advantages of the ogive will be demonstrated when the standardization of marks is described in a later section. Note, however, that the raw scores could easily be replaced by any quantile points (e.g. percentiles). This would have no effect on the shape of the ogive.

Finding the 'Central Tendency' of the Scores

It is often the case that frequency polygons, ogives or even the elementary histogram depict all a teacher needs to know in order to interpret the scores of children in relation to the group of scores to which they belong. Nevertheless, there are other kinds of information we may require. If we continue to think of the horizontal axis in all our graphs as a number line, we often need to know just where along that line the scores tend to occur. Referring back to the frequency polygon shown in figure 5.1 we can see that the scores tend to bunch together towards the higher values in the range. There is only one major hump corresponding to the class interval 36–37 but the majority of scores tend to occur close to that hump on either side of it. Three measures of central tendency are particularly useful in describing a distribution of this kind: (a) the mode; (b) the median; and (c) the arithmetic mean.

The mode

This is the most *frequently occurring* score. Adopting the mid-point of the interval we would say that the mode of the *grouped* data in table 5.3 is 36.5. Going back to the un-grouped data of table 5.2, the mode is 37. If all scores occur-red with equal frequency (a most unlikely event) the group of scores has *no mode.* If two scores which are not adjacent to one another occur with equal frequency we describe the distribution as bi-modal. Sometimes distributions have one *major* mode and several *minor* modes.

The median

This is the score which divides the distribution into halves such that half the scores are greater, half lower than the median. In other words it is the 50th percentile (P_{50}). Inspection of table 5.5 shows that it must occur somewhere between scores 33 and 34 since there are 47% of scores up to and including that interval. As a rough approximation to the median this method of inspection will often be sufficient for descriptive purposes. You can find the median by the method described for the calculation of percentiles but finding P_{50}, not P_{75} as in our example, alongside table 5.4. Using that method — the reader should check — the median is found to be 34.0. The results of the steps:

(1) $0.5n = 16$
(2) $L = 33.5$
(3) $16 - 15 = 1$
(4) $1/4 = 0.25, 0.25 \times 2 = 0.5$
(5) $33.5 + 0.50 = 34.0$

You will get away with less arithmetic if you have an odd number of scores without ties. In this case the median is the middle score when they are placed in rank order: for example, the scores 23, 28, 29, 33, 39 give a median of 29. If the scores are an even number of untied scores the median is half way between the two middle scores when these have been ranked: e.g., for the scores 36, 38, 41, 43, 49, 58

$$\text{median} = (41 + 43)/2 = 42$$

The arithmetic mean
The mean is by far the most useful measure of central tendency. There are in fact several means (the arithmetic mean; the geometric mean; the harmonic mean) but we are concerned here only with the *arithmetic mean* more commonly known as the familiar *average*. If we obtain a distribution of a large number (say several hundred) of scores, we shall almost certainly find that the mode (which can be obtained at a glance), the median and the mean are very close to one another. One difference between them, however, is that the mode and median are affected only little by extreme (or 'wayout') scores, whereas the mean is affected by them. This anticipates our need for some measure of variability as well as of central tendency in the full description and interpretation of scores.

The calculation of arithmetic mean poses no problems especially if a calculator is available: it is simply the sum of the scores divided by the number of scores. It is very useful, however, to use symbols to stand for these operations. The formula is:

$$\overline{x} = \frac{\sum\limits_{1}^{n} x_i}{n} \qquad [5.2]$$

where

$\overline{x}$ = arithmetic mean (pronounced 'x bar')

$\sum\limits_{1}^{n}$ = 'sum of'

(the subscript indicates where to start summing, i.e. 1, the first score, and the superscript where to stop, i.e. the nth score. These are normally taken as understood and will be omitted from future examples.)

x_i = the score of child i

n = the number of scores

Applying formula [5.2] to our data in table 5.1 we find that

$\sum\limits_{1}^{n}$ = 1052 n = 32

Hence

$\overline{x}$ = 1052/32 = 32.875

If our scores are grouped as in table 5.3 a very close approximation can be reached using formula [5.3]:

$$\overline{x} \cong \frac{\Sigma f_i \text{ (mid-point)}}{n} \qquad [5.3]$$

where

$\overline{x}$ = arithmetic mean

$\cong$ stands for 'approximately equal to',

Table 5.6 — Calculation of mean-grouped frequency data.

Frequency	Mid-point	f_i (mid-point)
2	42.5	85.0
2	40.5	81.0
4	38.5	154.0
5	36.5	182.5
4	34.5	138.0
3	32.5	97.5
2	30.5	61.0
2	28.5	57.0
3	26.5	79.5
2	24.5	49.0
2	22.5	45.0
1	20.5	20.5
		Σf_i (mid-point) = 1050

$$f_i = \text{frequency}$$

'mid-point' stands for 'mid-point of class interval',

$$n = \text{number of scores}$$

The product of the frequency and mid-points is shown in table 5.6. For table 5.6 the approximation to the mean is very close indeed:

$$\bar{x} \cong 1050/32 = 32.81$$

(compared with 32.87 for the ungrouped calculation).

In general, the greater the width of the class interval (only two points in our example) and the larger the number of scores in each, the poorer will be the approximation to the mean using this method. This is because the method assumes that the scores within an interval are evenly distributed throughout its length, which is never the case.

Let us just pause for a moment to compare the properties of our three measures of central tendency:

mean   takes all the scores into account but is influenced by the (possibly few) very high or very low scores;

Table 5.7 — A distribution of criterion-referenced scores.

Score	Frequency	
10	2	
9	4	'Masters'
8	5	Criterion score = 8
7	—	
6	—	
5	—	
4	—	
3	—	
2	2	
1	5	'Non-masters'
0	2	
	$n = 20$	

median   is to be preferred where an index relatively un-
          affected by extreme scores is required;
mode   is best where teachers wish to name the single score
          which best represents a group's performance. It is,
          however, very unsuitable in small groups.

A word of warning
It is, of course, possible to calculate mean, median and mode
for *any* set of scores or grades. But it is not always terribly
informative to do so. We can cite criterion-referenced scores
as an example. Suppose we have a ten item test for the attainment of an objective (with a specified mastery level of 80%).
During the course of a few weeks, 20 children were tested for
mastery and the scores obtained were found to be distributed
in table 5.7. Notice that the objective was such that children
either attained it or they failed to attain it by quite a considerable margin of scores. (Such a distribution is often found
in examination of students' mastery of statistics. Those who
find it easy, find it very easy; those who do not, find it very
difficult!)

Values for the central tendency of these scores are:

mean   = 5.35
median = 7.70
mode   = 8.0 and 1.0 (the curve is bimodal)

It is obvious that the mean and median of these scores tell you nothing very helpful about them. No child scores within two and a half units of the mean in either direction, for example. In this example the mode is probably the most descriptive value since it has two values and enables the recipient of this information to reconstruct a visual image of the shape of the distribution far more easily and accurately than either of the others, which are positively misleading. This is one reason why comparisons between average incomes in various countries in the EEC are not particularly meaningful in the absence of other measures of the shape of the distribution.

The Shapes of Distributions

If we look again at the frequency polygon for table 5.3 and redraw it somewhat idealistically, its general shape is something like the curve shown in figure 5.3 with its approximate mean (33) shown by the broken line.

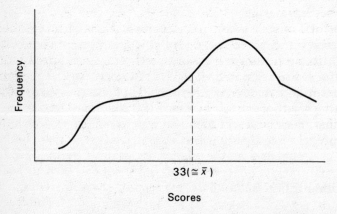

Figure 5.3   Smoothed frequency polygon for data in table 5.3.

This distribution is certainly not symmetrical about the line which represents its mean because the scores tended to bunch near the high end of the distribution. Such a distribution is known as a 'negatively skewed' distribution because its distortion is mainly at the low end of the range. Had the test been rather more difficult we might have expected scores to bunch near the low end. The curve would look something like that shown in figure 5.4.

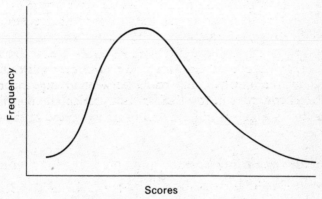

Figure 5.4   A positively skewed distribution.

The distribution is described as 'positively skewed' because its distortion is at the high end of the range.

One distribution which has been used extensively in test construction and in the interpretation of data in all branches of science and social science is the so-called 'normal distribution'. Its properties can be described mathematically but it is helpful at this stage to gain a visual idea of it. Its chief feature is that it is perfectly symmetrical about its mean, which also coincides with the mode and median. Its 'cocked-hat' shape is familiar to nearly everyone: normal curves belong to a family of curves having similar shape.

PROBABILITY AND THE NORMAL CURVE

A great deal is involved in a full understanding of the proper-

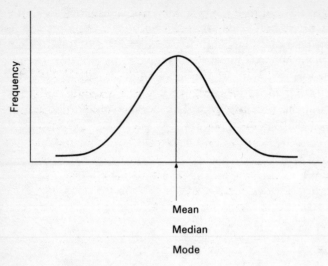

Figure 5.5   A normal distribution.

ties of the normal distribution and only a brief and intuitive idea can be given here. Nevertheless, teachers should try to grasp its fundamental properties since they are involved in the understanding of a great deal of measurement theory. This section can, however, be treated as a digression and readers may, if they wish, skip the text as far as the section on measures of variation (p. 154).

Readers will almost certainly have some grasp of the concept of probability. One basic concept is that of sample space. It describes the number of events that could have occurred. For example, a bag containing four white objects and six red objects has ten points in sample space. Every time one object is taken from the bag, a white object or a red object could be retrieved. Thus white objects occupy four points in a sample space (out of ten) and red objects six points in sample space (out of ten). Similarly blue, black, purple objects occupy *no* points in that sample space. Other everyday examples of events in sample space could be the number of people in a room (the points being occupied by men, women and children), the number of million passenger miles flown in one year by British Airways, the number of times a pedestrian crossing is used in an average day, and so on.

Formally, the probability of an event is the ratio of the number of sample points which are examples of that event to the total number of points in sample space. Thus the probability of a blindfold person drawing a white object from our bag would be

$$P \text{ (white object)} = \frac{\text{no. of white objects}}{\text{total no. of points}} = \frac{4}{10} = 0.4$$

Similarly the probability of drawing a red object

$$P \text{ (red object)} = \frac{\text{no. of red objects}}{\text{total no. of points}} = \frac{6}{10} = 0.6$$

Notice that the probability of drawing *either* a white or red object

$$P \text{ (white or red object)} = \frac{\text{no. of white and red objects}}{\text{total no. of points}} = \frac{10}{10} = 1.0$$

In other words, our blindfolded victim is certain to draw an object of one or other of these two colours because there are no objects of any other colour in the bag.

Interest in probability theory, and in particular the calculation of probabilities in gambling, led to the discovery in the late seventeenth and early eighteenth centuries of an equation for a curve which provided a good fit to the probabilities associated with coin tossing. Each time a coin is tossed one of two events take place (unless, of course, the coin is lost down a drain or is otherwise lost): it can be a head (H) or tail (T). Since two events are possible, sample space has two points and both probabilities $P(\text{H})$ and $P(\text{T})$ are equal to a half.

What could happen if two coins were tossed independently? Now we have four possibilities: HH, HT, TH, TT. Sample space contains four points and the associated probabilities are as follows:

$$P\text{ (HH)} \qquad = \tfrac{1}{4}$$
$$P\text{ (HT or TH)} \quad = 2/4 = \tfrac{1}{2}$$
$$P\text{ (TT)} \qquad = \tfrac{1}{4}$$

Many readers − and children who have studied 'modern mathematics' − will know that one neat way of showing what could happen (i.e. the number of points in sample space) is by a tree diagram. Such a diagram for our coin tossing example is given by figure 5.6.

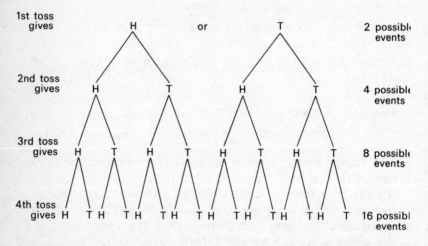

Figure 5.6   Tree diagram for probabilities of obtaining 'heads' and 'tails' in coin tossing.

What could happen if we tossed three coins independently (or of course the same coin three times?). There are now eight possibilities (i.e. eight points in sample space). Check that the probabilities are as follows by counting up.

$$P\text{ (HHH)} = 1/8 \text{ or } 0.25$$
$$P\text{ (HHT or HTH or THH)} = 3/8 \text{ or } 0.375$$
$$P\text{ (TTH or THT or HTT)} = 3/8 \text{ or } 0.375$$
$$P\text{ (TTT)} = 1/8 \text{ or } 0.125$$

Now we could toss ten coins independently (or the same coin ten times) and graph the probabilities of the possible events (figure 5.7). (There are, in fact, 1024 possible events, that is points in this sample space.) Here just the number of heads is shown.

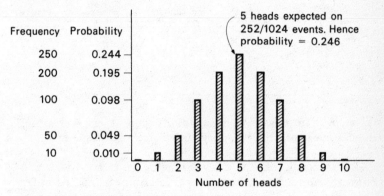

Figure 5.7 Distribution of probabilities of obtaining given numbers of 'heads' in ten tosses of unbiased coin.

A famous mathematician called De Moivre solved the problem of finding an equation to describe the line which nearly fits the tops of the columns. The actual formula is complicated and we shall not examine it here but the reader is asked to visualize the shape of the smooth curve which would fit the diagram. Imagine what would happen if an increasing number of coins were tossed and probabilities of the 'heads' calculated. Gradually the fit of the columns would come closer and closer to the smooth curve. You will, of course, by now have realized that there is no point in doing the actual tossing!

The equation derived by De Moivre yields a normal curve and it is indispensable to statisticians. It is more correct to speak of *a* normal curve than of *the* normal curve since its actual spread could easily be changed by an alteration to its scales. Distributions which are flatter than normal are called *platykurtic distributions,* those which are more peaked than normal are known as *leptokurtic distributions* (see figure 5.8).

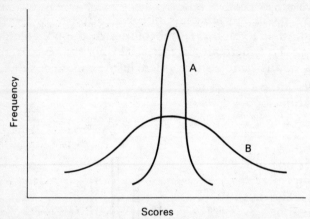

Figure 5.8   Varieties of the normal distribution: A, leptokurtic (small value for spread of scores); B, platykurtic (large value of spread).

This brief digression has been made in order to give the readers some idea of 'where the curve comes from'. To understand its use we have to study measures of variation, however.

Measures of Variation

The range

We have already met the simplest measure of variation: the inclusive range (p. 138). Though informative it can be misleading because its size is determined by just two scores in the group (the highest and lowest). Because of this limitation various other measures of range have been suggested but for some inexplicable reason they are seldom quoted. One is called the *semi-interquartile range.* In our example of quartiles (p. 139) we saw how the complete range can be divided into quarters using three values called quartiles. They are Q_1 (the point on the number line below which 25% of scores lie), Q_2 (50%) or the median and Q_3 (75%). The semi-interquartile (Q) range is given by:

$$Q = \frac{Q_3 - Q_1}{2} \qquad [5.4]$$

Whilst groups of scores which have similar values for the inclusive range need not be similar in any other respect (for
example in shape), if two distributions have similar values for
Q then they are likely to be similar in many respects. If a distribution is approximately normal then about 50% of the
scores lie between the median $\pm$ Q. Under these circumstances knowledge of Q and the median conveys a lot of information about the scores.

The variance
This is one of the central organizing concepts in the whole of
statistics. Recall the computation of the mean using equation
[5.2]. The mean uses every score in the group, unlike some
of the other measures discussed. Obviously the variation of a
single score can be determined by finding out how much it
differs (known as the 'deviation score') from the mean of the
group to which it belongs. Let us propose a small set of
scores to illustrate these points: to make the arithmetic
simple we shall use the scores of eight pupils on a spelling test
whose maximum score was ten (table 5.8).

The second column shows that the sum of the deviation
scores is equal to zero. This is always the case because the
sum of the positive deviations is cancelled out by the sum of
the negative deviations. This provides a check on the calculation of the mean. So merely adding the signed deviations
provides no idea of the spread of scores. We could achieve
this idea, however, by ignoring the signs and simply adding
up the absolute value of the deviation scores. We could then
divide by the number of scores and find the *mean deviation.*
In our example the sum of the deviation scores regardless of
sign is 16 and the mean deviation, therefore, 16/8 = 2. This is
not entirely useless since a large value for the mean deviation
indicates a large spread of scores.

For a variety of reasons, however, the mean deviation is
little used as a measure of variation. Instead, the *variance* is
greatly to be preferred. If the deviation scores are squared,

Table 5.8 — Marks out of ten for eight children on spelling test.

Score	Deviation score	Squared deviation score
8	8 – 5 = 3	9
5	5 – 5 = 0	0
3	3 – 5 = –2	4
4	4 – 5 = –1	1
9	9 – 5 = 4	16
6	6 – 5 = 1	1
2	2 – 5 = –3	9
3	3 – 5 = –2	4
$\sum_1^8 x_i = 40$	$\sum_1^8 (x_i - \overline{x}) = 0$	$\sum_1^8 (x_i - \overline{x})^2 = 44$

$\overline{x} = 40/8 = 5$

that is, $(x_i - \overline{x})^2$ is found for each score, the values in the final column of table 5.8 are obtained. If these are added over all scores, the sum of the squared deviations is found. In our example

$$\sum_1^8 (x_i - \overline{x})^2 = 44$$

This expression is known for short as the *sum of squares* (or SS). Dividing SS by the number of scores we obtain a value which is literally the mean of the squared deviations. This value is called the variance. In our example

$$\frac{\sum_1^8 (x_i - \overline{x})^2}{n} = \frac{44}{8} = 5.5$$

In general

$$\sigma^2 = \frac{\sum_1^n (x_i - \overline{x})^2}{n} \qquad [5.5]$$

is the formula for the variance, where

Table 5.9 — Calculation of variance of two groups of scores.

	Group A			Group B	
Scores	$(x_i - \bar{x})$	$(x_i - \bar{x})^2$	Scores	$(x_i - \bar{x})$	$(x_i - \bar{x})^2$
2	2 - 3 = -1	1	7	7 - 3 = 4	16
4	4 - 3 = 1	1	1	1 - 3 = -2	4
4	4 - 3 = 1	1	1	1 - 3 = -2	4
1	1 - 3 = -2	4	7	7 - 3 = 4	16
5	5 - 3 = 2	4	1	1 - 3 = -2	4
2	2 - 3 = -1	1	1	1 - 3 = -2	4
$\Sigma x = 18$		SS = 12	$\Sigma x = 18$		SS = 48
$\bar{x} = 3$			$\bar{x} = 3$		

σ^2 = variance (pronounced 'sigma squared')

$\sum_1^n$ = sum of, starting at the first score and continuing to include the nth score

x_i = raw score of ith child

$\bar{x}$ = mean score

n = number of scores

To reinforce these ideas, examine the two distributions given in table 5.9. They are the scores obtained by two groups of children (A and B) on a given test.

In the first place the means are the same but it is clear that the shapes of the distributions are very different. Whereas the inclusive range of the group A scores is five, that for group B is seven, but this will not make all that big a difference. In the second column for each group the deviation scores $(x_i - \bar{x})$ have been found, and in the third the squared deviation $(x_i - \bar{x})^2$. Adding these squares (to get SS) we find they are very different, 12 for group A, 48 for group B. Dividing by six (the number of scores in each group) we find that the variance in group A is only two whereas in group B it is eight. We can now see that the variance of the scores is four times as great for group B scores as for group A scores. Now if we had described each set of scores using only the mean and the range, the magnitude of the difference between the variability in the two sets would not have been so apparent.

Text book examples always involve easier arithmetic than is met in real life scores! In our two examples the mean and therefore the deviation scores are whole numbers. Where means are not whole numbers, however, squaring the actual deviations can involve tedium and accumulate error. A few lines of elementary algebra[3] show that

$$\Sigma\,(x_i - \overline{x})^2 \;=\; \Sigma x^2 \,-\,(\Sigma x)^2/n \qquad\qquad [5.6]$$

With this formula there is no need to calculate deviations: we can use the raw scores because

$$
\begin{aligned}
\Sigma x^2 \;&=\; \text{sum of squared scores}\\
(\Sigma x)^2 \;&=\; \text{sum of scores all squared}\\
n \;&=\; \text{number of scores}
\end{aligned}
$$

Applied to the scores in group A, we get

Scores	Squared scores
2	4
4	16
4	16
1	1
5	25
2	4
$\Sigma x = 18$	$\Sigma x^2 = 66$

Therefore

$$(\Sigma x)^2 \;=\; 324$$

---

[3] Actually only a slightly more complicated manipulation of $(a-b)^2$.

and so

$$\Sigma(x_i - \bar{x})^2 = 66 - 324/6$$
$$= 66 - 54$$
$$= 12 \text{ (as before)}$$

Thus

$$\sigma^2 = 12/6 = 2$$

Even without a calculator the arithmetic is very simple using the raw score formula for the sum of squares. Combining the final division by n into formula [5.5] to get the variance (σ^2) our formula becomes

$$\sigma^2 = \frac{1}{n}[\Sigma x^2 - (\Sigma x)^2/n] \qquad [5.7]$$

or

$$\sigma^2 = \frac{\Sigma x^2}{n} - \bar{x}^2 \qquad [5.8]$$

which is even simpler to use. In the example

$$\sigma^2 = \frac{66}{6} - 3^2$$
$$= 2$$

Readers who find an invitation to use symbols altogether too great a shock can try to visualize the concept of variance. Suppose we think of the scores in group A in table 5.9 as lying along a number line and then express them as deviations from the mean of the group. If we square the deviation score for the first child (-1^2) we get a square whose size is one square unit. This square can be drawn as shown in figure 5.7. Actually we have four children with deviation scores of one, so we must think of four superimposed squares each of area one square unit on the diagram. The fourth child in the list has a deviation score of minus two so the area of his squared deviation score is four square units. The size of the square for the fifth child in the list is also four square units. So, all told, we have four children with squared deviations of one square unit and two with squared deviations of four square units. The size of the average square, therefore, is two square units: this is the variance, indicated by the shaded area in the diagram. This is a visual demonstration that the variance in test scores is equal to the mean of SS (or average square).

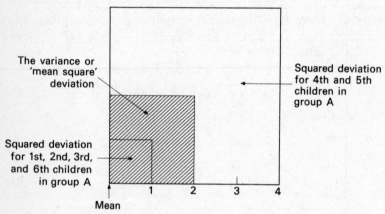

Figure 5.9   Illustration of 'variance'.

The standard deviation

Although the variance is an indispensable measure of variation and figures prominently in studies of overlap between two or more sets of scores, unlike the scores themselves it is a square measure. But we can very easily derive a measure of variation which is on the same linear scale as the scores themselves by finding the positive square root of the variance. Reference back to figure 5.9 shows that the resulting value would equal the base of the mean squared deviation: this is the definition of the standard deviation (σ) or 'root mean square deviation'.

Its formula would obviously be the square root of formula [5.5].

Hence

$$\sigma = \sqrt{\Sigma(x_i - \overline{x})^2/n} \qquad [5.9]$$

Readers are recommended to think of the standard deviation as the square root of the variance or as a linear (along a line) measure of the 'average variability' in a set of scores.

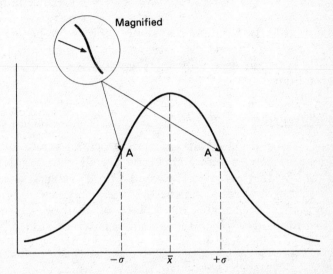

Figure 5.10   Normal curve showing the points of inflexion at $\overline{x} \pm \sigma$.

One important use of the standard deviation comes from its relationship with scores whose overall distribution is normal, or nearly so. Recall the shape of a normal curve (figure 5.10). If one were to put a magnifying glass on the points ringed one would see that there the shape of the curve changed from being convex to concave (at the point marked A). A change like this is known in mathematics as the point of *inflexion*. If a line is dropped perpendicular from this point to the horizontal axis it corresponds with the points on the scale which are one standard deviation above ($+\sigma$) and one standard deviation below ($-\sigma$) the mean respectively. If the distribution is normal three important properties of the standard deviation apply:

(1) Approximately 68% of the scores (area under the curve) lie between the mean $\pm\sigma$. Thus approximately 34% of the scores are between the mean $+\sigma$ and 34% between the mean and $-\sigma$.

(2) Approximately 95% of the scores lie between the mean $\pm 2\sigma$.

(3) Approximately 99% of the scores lie between the mean $\pm 3\sigma$.

Many important inferences about scores can be drawn from these facts if one can assume that the distribution of scores is approximately normal, as we shall see in the section which follows.

Standard Scores

When the author taught in secondary school it was quite common practice to determine yearly overall 'class positions' by awarding first place to the child whose aggregate marks across school subjects was highest. Occasionally, and in order to emphasize the greater importance of mathematics and English, the totals for these two subjects were doubled but little or no other manipulation of scores was undertaken. Some problems arose. In the years prior to the work of the Equal Opportunities Commission boys studied woodwork whilst girls took domestic science (now home economics). Unfortunately for the class list system, marks in woodwork were always much higher than marks in domestic science even where the least dexterous in the one was comparable to the most calamitous work in the other. Adding marks on very different scales of measurement, therefore, was very unfair, to say the least. One way in which the scores on disparate scales could have been compared was through the construction of 'standard scores', or by using the equivalent but slightly more cumbersome device of the 'z-score'. Percentile scores are used by some people for this purpose but their intervals are unequal (there may be as many as, say, nine points difference between the child ranked at the 95th percentile and the child ranked at the 90th percentile but only two or three marks difference between the child at the 50th

Table 5.10 — Calculation of z-scores for data in table 5.9.

	Group A			Group B		
Scores	$(x_i - \bar{x})$	z		Scores	$(x_i - \bar{x})$	z
2	-1	$-1/\sigma = -0.71$		7	4	1.41
4	1	$1/\sigma = 0.71$		1	-2	-0.71
4	1	$1/\sigma = 0.71$		1	-2	-0.71
1	-2	$-2/\sigma = -1.41$		7	4	1.41
5	2	$2/\sigma = 1.41$		1	-2	-0.71
2	-1	$-1/\sigma = -0.71$		1	-2	-0.71
SS $= 12$				SS $= 48$		
$\sigma^2 = 12/6 = 2$				$\sigma^2 = 48/6 = 8$		
$\sigma = \sqrt{2} = 1.41$				$\sigma = \sqrt{8} = 2.83$		

and 45th percentile). What is needed, then, is a way of converting scores to a common unit of measurement. This is accomplished by dividing the deviation score by the standard deviation of the group of scores. The effect of this on our woodwork and cooking scores is to translate the scores into deviations from their respective means (thus removing the first effect, i.e. that of the higher woodwork mean) and dividing by the average variability, thus adjusting for the differences in the spread of the scores.

This operation as a formula becomes:

$$ z = \frac{x_i - \bar{x}}{\sigma_x} \qquad [5.10] $$

where the symbols have the same meaning as before. Applied to our two groups of scores (A and B in table 5.9) it yields the results shown in table 5.10. We can see that the z-scores for groups A and B are now directly comparable. Thus the child who scores two in group A has a score which is 0.71 of a standard deviation below the mean; the child who scores seven in group B has a score which is 1.41 standard deviations above the mean, and so on.

Because the percentages of scores corresponding to different areas of the normal curve are known and z-scores are

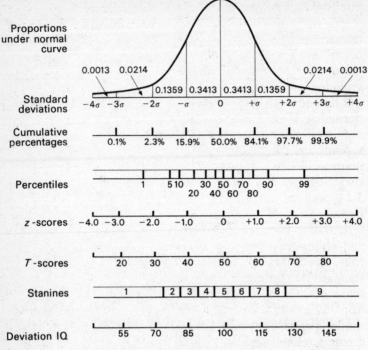

Figure 5.11   The normal curve and types of scale. From Seashore, H. G., 1955. Methods of expressing test scores. *Test Service Bulletin 39.* New York: The Psychological Corporation.

in units of the standard deviation one type of score can easily be translated into the other using figure 5.11.

One difficulty in the use of z-scores is that they involve decimals and negative signs. In practice in most published standardized tests in Britain, scores are given on scales which have a mean of 100 and standard deviations of 15. These are called *standardized scores*. To obtain them simply multiply the z-score by 15 and add 100. Thus a z-score of 1.0 becomes $100 + (15 \times 1) = 115$; a z-score of -3.0 becomes $100 + [15 \times (-3)] = 55$, and so on. There is nothing sacred about these particular values for the mean and standard deviation: any value could be chosen. But by convention values of 100 and 15 have been widely adopted for published tests. With published tests the scores are first *normalized,* that is, the scores of large numbers of pupils which form the norms are transformed in order to smooth out the irregularities which occur in actual frequency distributions, to make them 'normal'. A brief explanation of how this can be done is provided later in the chapter.

Classroom teachers will not usually wish to bother to normalize their scores but may, instead, translate the actual scores obtained into what is known as 'stanines'. These are a type of standard score closely related to z-scores. It is a nine-point scale with a mean of five and a standard deviation of two. Stanines are shown in the bottom line but one of figure 5.11 and are preferred by many people since they do not imply too great precision in scoring yet are sufficiently differentiating between pupils and easily understood by parents and children. On this scale, pupils whose stanine scores are four, five or six are found within the band captured by one standard deviation above and below the mean. A stanine score of eight or nine would be obtained only by about the 'top' 12 or 13% of pupils, and scores of one or two by a similar percentage 'at the bottom'. Readers may also come across a related scale known as 'T-scores'. They are on a scale with a mean of 50 and standard deviation of ten. Thus a z-score of +1.0 corresponds with a T-score of 60, a T-score of 35 with a z-score of -1.50, and so on.

Readers should study figure 5.11 carefully. Providing the assumption that the scores are normal, or nearly so, can be made, it shows how a score on any scale can be interpreted in terms of where it occurs on a normal curve. It demonstrates that the norm-referenced assessment of pupils gives meaning to a score only in terms of the scores obtained by a large number of similar pupils. The normal curve is also very important in probability theory and is closely bound up with deciding whether a particular observation — say the result of an experiment — is a 'chance' or 'real' occurrence.

The assumption that the normal curve represents a good approximation to the real life occurrence of biological data — such as height — is deeply embedded in western science. It is the case that where a large number of observations of natural phenomena are made their distribution is often near normal.

But whilst scores in scholastic tests often provide a reasonable fit to this curve it is very easy indeed to alter the distribution to achieve a different shape by the inclusion of items of different characteristics. By including a large number of easy items the curve can be 'shifted upwards' — that is, it can be negatively skewed — whilst, by the same token, a number of difficult items will produce a curve which is positively skewed. Near normal curves are known to result from tests whose items have a facility level (see chapter 4) of around 0.5; that is items which are answered correctly by about half the respondents. Obtaining such a distribution does not of course show that the *abilities* which are assumed to be responsible for the obtained scores are themselves normally distributed! Scaling the scores so that they are normal is done for convenience of interpretation only. As the first objection in chapter 3 argues, what is done for convenience should not be allowed to assume the properties of a natural law — not, of course, that any such laws have been identified in the social sciences!

Modern intelligence test scores (still, perhaps misleadingly, called 'IQs') are normalized standard scores: they have been constructed to correspond to the normal distribution and with mean 100, standard deviation 15 (16 in the case of the Stanford–Binet test). It is, therefore, nonsense to claim that they *demonstrate* the normal distribution of intelligence. Classical intelligence test interpretations used the concept of IQ first put forward by Stern for the comparison of scores obtained by Binet's famous tests. It is not the purpose of this section to go into detail about these developments since there are already many excellent accounts (e.g. Karmel and Karmel, 1978) but since much confusion about the IQ still exists we shall just point out that IQs (intelligence quotients) *used to be found* using the formula

$$IQ = \frac{\text{mental age (MA)}}{\text{chronological age (CA)}} \times 100 \qquad [5.11]$$

If a child is nine years old and achieved the average score for nine year old children on the test then his IQ was 100:

$$IQ = \frac{9}{9} \times 100 = 100$$

A second child, also nine, whose score was as high as the average for 12 year olds, however, had an IQ of 133, and so on

$$IQ = \frac{12}{9} \times 100 = 133$$

One of the problems with this method lay in the unfortunate misinterpretations which became attached to the concept of 'mental age'. Firstly it is merely a ratio of a score on a test to age and describes only a comparison between the testee and the average of a number of other testees at a similar or different ages. Although it is still common for some criminals to be described at their trial as having a 'low mental age' it would be wholly misleading to assume that their accumulated experiences and mental lives were in any way comparable to those of the young children with whom their performances on the solution of a few abstract puzzles was being compared. For statistical reasons, too, the classical method of obtaining the IQ has given way to use of the normalized standard score. Unfortunately, the terminology has not been standardized! Wechsler intelligence scales (WAIS, the adult scale and WISC, the children's scale) employ the term 'deviation IQ', but this is merely a way of retaining a link with its historical antecedents whilst adopting the modern practice of using standardized scores. It is not anticipated that teachers will have much use for intelligence tests but the moral is clear: make sure the manual of any published tests being used is explicit in its description of the type of scale being used and the inferences about the norm-referenced description of a child's performance permitted by it.

Normalizing Scores

The relationships we have been discussing between the various types of scales apply only when the distribution of raw scores is normal. The construction of published tests of

Table 5.11 – Calculation of normalized scores from data in table 5.2.

Raw score	f	Cumulative f	Cumulative f below score + ½f	Proportion	Value of z in normal curve	Rounded T-score (10 × z) + 50	Standardized score (15 × z) + 100
43	1	32	31.5	0.9844	2.15	72	132
42	1	31	30.5	0.9531	1.68	67	125
41	1	30	29.5	0.9219	1.42	64	121
40	1	29	28.5	0.8906	1.23	62	118
39	2	28	27.0	0.8438	1.10	61	117
38	2	26	25.0	0.7813	0.78	58	112
37	3	24	22.5	0.7031	0.53	55	108
36	2	21	20.0	0.6250	0.31	53	105
35	2	19	18.0	0.5625	0.16	52	102
34	2	17	16.0	0.5000	0.00	50	100
33	2	15	14.0	0.4375	-0.16	48	98
32	1	13	12.5	0.3906	-0.28	47	96
31	1	12	11.5	0.3594	-0.36	46	95
30	1	11	10.5	0.3281	-0.45	46	93
29	1	10	9.5	0.2969	-0.53	45	92
28	1	9	8.5	0.2656	-0.63	44	91
27	2	8	7.0	0.2188	-0.78	42	88
26	1	6	5.5	0.1719	-0.95	41	86
25	1	5	4.5	0.1406	-1.08	39	84
24	1	4	3.5	0.1094	-1.23	38	82
23	1	3	2.5	0.0781	-1.42	36	79
22	1	2	1.5	0.0313	-1.86	31	72
21	1	1	0.5	0.0156	-2.16	28	68
	32						

ability and achievement takes great care to ensure that the raw scores on which the norms have been based have been normalized from a large sample of children. When using standardized tests (mean 100, standard deviation 15) teachers can be confident that a score of 130 indicates that the child's performance is at a level which would be exceeded by less than 2½% (2.27% precisely) of similar children, and so on. In interpreting a score in a class of, say, 30 children it is often convenient to translate it into a z-score (or one of its derivatives) and to report this score as if it were a member of a normal distribution. Obtaining some sort of standard score is, of course, necessary in all cases where overall class lists based on the summation of several scores are required. But with a class of the size usually met in schools a normal distribution is extremely unlikely, to say the least. With such a small group there would be little point in normalizing them because, amongst other reasons, there would be far too few children near the tails of the distribution (i.e. very high or very low scorers) to provide the necessary information.

An approximate and simple method of normalizing is illustrated in table 5.11 using the data of table 5.2. Although one would not normally bother to normalize only 32 scores the method is applicable to larger distributions. The steps in the normalizing procedure are:

(1) Record the raw scores in descending order and tabulate the frequences (columns one and two).
(2) Record the cumulative frequences upwards (column three).
(3) For each raw score, record the cumulative frequency *below* the score and add half the frequency in the row corresponding to the raw score. Place the result in column four. For example, the cumulative frequency up to (i.e. below) raw score 33 is 13. The frequency of score 33 is two: therefore the entry in column four is 13 + (½ x 2) = 14.
(4) Express the cumulative frequency in row four as a proportion of the total number of scores. Record the result in column five. For example, the cumulative frequency up to and including raw score 37 in column four is

22.5. There are 32 scores, therefore the proportion is 22.5/32 = 0.7031.

(5)   Consult the table of areas under the normal curve for given z-score values (see the appendix) to find the value corresponding to the proportions. For example, the proportion corresponding to raw score 40 is 0.8906. This means that 0.8906 of the normal curves area is below the value for z. Since the normal curve is symmetrical *half* the area (0.5000) is below the mean — which is z-score 0.000. Therefore the area *between* the mean and 0.8906 is 0.8906 – 0.5000 = 0.3906. Inspection of the table shows that 0.3906 corresponds with a z-score of 1.23. (Actually 0.3907 corresponds to a z of 1.23, but go to the nearest value.) It is a little trickier to read the table for negative z-scores but the logic is the same. For example, the proportion corresponding to raw score 26 is 0.1719. We are now dealing with that half of the normal curve which is *below* the mean since 0.1719 is less than half (0.5000). Therefore the proportion of the area between the mean and the z-score which contains 0.1719 of the score is 0.5000 – 0.1719 = 0.3281. The nearest entry in the table to this value is 0.3289: it gives –0.95 as a value for z. Place the entries in column six.

(6)   The z-scores are now normalized. To remove the negative signs decide which scale is required and use the appropriate formula at the top of the column. Column seven shows T-scores (mean 50, standard deviation ten) column eight standardized scores (mean 100, standard deviation 15).

Inspection of the resulting standardized scores or the T-scores shows that normalization has compressed the scale in some places but elongated it in others. We can see the disadvantages of having only a small number of scores. In the middle of the range a difference of one between raw scores yields a corresponding difference of only two in the standardized score whereas a difference of one in raw scores at the extremes of the range yields a difference in standardized score of seven at the top and four at the bottom end of the distribution. For this reason published tests standardize their scores by using much larger samples and more sophisticated methods of normalization at the extremes. The method described, however, should be sufficient for most purposes where teachers wish to normalize scores. Ideally, scores on two distributions are only directly comparable where both are normal and have the same standard deviation.

Use of Norms

Following the method will give some insight into the construction of norms. Clearly standardized scores in our sample of 32 children are totally inadequate to constitute worthwhile norms for interpretation. But what makes norms adequate? The purpose of norms is to provide a reference frame by which to compare the scores of our children with scores by similar children elsewhere. Mere size of the standardizing sample is not the only attribute to look for: if the sample was very different in composition from the children using the test little would be learnt. Tests which are sold for wide geographical use may not quote meaningful national norms. An enormous sample of children in the south-east of England would not be a 'national sample', for example, so teachers should look to the manual to see whether a full description of the sample is given. Schools could well be recommended to develop local norms especially in relation to achievement tests which reflect local teaching objectives. These could be revised from time to time. Careful study should also be made of the year in which the norms were produced. There is an inevitable timelag between original publication and use, such that some may be so much out of date as to be inapplicable. Teachers should also ask themselves whether they have need of norms at all: in some instances, say where the ablest children in the group are to be identified, norms are unnecessary.

Karmel and Karmel (1978) have listed nine things to look out for in the manual by which to judge whether the normative data are adequate. They are (Karmel and Karmel, 1978, 96—7):

(a)   the scales used for reporting the scores should be thoroughly explained;

(b)   standard scores should be used for reporting raw scores;

(c)   conversion tables should be provided;

(d)   norms should be published in the manual at the time of distribution;

(e)   the normative group should be clearly defined and described;

(f)   standard scores should reflect the distribution of scores in a reference group that is appropriate for the comparison you wish to make;

(g)   the method of sampling schools and pupils which constitute the norms should be fully reported;

(h)   achievement test norms should report the number of schools as well as the number of children tested;

(i)   variance in scores because of such variables as age, sex and amount of education should be reported.

Very few manuals consulted by the writer pass muster on all these aspects. In the past there has undoubtedly been what Seashore and Ricks (1950) have called the 'lumping together of all the samples secured more by chance than by plan', but standards of sampling have improved. Nevertheless, if test constructors do not provide all the information required by the nine principles above teachers may, with justice, adopt a sceptical attitude to the value of the norms presented.

Measurement of Relationships

The product-moment correlation

Many occasions arise in which measurement of the relationship between two sets of scores is needed. The two sets of scores could be the scores obtained by the same group of children on two different forms of the same test as is often necessary, as we shall see in chapter 6, in the study of *reliability*. Similarly, we might be interested in finding the relationship between a test and a criterion test taken much later. One obvious instance of this is where an examination taken at age 11 was held to predict later performance in school. This relationship needs to be examined in studies of the validity of the test (see chapter 8). An equally important application would be in studies of how well a test which claims to measure 'attribute X' overlaps in the information it provides with a second test which also claims to measure the same attribute. A still more complicated application is in the study of the relationship between several sets of scores in an attempt to identify and name a smaller number of 'underlying abilities' responsible for the performances — for example a number of tests which appear to require the mental manipulation of shapes to see whether the performances can be explained in terms of a single ability which could be labelled 'spatial visualization'.

Teachers will almost certainly have tried to intuit relationships between variables. Some are convinced that pupils better than average in one school subject or activity are also better than average in another. Some may claim to have recognized a tendency for pupils of certain 'home backgrounds' to do better than pupils from others. Still more may expect higher achievement scores from pupils whose parents have attained higher educational standards. We are not concerned here with the validity of these impressions but merely to point out that they are examples of relationships which teachers suspect might exist. The purpose of calculating correlations, however, is to replace subjective impressions of this kind with more precise indexes which actually measure the strength of the relationship.

Before the advent of computers, the first step in the examination of a correlation between two variables was to display the relationship on a type of graph known as a 'scatter diagram'. If numbers are not too large this method still repays study. Suppose a teacher has obtained scores for ten children (we shall keep the numbers small for simplicity's sake) on two tests of, say, comprehension. Following convention we shall label one test 'X' the other 'Y': the scores, denoted by x and y respectively, are given in table 5.12. These scores are then plotted to form a scatter diagram (figure 5.12, with x on horizontal, y on vertical axis, by convention).

The relationship between the two sets of scores is a perfect one as shown by the straight line which joins the points.

Table 5.12 — Scores of ten children on two tests of comprehension: perfect positive correlation.

Child	x	y
A	28	23
B	25	21
C	22	19
D	19	17
E	16	15
F	13	13
G	10	11
H	7	9
I	4	7
J	1	5

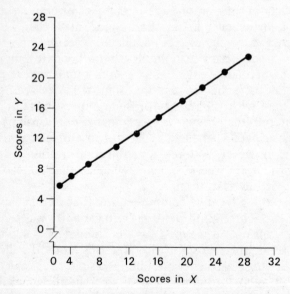

Figure 5.12   Scatter diagram for data of table 5.12.

Moreover it is *positive* because the highest score on X is paired with the highest on Y, the second highest on X with the second highest on Y, and so on through the list. Mathematically its strength is +1.0.

Table 5.13 — Scores of ten children on two tests: moderate positive correlation.

x	y
28	21
25	13
22	23
19	13
16	15
13	21
10	12
7	17
4	11
1	9

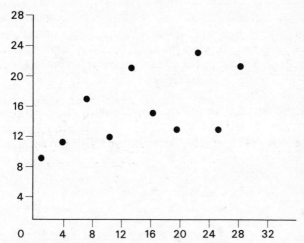

Figure 5.13   Scatter diagram for data of table 5.13.

Suppose these two lists had been inversely related: that is the *highest* score on X is paired with the *lowest* score on Y, the second highest on X with the second lowest on Y and so on. Once again the relationship would have been perfect and all points would be on a straight line but this time the line would have been sloping from top left to bottom right. In this case the relationship is described as being 'perfect negative' and mathematically its strength is −1.0.

Now the relationships between two sets of scores in real life are never perfect, either positive or negative. More often test scores in school subjects are paired something like the relationship shown in table 5.13. Figure 5.13 shows the relevant scatter diagram.

It is obvious from this scatter diagram that the relationship is far from perfect, but if one were to draw the line which best represents the plot it would tend to run from top right to bottom left. This shows that whilst there are individual exceptions, the tendency in the scores in the group as a whole is for higher than average scores on X to be higher than average on Y. In fact the correlation calculated from these data is +0.56. We would call this a positive relationship but only of moderate strength.

We shall not bother to quote actual sets of data for figure 5.14. Figure 5.14(a) shows no relationship between X and Y since one finds as many children who are 'high on X, low on Y' as one finds children who are 'low on X, high on Y'. This scatter diagram illustrates a zero-order relationship, correlation 0.00. Figure 5.14(b) shows a definite relationship but it is certainly not one that can be described by a single straight line. Although the actual measurement of the correlation is zero we would not wish to say there is no relationship since it is curved (more properly, 'curvilinear'). It is typical of the

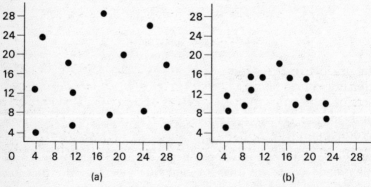

Figure 5.14   Scatter diagrams showing two reasons for zero correlation: (a) no relationship between X and Y; (b) curvilinear relationship between X and Y.

theoretical relationship between test performance (Y) and anxiety (X) since performance improves with a moderate amount of anxiety (up to anxiety score 12 to 15) but decreases thereafter.

Readers will have gathered from the above that a correlation can be thought of as the closeness of the fit between the points and a *straight* line. Perfect correlation is said to exist when points fall *on* the straight line which can slope positively or negatively. The further the points lie away from a straight line the smaller the correlation until, where the points make a roughly circular pattern, the correlation is zero.

Provided the scatter plot does not indicate a curvilinear relationship, the device which provides the most useful index of the strength of the relationship between two sets of scores is the so-called Pearson product-moment correlation. If the scores on both variables are thought of as having been transformed to z-scores (formula [5.10]) the formula for the product-moment correlation coefficient is

$$r_{xy} = \frac{\Sigma z_x z_y}{n} \qquad [5.12]$$

where

$$r_{xy} = \text{the correlation between scores } x \text{ and } y$$
$$\Sigma z_x z_y = \text{the sum of the products of the z-scores}$$
$$n = \text{the number of pairs of scores}$$

In practice this formula is rarely used since it is computationally clumsy and can yield rather a lot of error if the two sets of scores run to several places of decimals. Many moderately priced calculators provide a direct computation of the product-moment correlation but a fairly convenient raw score version of formula [5.12] can be derived by simple algebra. It is:

$$r_{xy} = \frac{N\Sigma xy - (\Sigma x)(\Sigma y)}{\sqrt{\{[N\Sigma x^2 - (\Sigma x)^2][N\Sigma y^2 - (\Sigma y)^2]\}}} \qquad [5.13]$$

where Σxy = the sum of the products of the raw scores
   Σx = the sum of the x scores
   Σy = the sum of the y scores
   $(\Sigma x)^2$ = the sum of the x scores 'all squared'
   $(\Sigma y)^2$ = the sum of the y scores 'all squared'
   Σx^2 = the sum of the squared x scores
   Σy^2 = the sum of the squared y scores

Use of this formula in calculating r_{xy} is demonstrated in table 5.14.

This correlation is positive but low. If we square 0.368 we get the proportion of the variance in mathematics scores which can be predicted from the English scores (0.135). This can be interpreted to mean that only 13.5% of what is measured by the test of English enters into performance in mathematics. Using these English scores would not make a very good job of predicting mathematics achievement; in fact, because we had only 12 pupils in our example, the correlation is *not significantly different from zero*. If you plot the scattergram you can see that the points provide a very poor fit indeed to a single straight line. In fact the value for the correlation where only twelve pairs of scores are involved would have to reach ±0.57 before a statistician would claim that the correlation was signicantly different from zero. Notice that a correlation of −0.57 indicates the same *strength* of relationship as a correlation of +0.57 but differs only in direction. Notice, too, that a correlation of 0.80 is not indicative of a relationship that is twice as strong as a correlation of 0.40. In fact the correlation of 0.80 allows 64% of the variance in one test to be predicted from the other (0.80^2), whereas only 16% is possible for the correlation of 0.40. From this point of view, then, the strength of the relationship is proportional to the *square* of the correlation coefficient.

It is not the purpose of this section to provide any more detail about correlation coefficients than is necessary for an understanding of basic measurement theory but one common misconception about the inferences that can be drawn should be pointed out here. In a nutshell it is: correlation does not indicate causation. All that the correlation coefficient tells us

Table 5.14 — Calculation of the product-moment correlation between an English and a mathematics test.

Pupil	English test x	Mathematics test y	x^2	y^2	xy
A	38	30	1444	900	1140
B	25	18	625	324	450
C	35	26	1225	676	910
D	22	17	484	289	374
E	40	17	1600	289	680
F	42	26	1764	676	1092
G	41	16	1681	256	656
H	41	37	1681	1369	1517
I	37	21	1369	441	777
J	30	16	900	256	480
K	31	37	961	1369	1147
L	41	37	1681	1369	1517
n=12	Σx=423	Σy=298	Σx^2=15415	Σy^2=8214	Σxy=10740

Using formula [5.13]

$$r_{xy} = \frac{(12 \times 10740) - (423 \times 298)}{\sqrt{\left\{ [12 \times 15415 - (423)^2][12 \times 8214 - (298)^2] \right\}}}$$

$$= \frac{128880 - 126054}{\sqrt{[(184980 - 178929)(98568 - 88804)]}}$$

$$= \frac{2826}{\sqrt{(6051 \times 9764)}}$$

$$= \frac{2826}{7686.48}$$

$$= 0.368$$

is the strength and the direction of the linear relationship between the two sets of scores, not that one variable causes the other.

The rank order correlation

Where the two sets of scores are on an interval scale the method described above is appropriate for measuring the strength of the relationship. But we have already seen that rank orders can be used to indicate the relative position of children in a list and it is easy to correlate two sets of ranks using Spearman's rank order correlation (usually abbreviated ρ (rho) and sometimes r_S if formula [5.13] or one of its variants is used.

A very simple formula is used to calculate ρ it is

$$\rho = 1 - \frac{6\Sigma d^2}{N(N^2 - 1)} \qquad [5.14]$$

where

Σd^2 = the sum of the squared differences between ranks
N = the number of pairs of ranks

The use of this formula is illustrated for the data in table 5.15 but here ranks have been substituted for the raw scores. Assigning 'one' to the highest on each test, 'two' to the next highest and so on to rank 12 and giving the mean of the ranks covered in cases of a tie occurring, we have data as shown in table 5.15.

Notice in the above list that a considerable number of tied ranks has occurred especially in the mathematics test (which was not a terribly good discriminator between pupils' achievements). When tied ranks occur, the resulting answer is not a particularly good approximation to r_S. In this event it is probably simplest to calculate a corrected r_S using the formula for the product-moment correlation r_{xy} (formula [5.13]) but replacing the scores by the ranks assigned. Readers should check that the summary data for computation of r_{xy} from table 5.15 are as follows:

$$\Sigma xy = 551.5$$
$$\Sigma x = 78$$
$$\Sigma y = 78$$
$$\Sigma x^2 = 648$$
$$\Sigma y^2 = 646.5$$

Table 5.15 — Calculation of the rank order correlation, ρ.

Pupil	Rank order on English test X, R_X	Rank order on mathematics test Y, R_Y	$d_{R_X - R_Y}$	$(d_{R_X - R_Y})^2$
A	6	4	2	4
B	11	8	3	9
C	8	5.5	2.5	6.25
D	12	9.5 =	2.5	6.25
E	5	9.5 =	-4.5	20.25
F	1	5.5 =	-4.5	20.25
G	3 =	11.5 =	-8.5	72.25
H	3 =	2 =	1	1
I	7	7	0	0
J	10	11.5 =	-1.5	2.25
K	9	2 =	7	49
L	3 =	2 =	1	1

$$\Sigma d^2 = 191.5$$

$$\rho = 1 - \frac{6 \times 191.5}{12(12^2 - 1)}$$

$$= 1 - \frac{1149}{1716} = 1 - 0.6696$$

$$= 0.330$$

By substitution into formula [5.13] we get

$$r_S = \frac{(12 \times 551.5) - (78 \times 78)}{\sqrt{\{[12 \times 648 - (78^2)][12 \times 646.5 - (78^2)]\}}}$$

$$= \frac{6618 - 6084}{\sqrt{[7776 - 6084)(7558 - 6084)]}}$$

$$= \frac{534}{1682.98}$$

$$= 0.317$$

Notice that the presence of ties tends to inflate the correlation coefficient but that the correction exerts only a relatively small effect. Generally, correlation between ranks tends to be a lower estimate of the strength of the relationship than the product-moment correlation between the raw scores on which the ranks are based.

At this point it is necessary only to point out that there are other types of correlation coefficient for use with different types of data. Most of the teachers' needs in dealing with test results are met by one or other of the two methods described. Note, however, that there is no such thing as *the* correlation between two tests and that the use of different methods produces different values. Tables have been prepared and are included in most basic statistics text books which give the probability that an obtained result is a chance occurrence. By convention, two cut-off points, or levels of significance, have been adopted by which to decide these probabilities. These are the 0.05 and 0.01 levels of significance. The former indicates that the result you have obtained would be expected by chance in only five cases out of 100, the latter only once in 100. Thus in the first instance you are taking the risk that five times out of 100 you will report a chance difference as a real one, and so on. The sample size is important. For example, if you have a sample of 20 pairs of scores the product-moment correlation has to reach ± 0.43 and ± 0.55 to be declared significant at the 0.05 and 0.01 levels respectively.

SUMMARY

In this chapter the reader has been introduced to some of the basic 'statistical' ideas in the use and interpretation of tests. If topics of a similar nature to those in chapter 4 are also included you should by now be conversant with the following principal ideas:

(1)   If measurement is defined as 'the assignment of numbers to objects or events according to rules', two main types of scale are achieved by most assessment in

education: these are the *interval scale* and the *ordinal scale*. In interval scales, distances between scores can be interpreted whereas in ordinal scales only the order of scores can be interpreted. Most measurement in physical sciences is on *ratio* scales which have a zero point as well as order and interval. Sometimes a number is nominally assigned to a characteristic of a person, '0' for male '1' for female. This is occasionally known as a *nominal* scale but it has neither order, interval nor zero point.

(2) Because scores in education have no zero point they can be interpreted only in relation to a larger number of scores obtained by a group of children.

(3) How to tabulate frequency distributions, and how to find and use some very simple summarizing indices such as the *inclusive range, quantiles* (percentiles, deciles, etc.); how to construct and use an *ogive.*

(4) The characteristics of *three measures of central tendency* — mean, median and mode — and their general *lack* of applicability to criterion-referenced scores.

(5) The distribution of scores for large groups can be described by a smoother curve almost fitting the tops of the histogram or smoothing out the frequency polygon. The resulting shapes can be skewed negatively or positively, can have a single mode, several modes or no mode and vary in their degree of similarity to the normal distribution.

(6) Two sets of scores may have similar means but very different shapes. The need for the measurement of the amount of variation in a set of scores (individual differences in the scores) is met by the calculation of the *variance* (a squared index) and the *standard deviation* (a linear index). Methods of calculation of these values have been demonstrated.

(7) Where a distribution of scores is normal the percentages of scores which fall between the mean and units of the standard deviation along the horizontal axis are known.

(8) Where the standard deviations of distributions are different no meaningful comparison can be made between

a raw score on one distribution and a raw score on another. For this reason standard (or 'z') scores may be calculated.

(9)   In a normal distribution, a direct conversion between various types of standard scores (including percentiles, stanines and 'T-scores') can easily be made (figure 5.11).

(10) Because percentages of scores in various segments of a normal curve are known, distributions which are not normal can easily be normalized.

(11) Published norms are often of variable quality. Because of this, certain fundamental questions about the appropriateness of norms to the children tested by the teacher need to be asked.

(12) The use and interpretation of two types of coefficient of correlation (the Pearson product-moment coefficient for interval scores and the Spearman rank-order coefficient for ordinal scores).

A more recent method for describing and interpreting test scores seems to be gaining ground in education. Sometimes referred to as 'objective' or 'sample free' measurement, it is introduced in chapter 10.

6

Reliability of Tests

This chapter presents one of the most important concepts in assessment theory. It is rather technical and requires that the reader understand some pre-requisites. These have in fact been dealt with in chapter 5 so readers should make certain that the concepts of *mean, variance, standard deviation* and *correlation* have been grasped if they are to make intelligent use of the material in chapter 6. Other important ideas about measurement will be introduced in contexts which teachers will recognize as familiar classroom applications.

Basically, the chapter attempts to deal with the problem of the consistency of an assessment. The first section examines the concepts of errors of measurement and shows that the results or scores of a test vary both within an individual at different times as well as between individuals. Some sources of variance in test scores are identified and a distinction drawn between 'true' and 'error' variance. The problem of estimating reliability is seen as that of differentiating these types of variance, and several methods of doing so are described with examples. Readers are then shown how to use these results in the estimation of a child's true score and the size of the error in the estimate as well as how to decide whether scores by two children on the same test represent a real or a chance difference in the ability measured. Some special problems in the reliability of open-ended or essay type assessment are discussed in chapter 7 where a method of estimating the reliability of criterion-referenced tests is described. Finally, the importance of the concept of reliability for teachers who construct their own tests or use those of others is summarized.

ERROR IN TEST SCORES

The essential problem in the study of reliability is to determine the extent to which test scores are in error. Suppose a test which claims to measure reading comprehension has been given to a class of children. On the test, which has a mean of 50 and a standard deviation of ten, John scored 48 and Mary 52. From the raw scores (the scores actually obtained following marking) it is obvious that Mary's score was the higher, but not by a very large amount. Before teachers conclude that Mary's reading comprehension (which is slightly above average) is better than John's (which is only just below average) they will need to know how much error is present in the measurement for it is quite possible that on a second testing occasion John's score would be higher than Mary's, thus reversing the conclusion if hastily made. The important point is that error is *always* present even when we measure the same attribute several times, but the results of a test are of little use to us unless we find some consistency in them. It really would not be at all helpful to have to conclude that Peter's arithmetic *ability* was average for his age on Wednesday, outstanding on Thursday, but well below average on Friday even though we expect *some* fluctuations in performance! Even where we are measuring an attribute known to be fairly unstable (for example a pupil's motivation) we ordinarily expect a certain amount of consistency if we are to make any use of the results of the assessment. We normally estimate the reliability of a test using correlation and we can think of the result as indicating the degree to which a test would be expected to give a similar result on a number of occasions.

INTRA-INDIVIDUAL VARIABILITY

An understanding of reliability can be gained by examining what would be expected to happen if John and Mary took the same test of reading comprehension a number of times. We would, of course, expect the scores to vary from occasion to occasion for all children (unless, of course, the test was so easy that John, Mary and the other children got every answer right each time, but even here boredom might set in so that they made careless mistakes). The very fact of John and Mary taking the test would alter their performance, but if we were to imagine that they took it 50 times then 50 estimates of what is known as their *true score* would be obtained. These estimates could be plotted on a graph, one for John and one for Mary, and would probably resemble an approximation to the normal curve. Each curve would have a mean value and a spread of scores around it. Because we would think of that mean as being the best single estimate we could obtain of the true score we would interpret the curve as indicating the *error* in the scores. As before, the positive square root of that variance would be the standard deviation of the error. A similar example of variation in scores would apply if we were to draw the distribution of results when 50 children independently measured the length of the top of teacher's desk. Notice, however, an important difference. In our example of the reading comprehension test the variability we are measuring occurs in the scores obtained by a *single* child (John or Mary). For this reason we are measuring an *intra-individual* variation. This is expressed as a standard error of measurement and is explained in a later section.

INTER-INDIVIDUAL VARIABILITY

For obvious reasons the same test cannot be administered a large number of times to the same pupil but, fortunately, classroom use of tests is often satisfied by an alternative approach to the estimation of reliability. Methods of doing so will be explained more fully later in the chapter but it is useful to get an overall view here. Whereas the first approach described above implies that a reliable test is one which gives a similar score for a child on a number of separate occasions, the second approach assumes that a test is a reliable one so long as it places a *group* of children in a similar rank order each time it is used. One way of estimating this is to obtain two measures for each child in the group and to compare the two sets of scores obtained. If we assume that any similarity between the two *sets* of scores obtained is because of the relatively stable differences between children in the attribute (reading comprehension) being measured, the variation between the two rank orders is assumed to result from the other sources ('chance'). The amount of variation then indicates the size of the errors due to chance. Unlike our first approach where we are concerned with the variation in scores of single children on repeated testings, here we are examining the size of the variation *between* children: in other words our approach to reliability is now by studying *inter-individual* variation.

Whichever approach is adopted it should serve to remind the teacher that raw scores are not precise. In order to interpret them intelligently we *must* be able to estimate the size of the error inherent in the score. Even where tests are claimed by publishers to be exceptionally reliable (for example intelligence test scores), the conclusion should be a tentative one with a stated margin of error attached to it. One of the reasons for the decline and near death of selection at 11 years of age was that mistakes were inevitably made in placement particularly at or near the cut-off point. Given that no test is completely reliable, an intelligent choice will be to select the one which provides the most dependable estimate of the ability or performance the teacher seeks to measure. Although no teacher would wittingly use a test whose reliability is little better than zero, teachers are frequently using tests whose reliabilities are unknown.

THE SOURCES OF VARIANCE IN TEST SCORES

There are several methods for estimating the reliability of a test but their usefulness depends upon the type of test used and the purpose to which it is put. For example, if teachers wish to assess a child's performance in its own right, to diagnose the child's strengths and weaknesses or to identify the amount of learning that has taken place over a period of time they will probably have little interest in comparing one child with another. In such a case a criterion-referenced test (chapter 3) will probably be used. The ideas about reliability discussed in the next sections are not particularly helpful in estimating the reliability of that type of test, however. This is partly because a criterion-referenced test which gave all children the same score might, in some circumstances, be useful but there would be no variance in the scores obtained. If the teacher is interested in making differentiations between pupils (either for placement or in the end-of-year assessment) a test which spreads the children out over a number of score values is obviously required. But not all the variance in such scores is of equal interest since it arises from a number of sources only some of which refer to the abilities or performance being assessed.

The sources of variance in scores may be classified into six main types. Briefly, they are as follows.

Stable and General Features of Children

This refers to the more or less permanent and general characteristics of the children taking the test. They include the level of ability on general traits needed for performance in a number of tests (e.g. the ability to read) general test-taking skills (contrasting the 'test-wise' with the 'test-naive' child) and the ability to comprehend and execute instructions.

Stable but Specific Features of Children

This refers to the more or less permanent but specific features of the children. They include the ability specifically required by the test and any peculiar to actual test items (e.g. the child's familiarity with certain facts but not others).

Unstable and General Features of Children

This source refers to temporary but general characteristics of the child. These are the features associated with the child's state of health, motivational level and anxiety which affect his performance throughout the test.

Unstable but Specific Features of Children

This source refers to temporary but specific characteristics of the child. For example, the ability to 'catch on' in items where particular tricks may lead to the correct solution. They also include brief fluctuations in memory or attention ('careless errors') which frequently occur during test taking.

Features Outside the Child during Assessment

Systematic or chance fluctuations which affect the administration of the test are meant here. These include the conditions of testing, the clarity of the tester's instructions, freedom or otherwise from distraction, the presence of disruptive children or any features of the administration which interact with the children taking the test. (The sex or race of the tester may be relevant here.)

Other Sources

These refer to chance variance (that is, variance not accounted for by any of the five sources above). The most pervasive source of this type of variance is probably guessing.

It is an obvious problem to decide which of the above sources of variance are of chief interest to the test user. Although guessing seems a relatively pure form of error variance teachers may not object to its contamination of the raw scores on the grounds that pupils whose general level of ability (first source) is high are likely to be better guessers than others. Most users of tests would probably argue that the first and second sources are of special interest in the measurements they wish to make and that these, therefore, properly constitute 'true' variance. The size of these components can be minimized. For example, differences in the comprehension of instructions and in test-wiseness (first source) may be partly overcome by careful instructions and the use of practice items which provide an opportunity for all children to get the 'feel' of the tests. Nevertheless, other sources of variance would not be acceptable as being of systematic interest, for example, if the particular format or layout were a source of error in measuring the attribute in question (fifth source). In practice, most test manuals quote coefficients of reliability which help the user distinguish the true only from the undifferentiated error variance. Quite recently Cronbach and his colleagues (1972) have produced methods by which the error variance may be differentiated, that is, separated into a number of different components. The next sections are devoted to the basic problems of obtaining, using and interpreting reliability coefficients in published and teacher-made tests.

WAYS OF ESTIMATING RELIABILITY

Although a child's obtained score will vary from test to test and from time to time on the same test, his or her true score on the attribute in question would remain the same provided the occasions are close together. Cattell (1973) has described this reliability as the *dependability* of the test. It is applicable if the testings are close enough together (say, about one month) for a little or no change to be expected by learning or maturation. Any variation in actual score, therefore, is by definition 'error'. Cronbach (1971) has pointed out, however, that the meaning of error depends upon the purposes of testing. If the purpose is to assess a child's temporary condition at the time of testing then scores which vary are the goal of the assessment. However, where the score is obtained as a measure of a relatively stable attribute such as an ability, transient variation is undesirable. This raises the obvious question, already referred to: 'Which sources of variance in scores are properly regarded as error variance?' The answer is, of course, implied above: 'It all depends on the purpose of the assessment'. Given that the concern of the book is to deal with assessment within the cognitive domain, especially of ability and learning performance, it is fairly clear that we are interested in the assessment of relatively stable attributes of the child which inform our decisions in an educational context. Instability from occasion to occasion and test to test is, therefore, properly thought of as error. If teachers are interested in a systematic study of the change or growth in pupils' abilities, then a test—retest design will be adopted with a large enough interval between testings for growth to be observable. Periods of less than one year are not likely to be of much interest in this connection.

In theory we could construct a large number of forms of a

test all designed to measure the same attribute. If we then gave all these forms to a group of children, we would assume that for a single pupil his or her true score for the attribute would be the same on every form of the test. The difference between the true score and obtained score would vary from test form to test form but would always constitute the error. As we make no attempt in this approach to reliability to differentiate the types of error we can write the equation (for each pupil):

$$x_i = T + e \qquad [6.1]$$

where

x_i = obtained score by the ith child
T = the unknown true score
e = the error score, which can be positive or negative

It is then assumed that for any one child the mean error over *all* forms of the test is zero. In other words, though the error on some forms of the test will be positive (i.e. will inflate the score above the true score), on other forms it will be negative. We further assume that the size of the error in one form of the test is uncorrelated with the error in another. Under these conditions the child's true score is *estimated* simply as the mean of his or her obtained scores because the error scores will cancel one another out to give zero for the error for each child.

Think of the entire group of children taking the test. Since each child would have his or her own 'personal equation' (equation [6.1]) the variance of the obtained scores can easily be shown by simple algebra to be the sum of two component variances, true variance and error variance. As a formula:

$$\sigma^2_o = \sigma^2_t + \sigma^2_e \qquad [6.2]$$

where subscripts o, t and e stand for obtained score, true and error scores respectively. Formally, the reliability coefficient is given as the proportion of obtained (total) variance which is true variance, that is

$$r = \frac{\sigma^2_t}{\sigma^2_o} \qquad [6.3]$$

Unfortunately for our formula σ^2_t is by definition unknown and unobservable! The difficulty, however, is a minor one. From equation [6.2],

$$\sigma^2_t = \sigma^2_o - \sigma^2_e$$

so formula [6.3], by substitution, becomes:

$$r = \frac{\sigma^2_o - \sigma^2_e}{\sigma^2_o} \qquad [6.4]$$

By now the reader will probably have had enough of these abstract ideas and we turn to ways in which the reliability co-efficient (r) can be estimated. Before doing so, however, we must distinguish the reliability *index* (r_i) from the reliability *coefficient* (r) although these terms are often (incorrectly) used interchangeably. The reliability *index* is the correlation between the true scores and the obtained scores. The reliability *coefficient* is the proportion of variance in the obtained scores which is predictable from the true scores. In words, the relationship between the index and the coefficient is that the square root of the reliability coefficient is equal to the reliability index. As a formula, $\sqrt{r} = r_i$ or

$$r = r_i^2 \qquad [6.5]$$

The two fundamental types of reliability and their various methods of estimation are shown in table 6.1. For type 1 in table 6.1, the difference in emphasis between dependability and stability has been pointed out by Cattell (1973) although both are obtained by the test—retest method. *Dependability* refers to the test—retest correlation obtained from two

Table 6.1 — Types of reliability coefficient.

Type	Name	Description	How obtained
(1) Dependability or stability	(a) test—retest coefficient	Estimates stability of scores over time	By correlating scores obtained on same test administered twice to same group of children
(2) Consistency	(i) *Internal equivalence or homogeneity*		
	(a) split-half coefficient	Estimates agreement between scores on two halves of a test	By correlating scores obtained on the two halves of a test
	(b) Kuder—Richardson coefficient	Estimates agreement between all items within a single test	By calculating proportion passing and failing each item and total test variance
	(ii) *Parallel forms equivalence*		
	(c) alternative forms coefficient	Estimates agreement between two equivalent measures of the same ability	By correlating scores obtained on two equivalent forms of a test

occasions which are close together whereas *stability* applies to the test—retest correlation obtained after a longer time (say more than one month) has elapsed between the two occasions. This distinction is made to distinguish between the different sources of fluctuation that would be expected to occur over the longer period but which would be absent from the shorter.

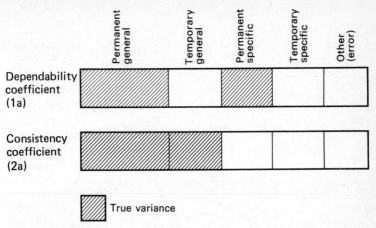

Figure 6.1   Sources of true variance in the types of reliability estimate.

At first sight this may appear confusing. Yet it is to be expected. The sources of variance which overlap to give the correlation between the two halves of the same test (type 2ia in table 6.1) will be different from those responsible for the correlation between scores obtained on the same total length test used on two occasions (type 1a). This is illustrated in figure 6.1 for a dependability coefficient obtained from two administrations of the same test taken seven days apart and a consistency coefficient of the split-half type. To simplify we classify the sources of variance as 'general', 'specific', 'permanent' and 'temporary' variance and can see from the diagram that the dependability coefficient includes as true variance different portions from those included in the consistency coefficient.

All these methods yield coefficients which are expressed as numbers which range from 0 to 1.0. A test with perfect reliability would obviously yield a coefficient of 1.0. By definition (formula [6.3]) the coefficient expresses the proportion of variance in the obtained scores that is attributable to differences in true scores. Thus a value for the reliability of 0.89 means that 89% of the differences in obtained scores occurs because of differences in true scores. A reliability of 0.64 means that 64% is true variance and so on. Quite obviously the error of measurement is given by the simple formula

$$\text{error} = 1 - r \qquad [6.6]$$

A reliability of 0.89 indicates 11% error of measurement and 0.64 an error of measurement as high as 36%.

The Test—Retest Estimate

This is probably one of the easiest to obtain since it involves only two administrations of the same test to a given group of children. Each child obtains a pair of scores (X, Y) which are then used to calculate the correlation coefficient as already described in chapter 5. This correlation is then the reliability estimate. If the value is high it confirms that a child high in the ability tends to be highly placed on both administrations of the test, and vice versa. Referring to figure 6.1 it can be seen that temporary factors, especially the child's health and motivational level, may serve to lower the reliability estimate obtained in this way because they are not sources of true variance. Quite obviously this estimate will also vary with the time interval separating the two administrations. If it is short, the child may recall earlier answers and reproduce them; this may inflate the coefficient. If it is long, the tester will not know whether the reliability is low because of measurement error or whether there are genuine individual changes due to learning or maturation in the ability being assessed by the test. Herein lies the value of Cattell's distinction between dependability (symbolized r_d) from immediate retest and the stability (r_s) from retest after a month or two, the *constancy* of the attribute being measured (r_c) is given by the formula

$$r_c = \frac{r_s}{r_d} \qquad [6.7]$$

This has proved a most helpful formula in demonstrating the size of the fluctuations which can occur in traits which, it used to be thought, change comparatively little during a person's lifetime, for example in intelligence (see second objection in chapter 3).

The Split-half Estimate

This is calculated in exactly the same way as the test—retest coefficient only this time the x and y scores for each child are the scores on the two halves of the test. Teachers will probably find this the most convenient to calculate since only one form of the test has to be used. A test can be split into two halves in a number of ways. It is usually accomplished at random or by taking half-tests composed of odd and even items. If several items together make up a unit (as would be the case where more than one question refers to the same paragraph or to the same map) it is preferable to divide the test into odd and even *units* rather than odd and even items within units, since the latter are likely to involve some of the same response elements and may inflate the reliability coefficient. Having obtained a score for each pupil on the two subdivisions (X, Y), they are then correlated as before. Notice, however, that each subdivision of the test is only half as long as the complete test. In order to estimate the reliability of the full test, therefore, the Spearman—Brown prophecy formula is used:

$$r_{ft} = \frac{2r_{\frac{1}{2}t}}{1 + r_{\frac{1}{2}t}} \qquad [6.8]$$

where subscripts ft and ½t stand for full test and half-test respectively. Suppose a test consisting of 20 items has a reliability of 0.82, what reliability would be expected if 40 items had been used? Using formula [6.8] :

$$r_{ft} = \frac{2 \times 0.82}{1 + 0.82} = 0.90$$

Kuder—Richardson Estimates

This is really a family of methods which do not involve a division of the test or the calculation of a correlation. It assumes that each item in a test measures the same general ability and requires that each item be scored as a dichotomy,

Table 6.2 — Item score matrix for ten children on a ten-item test.

Child	Item										Total	Odd score	Even score
	1	2	3	4	5	6	7	8	9	10			
A	0	0	0	0	0	0	0	0	0	0	0	0	0
B	1	0	0	0	0	0	0	0	0	0	1	1	0
C	1	0	1	0	0	0	0	0	0	0	2	2	0
D	1	1	1	0	0	0	0	0	0	0	3	2	1
E	1	1	0	1	0	0	0	0	0	0	3	1	2
F	1	1	1	0	1	0	1	0	0	0	5	4	1
G	1	1	1	1	1	1	0	0	0	0	6	3	3
H	1	1	1	1	1	1	0	0	0	0	6	3	3
I	0	1	0	1	1	1	1	1	1	0	7	3	4
J	1	1	1	1	1	1	1	1	1	1	10	5	5
Total	8	7	6	5	5	4	3	2	2	1	43	24	19
Proportion of ones (p)	0.8	0.7	0.6	0.5	0.5	0.4	0.3	0.2	0.2	0.1			
Proportion of zeros (q)	0.2	0.3	0.4	0.5	0.5	0.6	0.7	0.8	0.8	0.9			
pq	0.16	0.21	0.24	0.25	0.25	0.24	0.21	0.16	0.16	0.09			

$1.97 = \Sigma pq$

that is either 'right' or 'wrong'. The easiest to use is usually known as 'formula 20'. It is

$$r = \frac{n}{n-1} \left(\frac{\sigma_0^2 - \Sigma pq}{\sigma_0^2} \right) \qquad [6.9]$$

where

n = number of items in a test
p = proportion passing (1) an item
q = proportion failing (0) an item
σ_0^2 = variance in test scores

Its underlying argument is a little difficult to describe. The term Σpq is the sum of the variances of all items and σ_0^2 is the total test variance. The difference between the two (technically the sum of the covariances) can be thought of as indicating how much agreement or overlap there is between scores in the items. Since overlap between items is assumed to be because of the same general ability, this is where the true variance is to be found. This definition then fulfils the requirements for a coefficient of reliability. Its calculation is shown using the scores of ten children on a ten-item test with items arranged in order of difficulty as an item-score matrix (table 6.2) following Guilford and Fruchter (1973, 411). The reader should check that the variance of the scores (σ_0^2) is equal to 8.41 and the standard deviation 2.90. Substituting in formula [6.9]

$$r = \frac{10}{9} \left(\frac{8.41 - 1.97}{8.41} \right) = 0.85$$

When all the items are of roughly equal difficulty we can get an approximation to the value for the reliability using an even simpler formula. It uses only the number of items (n) the mean ($\bar{x}$) and the total test variance (σ_t^2):

$$r = \frac{n}{n-1} \left(1 - \frac{\bar{x}(n-\bar{x})}{n\sigma_0^2} \right) \qquad [6.10]$$

Since the mean score is 4.3, substitution in formula [6.10] gives us:

$$r = \frac{10}{9} \left(1 - \frac{4.3\,(10 - 4.3)}{10 \times 8.41} \right) = 0.79$$

The reason why the values of r obtained from formulae [6.9] and [6.10] differ is that the items in our test were of different degrees of difficulty, the easiest being item one and the hardest item ten. Even here, however, the approximate method yields a quite similar value to that using 'formula 20' (equation [6.9]). Where items are not scored dichotomously (as right or wrong), the coefficient α (alpha) developed by Cronbach may be used. It is very similar to the Kuder–Richardson (KR) 'formula 20' (equation [6.9]):

$$\alpha = \frac{n}{n - 1} \left(1 - \frac{\Sigma s^2}{\sigma_0^2} \right) \qquad [6.11]$$

The meaning of the symbols is as before, but Σs^2 is the sum of the variances of the single items. It yields exactly the same result as formula [6.9] if applied to the dichotomous data of table 6.2.

It is interesting to see what would have happened if we had calculated the reliability coefficient using the split-half (odd–even) method. Total test scores have been appropriately subdivided to the right of table 6.2 and the correlation, calculated using what by now will be a familiar method, is 0.72. This estimate is lower than the higher KR coefficient because it is based on only one of the many ways in which the test could have been subdivided.

Alternative (Parallel) Forms Estimate

This method is more difficult for the teacher to carry out since it requires the construction of two tests which have similar content. It is difficult in practice to fulfil criteria by which tests may be considered parallel. They should, however, contain the same number of items designed to cover the same content, be of similar difficulty and be arranged in the same format. Instructions and conditions of administration should be comparable. Although it has certain disadvantages (for example, scores are susceptible to practice effects as in test–retest reliability) the parallel forms method can, unlike the other methods described, be used to estimate the reliability of speed tests (a speed test is one which is made up of relatively easy items which most children would be expected to get right but for the fast conditions under which they are administered). The parallel forms reliability coefficient is simply the correlation between the scores obtained by the same children on two different forms of the same test. The correlation, of course, is calculated as shown in chapter 5.

STANDARD ERROR OF MEASUREMENT

This is the most useful concept in reliability theory to the teacher. Formula [6.3] reminds the reader that reliability is defined as the ratio of true variance and obtained variance:

$$r = \frac{\sigma^2_t}{\sigma^2_o} \qquad [6.3]$$

Use of the most elementary algebra shows that formula [6.2] in this chapter can be rewritten for σ^2_t as follows:

$$\sigma^2_t = \sigma^2_o - \sigma^2_e \qquad [6.12]$$

If we substitute [6.12] into [6.3] we get:

$$r = 1 - \frac{\sigma^2_e}{\sigma^2_o} \qquad [6.13]$$

This is another expression for the reliability.

Now the standard error of measurement is actually the standard deviation of the error, so we want to derive a formula for the latter. This can easily be done by rearranging formula [6.13] and taking the square root. Solving [6.13] for σ_e we get:

$$\sigma_e = \sigma_o \sqrt{1 - r} \qquad\qquad [6.14]$$

We have now got a simple formula for the *standard error of measurement* (σ_e). This is usually indicated by the symbol SE_m which we shall be adopting from now on.

Some Uses of the Reliability Coefficient

If two tests have approximately equal standard deviations the one with the higher reliability coefficient gives the better estimate of a child's true score.

Example

Suppose we have two English tests each having mean 50 and standard deviation ten. Test A has a reliability of 0.96 and test B one of 0.64. Suppose Mary scored 56 on test A and Tony 56 on test B. How closely do these lie to the true scores? We can obtain a fair approximation of the answer to this question as follows.

Using the general formula for the standard error of measurement (formula [6.14]) we can now see its value.

Mary's score on test A (r = 0.96)

Steps in the argument are as follows:

(1) If 0.96 is the reliability estimate (the proportion of true variance), then 1 – 0.96 (4%) is error variance.
(2) The standard error of measurement is, therefore, $\sqrt{0.04}$ = 0.2 of the standard deviation of the obtained scores (i.e. 0.2 x 10 = 2 points).
(3) Since roughly two-thirds (68%) of scores lie between true score ± one standard deviation (see section in chapter 5 on the normal curve) the odds are two to one that Mary's obtained score would not exceed 56 plus two nor fall below 56 minus two points on repeated testing.

(4)   If we want to be more confident we can use the fact
      that 95% of scores lie between the mean and ± two
      standard deviations. In this case the odds are roughly 19
      to one that Mary's obtained score would not exceed 60
      nor fall below 52 points. These are sometimes known as
      the 95% confidence intervals for the true score. To be
      strictly accurate, the 95% confidence interval is the ob-
      tained score ± 1.96 SE_m but it is easier to remember to
      use two for most practical purposes.

Tony's score on test B (r = 0.64)
Using the same argument the standard error of measurement
for test B is 0.6 of the standard deviation (i.e. six points).
The 68% confidence interval, therefore, is from 62 to 50
points (compared with from 58 to 54 for Mary) and the 95%
interval from 68 to 44 points (compared with 60 and 52).

   Notice that the measurement error is a function of the
reliability and the standard deviation of the test. To give you
some idea of their interdependence look at table 6.3. The
body of the table shows the value of the standard error of
measurement for different standard deviations and reliabilities. Notice that standard errors for the test with high reliability (5% error variance) are less than half as large as those
for low reliability (25% error variance).

The Interpretation of the Standard Error of Measurement

The most helpful way of using the standard error of measurement to apply to an individual child is to think of it as the

Table 6.3 — The relationship of standard error of measurement to the
standard deviation and reliability estimate.

Standard deviation	Reliability		
	0.95	0.85	0.75
30	6.7	11.6	15.0
20	4.5	7.7	10.0
10	2.2	3.9	5.0

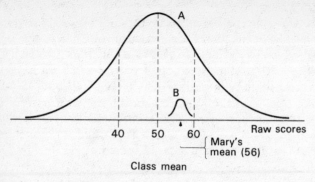

Figure 6.2   The distribution of an individual child's test scores (B) with that of all children taking the test (A).

standard deviation of the child's distribution of test scores on a large number of administrations. In figure 6.2 curve A shows the distribution of scores for *all* children taking the test, curve B shows the distribution for *one* child over several occasions. In our example the standard deviation of the large curve is ten but the standard deviation of the small curve is only two when $r = 0.96$.

Although this method applied to an individual's score gives us a reasonably approximate answer to the question: 'What are the limits within which Mary's or any individual's true score is expected to lie?', it is not a strict interpretation. It would be more correct to conclude that 68% of *all* true scores are likely to be within the limits $\pm SE_m$ and 95% within $\pm 1.96SE_m$ of the obtained score. In other words, 32 out of 100 children or only five out of 100 children taking this test would be expected to have true scores *outside* these respective intervals rather than that any *one* child's true score would be inside these intervals 68 or 95 times in 100 testings.

The higher the reliability coefficient the closer the obtained score to the true score.

When we know the reliability in a group of children we can *estimate* a child's true score using the simple formula:

$$T = \bar{x} + r(x_i - \bar{x}) \qquad [6.15]$$

where

T = true score
$\bar{x}$ = group mean
r = reliability coefficient
x_i = raw score of ith child

This formula assumes that the true scores have a linear relationship with the raw scores and it is known as the 'least squares equation' (see Lord and Novick, 1968).

Example
Suppose Peter scored 48 on a science test (reliability 0.89) on which his year group's mean was 40 and standard deviation eight points. His estimated true score is:

$$T_{Peter} = 40 + 0.89(48 - 40)$$
$$= 47.12$$
$$\cong 47$$

The higher the reliability the more confident we can be that the difference between two scores in the same group of children is real.

Suppose John and Helen were among the age group of 120 pupils who took the above science test and they scored 42 and 46 marks respectively. Is the difference between these scores large enough to be considered real, i.e. unlikely to have arisen by chance? Steps in the argument are:

(1)   Standard error of measurement is

$$SE_m = \sigma\sqrt{1 - r}$$
$$= 8\sqrt{1 - 0.89}$$
$$= 2.65$$

(2)   We now know that 2.65 is the estimated size of the

standard deviation which would be expected in John's and Helen's scores if they each took the test a large number of times. But we need to know what would be the standard deviation of the *differences* between a number of *pairs* of scores (one for John, one for Helen) if these were obtained. A formula for this value, known as the *standard error* of the difference (SE_d), is given by

$$SE_d = \sqrt{2SE_m^2} \qquad [6.16]$$

Thus

$$SE_d = \sqrt{2 \times 2.65^2}$$
$$= 3.75$$

(3) When we express the ratio of the difference between the scores and the standard error of their difference we get what is known as a *t-ratio*. Obviously the larger the difference between two scores compared with the standard error of their difference, the more confident we can be that the difference is a real (as opposed to a chance) one. We find the *t*-ratio, using the formula:

$$t = \frac{x_1 - x_2}{SE_d} \qquad [6.17]$$

Thus

$$t = \frac{46 - 42}{3.75}$$
$$= 1.07$$

(4) Now see if the value for *t* equals or exceeds the value in table 6.4. The obtained value for t_{120} (1.07) is less than 1.98. This means that a pair of scores whose difference is four (Helen scored four marks more than John) could have occurred by chance *more often* than five times in 100. We have no grounds for concluding that the difference is *un*likely to have occurred by chance. For all

Table 6.4 — Values for *t* required for significance.

		Significance level	
Size of group		5%	1%
20		2.09	2.85
30		2.04	2.75
40		2.02	2.70
60		2.00	2.66
Look for group size minus 1 120		1.98	2.62

practical purposes, therefore, John and Helen do not differ in science ability as measured by this test.[4]

We can extend the above ideas to calculate how large the difference between two scores must be for it to be unlikely to have arisen by chance. To have occurred by chance only five times in 100, the value for *t* must be equal to or greater than 1.98 (see table 6.4). Hence

$$1.98 = \frac{\text{size of difference}}{3.75}$$

therefore

$$\text{size of difference} = 1.98 \times 3.75$$
$$= 7.25$$

On our test, assuming no fractions of one in the scoring and with this size of group, therefore, a difference between any two scores of about seven points would need to exist before we could conclude that the odds were 95:5 (19:1) in favour of this being a real, rather than a chance, difference. (Notice that in all these calculations the *reliability, standard deviation* and *group size* are needed.) In all these applications we have used the same estimate for the standard error of a given test

[4] Full tables for *t* can be found in most basic statistical texts, usually in an appendix.

by which to interpret and calculate confidence intervals for each child's score on that test. This is probably what all teachers will be able to do for their home-made tests, but it can be shown that the actual value for the standard error of measurement varies at different points along the test's range. If the reliability is calculated for a very large group of children, then different standard errors at different score points can be presented. Some published tests do indeed report different standard errors for different obtained scores. If a really crucial decision were to be taken about the confidence intervals for a given score, a teacher could use an alternative procedure proposed by Lord (1957) which enables the computation of intervals for each child. The formula is

$$SE_m \cong \sqrt{\frac{1}{n-1} \, x_i \, (n - x_i)} \qquad [6.18]$$

In this formula

$$
\begin{aligned}
SE_m &= \text{the standard error for an individual} \\
x_i &= \text{the obtained score for that individual} \\
n &= \text{the number of items in the test}
\end{aligned}
$$

The methods described so far are applicable to finding the reliability of tests for which scores are available. Rather different problems are experienced with essay type tests, and it is with these that chapter 7 is concerned.

7

Reliability of Essays, 'Short Answers' and Criterion-referenced Tests

RELIABILITY OF ESSAYS

Essays are open-ended examinations in the sense that the titles or questions set require the writers to recall, organize and present material selected by them as relevant in answering the question. No right or wrong answers to this type of test exist (except, of course, in the factual content of the essay). Unlike standardized tests, in which the score for each child may be regarded as a value on an interval scale, essays or open-ended ratings are on an ordinal scale only. Quite erratic variation in the scoring often occurs when teachers mark essays but some of the ways in which greater agreement can be obtained by reaching consensus, before marking, as to the number and nature of the criteria to be employed in the assessment were described in chapter 4. Nevertheless, so long as methods of assessment which permit the individual differences between markers to influence results continue to be used, there is always certain to be less than perfect agreement amongst even the most well intentioned and conscientious of judges.

The problem of the reliability of such marks can be investigated in three ways.

Method 1

We can think of the true score on an essay type examination as the mean of the assessments of all qualified raters and the reliability of the assessment as the mean correlation between the marks given by the teachers rating the essays. This value could be called the coefficient of concordance (between the examiners).

Method 2

We can construct two equivalent forms of the essay and administer it to all the children with a suitable time interval to prevent boredom. Each rater would read all the answers to both forms and a correlation between grades on the two forms would constitute an estimate of reliability. This is obviously similar to the parallel form estimate (type 2c in table 6.1) already discussed and is the method preferred by Cureton (1966).

Method 3

We can estimate the *self-consistency* of individual raters. Each teacher would be asked to mark the same essays twice with a time interval between them and the correlation between the two sets of marks calculated. This exercise is often salutary for the marker concerned but a high correlation could indicate only that the examiner is consistent in his prejudices. The 'mark—remark' or 'self-consistency' coefficient obviously yields no information whatever as to how close each mark is to the true score and is, therefore, of limited use.

Only method (2) corresponds with the reliability estimates for objective tests already discussed in table 6.1. The other two methods refer to the consistency between *markers* or within a *single marker* on different occasions. In them the error attached to the ratings refers to the variability between raters or within a single rater whereas true reliability refers to the variation in the ability or attribute being assessed. Because of this it is somewhat misleading to group the three types of coefficient under the single heading of 'reliability' although this is frequently done. We shall distinguish them by describing them as: (1) coefficient of concordance, (2) coefficient of reliability, (3) coefficient of self-consistency, respectively. Whilst each has its value, the teacher should note that it is their meaning and, therefore, the inferences that can be made from them which differ. It is only using method 2 that one could defensibly calculate a standard error of measurement, for example.

Table 7.1 — Marks given by three raters for ten children's essays.

Child	Marker		
	1	2	3
1	10	8	13
2	3	5	16
3	12	4	9
4	5	11	17
5	7	17	15
6	14	6	9
7	11	12	10
8	9	14	14
9	16	9	11
10	4	15	13
Total	91	101	127
Mean	9.10	10.10	12.70
Standard deviation	4.11	4.20	2.72

We illustrate below a simple method for obtaining an estimate of the reliability in the sense of method 1 of essay type examinations which avoids making very strong assumptions about the nature of the measurement made. It follows Lord and Novick (1968) who propose that the most effective way of studying essay marks is to transform all observed scores into rank orders and to see how consistently a number of markers agree as to the relative merits of the children's work: that is, to obtain an estimate of concordance. The layout in table 7.1 illustrates the marks given (out of 20) by three hypothetical markers for ten children.

Unfortunately these teachers had failed to agree their marking criteria beforehand such that child two, who is an appalling speller, is penalized by markers one and two but evaluated highly for content by marker three who is indifferent to spelling deficiencies! Notice also that the markers are using different implied scales. Not only are the mean values different but, more importantly, so are the standard deviations. Marker three is most generous and also makes less

Table 7.2 — Marks in table 7.1 transformed to rank order.

| Child | Marker | | | Sum of ranks |
	1	2	3	
1	5	7	6	18
2	10	9	2	21
3	3	10	10	23
4	8	5	1	14
5	7	1	4	12
6	2	8	9	19
7	4	4	8	16
8	6	3	3	12
9	1	6	7	14
10	9	2	5	16

differentiation amongst individual children than the other two markers. It would clearly make no sense to claim that the mean of the three scores for each child estimates the true score if the three markers are using different scales.

In table 7.2 each marker has placed the scripts in rank order. These values can now be used to calculate the correlations between each pair of markers (r_{12}, r_{23}, r_{13}). Using the procedure described in chapter 5 we find the following values:

$$r_{12} = -0.32$$
$$r_{23} = +0.38$$
$$r_{13} = -0.81$$

Thus the average correlation, $\bar{r}$, is given by

$$\bar{r} = \frac{-0.32 + (+0.38) + (-0.81)}{3}$$

$$= -0.25$$

Remember that a positive correlation indicates that there is a tendency for children who receive an above average mark from one rater to receive it from the other. A negative correlation shows the tendency for children rated above average by one marker to be rated below average by the other. The more cases there are of the former, the higher the concordance between the two raters. Marker one is obviously employing very different criteria from the other two markers. In fact, if marker one rates a child as above average, the other two seem more likely to rate his score lower than average: this is suggested by the negative correlations. Markers two and three have achieved some agreement, but it is not very strong. If a result such as this was obtained, it would be very difficult indeed to know what meaning could be attached to the scores given and the teachers clearly have a lot of collaboration to do before marks are given in the future for this kind of work!

It is not very likely that teachers will find time to have the work graded by more than three independent raters. In this case only three correlations and their average need be calculated. There is, however, a similar technique available which provides a measure of the *overall* agreement between a number of judges: it will be illustrated briefly using the same data.

Some understanding of how this method works can be given by thinking of what would have happened if the raters had been in perfect agreement — a most unlikely event! In this case they would each have ranked the ten children in exactly the same order: one child would have received three ranks of one, a second child three ranks of two, and so on. The 'top' child would have obtained one + one + one = three, the 'second' child two + two + two = six and the 'bottom' child ten + ten + ten = 30. Notice that these constitute a series as follows: number of raters; two x number of raters; . . . number of children x number of raters. If we say we have k raters, our series will be $k, 2k, 3k, 4k, . . . , 10k$. It is obvious from our data that we get nothing like this series. In fact our lowest sum of ranks (child five) is 12, and highest 23 (child three). Now we know what the average sum of ranks per child is. The sum of the ranks is given by

$$k \left(\frac{n}{2}(n+1) \right)$$

and in this case $k = 3$ and $n = 10$. Thus the sum of ranks is

$$3 \left(\frac{10}{2}(10 + 1) \right) = 165$$

and so the average sum of ranks is 165/10 = 16.5. (Gauss, the famous mathematician, is said to have discovered that the sum of a series is ½n (n + 1) (i.e. the term in large parentheses above) at the age of six years since he saw that the first number plus the last (1 + n) equals the second number plus the second from last and so on and that these will be half as many pairs (½n) as there are numbers: so teachers, don't give up!) It is very easy therefore to find the variance in the sum of the ranks exactly as we find the variance in any other set of scores. Refer back to table 5.8 where you will see that the deviation for any child is given by the difference between the child's score and the mean of the group. Therefore the deviation for child one in table 7.2 is given by (18 − 16.5), for child two (21 − 16.5) and so on. Squaring these values, summing over all ten children and dividing by the number of children therefore gives us the actual variance in the ranks (s^2). This is then expressed as a proportion of the variance which would be the case if perfect agreement were obtained, actually equal to $1/12k^2 (n^3 - 10)$. The coefficient of concordance (W) which indicates the strength of the overall agreement between three judges can now be obtained. It is given by:

$$W = \frac{s^2}{1/12k^2 (n^3 - 10)} \qquad [7.1]$$

$$= \frac{124.5}{1/12 \ 3^2 (10^3 - 10)}$$

$$= 0.17$$

Notice that we use W where the concordance is measured between *more than* two raters, r where it is between only two raters. W is closely related to the average correlation between judges ($\bar{r}$) already obtained. To be exact, the relationship between them (W and $\bar{r}$) is given by:

$$\bar{r} = \frac{k(W) - 1}{k - 1} \qquad [7.2]$$

W can only take values ranging from 0 to +1 whereas the correlation can, of course, take values ranging from -1 to +1. To check that formula [7.2] holds substitute $W = 0.17$ and $k = 3$ from our example:

$$\bar{r} = \frac{3(0.17) - 1}{3 - 1} = -0.25$$

which agrees with the value already obtained.

There are other methods of assessing the reliability of essays depending upon the purpose of the marking, but these are not referred to here. Examples of reliabilities obtained for essay marking have been given by Gosling (1966). A large number of rating scales and procedures have been adopted so it is difficult to compare the results obtained. A selection of values reported is given in table 7.3.

It is clear from table 7.3 that interest has persisted for a very long time and that values of the coefficients vary with the procedure adopted. It is possible by careful preparation of marking schemes, the training of examiners and the use of multiple marking that is both analytic and impressionistic to increase the reliability of the essay as a technique for the evaluation of learning. Teachers are unlikely to have the time or resources for such elaborate schemes and will probably come to rely more heavily on alternative tools of assessment where more objective standards may be achieved.

It is instructive for teachers to examine the coefficients listed in table 7.3 to see whether much value can be gained from such results. In the first place, only the type of estimate made by Finlayson would permit the teacher to estimate the size of the error component in each grade awarded. To do this, the standard deviations would also be required. But a coefficient as low as 0.60 would indicate that a large margin of error is present. The other coefficients are of concordance (agreement between markers) and of self-consistency (agreement between the same marker on a number of occasions on which the same answers were marked). To take the latter first, consider situations (c) and (k). They demonstrate that very large discrepancies can exist within a single marker. Such

Table 7.3 — Some examples of reliability of essay tests.

Situation	Value of coefficient	Type	Source
(a) British university scholarships	0.51	concordance	Hartog and Rhodes (1936)
(b) School compositions	0.25 to 0.59	concordance	Cast (1940)
(c) School certificate essays	-0.04 to 0.95	self-consistency	Hartog (1941)
(d) American university qualifying exam	0.55 to 0.83	concordance	Stalnaker (1934)
(e) School exam	0.66	self-consistency	Phillips (1948)
(f) Grammar school entrance	0.72 to 0.88	self-consistency	Nisbet (1955)
(g) Primary school	0.60 to 0.80	parallel forms	Finlayson (1951)
(h) Students	0.55 to 0.77	concordance	Vernon and Millican (1954)
(i) Australian university students	0.60 to 0.89	concordance	Dunstan (1959)
(j) O level biology	0.64	concordance	Head (1966)
(k) Biology exam (Australia)	0.35 to 0.79	self-consistency	Lucas (1971)

fluctuations may be so large that it would be most unwise to draw conclusions about the children from them, not to say grossly unfair! The best use that teachers can make of this co-efficient is to check their own consistency and correct if it necessary. Though the high values suggest that greater self-consistency can be attained they do not show that it is objec-tive or even fair. For this reason it is recommended that these types of estimate are used to check the marking procedures and only indirectly to draw inferences about children's work. In any case essays are almost always so unreliable that their proper place seems to be as part of a programme of assessment, but always marked by more than one teacher, among other alternative assessment techniques.

To turn to the concordance estimates (they are all, in fact, average correlations rather than values for W). As such they show the average agreement amongst pairs of markers. Notice that even the highest (0.89) reveals considerable disagreement. A correlation of 0.71 between the sets of marks by two judges indicates that only 50% of the individual differences in one marker's list can be predicted from the other's list! Knowing that the same teacher's marks vary from time to time and that different teachers' marks vary is 'common sense', but quantification of the error will often emphasize the dangers inherent in educational decision making on the basis of essay marks. It is not possible to specify a cut-off point by which to decide whether to accept or to reject the marks as meaningful. But if the teachers concerned have agreed on a marking schedule, have practised its use and are satisfied that the essay is a valid method of assessment, any set of results which yields a mean correlation between markers of less than 0.80 must be regarded as unsatisfactory, and deserves the report 'could do better'!

RELIABILITY OF CRITERION-REFERENCED TESTS

It must by now be clear that the concept of reliability discussed so far can be applied only to tests in which variance exists. Given the definition of reliability, it is obvious that if a test failed to distinguish between children (say if all children in a group got the same mark) it would be impossible to differentiate zero variance into true and error components! Although such a test would be useless as a norm-referenced instrument it is not entirely valueless in the assessment of criterion-referenced learning. Remember from chapter 3 that the purpose of criterion-referenced testing is usually to classify learners into 'masters' or 'non-masters' of an objective so that the teacher may decide whether a pupil is ready to move on to the next objective or whether it would be advisable to spend longer on related learning in order to overcome the deficiency identified. In this usage teachers would ordinarily be delighted to find that all children in a group exhibited mastery of a given objective! In such a case the facility of the item would be 1.0 whereas we saw in chapter 4 that items with facilities of around 0.5 may be expected to maximize the variance.

Because criterion-referenced tests are designed to assess how closely a child's performance approaches the objective there is little point in determining the variance of the mean score as this would only give us an idea of the relative performance of the pupils. Instead we need to know how many individuals achieve mastery of the given objective where mastery has been defined in terms of a prescribed score (say 80 or 90%; the decision is arbitrary) on the criterion test. The methods of estimating reliability for norm-referenced tests which depend on the existence of variance, therefore, are not entirely applicable to criterion-referenced tests since their purpose is different. Because of this, there is as yet no universally agreed method for estimating the reliability of criterion-referenced tests. However, some people have attempted to obtain a reliability coefficient for criterion-referenced tests which is analogous to those for norm-referenced tests. Livingston (1972), for example, has provided a formula recommended by some writers (e.g. Mehrens and Lehmann, 1978, 107). In practice this method has been found to be unsatisfactory because it yields higher criterion-referenced reliability the greater the distance between the criterion score and the mean score. For theoretical reasons, too, the coefficient obtained in this way cannot be used to estimate whether or not a true score falls below or above a given criterion value and is of limited value.

If measurement theorists, then, are unable to provide a satisfactory method for estimating the reliability of criterion-referenced tests what can teachers do to improve the reliability of those they have constructed? Perhaps the best and simplest advice that can at present be offered is to reinterpret the concept of reliability for criterion-referenced tests in terms of the consistency with which a test makes a decision

Table 7.4 — Pupils achieving mastery state on two administrations of the same test.

2nd administration 1st administration	Masters	Non-masters	Total
Masters	33 (a)	2 (b)	35
Non-masters	7 (c)	8 (d)	15
Total	40	10	50

about the 'mastery state' of the pupils taking it. Normally a criterion-referenced test programme contains a number of objectives and a number of items per objective. If the objectives are relatively independent of one another there is no reason to suppose that a child who achieves the criterion score on one will necessarily achieve it on another. In this sense, then, there are as many reliabilities as there are objectives within a test. Suppose, however, as will ordinarily be the case, a given objective is assessed using a number of items, these items will constitute a test in its own right. Following a single administration, children would be classified as masters or non-masters of that objective. Let us suppose, in order to make the arithmetic easy, that 50 children take the test (not necessarily all at the same time) and as a result 35 of these reach the criterion score. In other words 35/50 are classified as masters, 15/50 as non-masters. On a second testing with the same items the corresponding numbers are 40/50 and 10/50 respectively. By plotting a simple table like table 7.4 the teacher can compare the numbers of children classed as having the same or different mastery status by the two administrations.

Quite obviously the size of the entries in cells (a) and (d) relative to those in cells (b) and (c) indicates the agreement between the two administrations. From these a simple index of *consistency of classification* can be stated. Using the symbol k (to remind ourselves that its interpretation is different from that of the usual reliability coefficient) it is:

$$k = \frac{P_o - P_e}{1 - P_e} \qquad [7.3]$$

where

P_o = the observed proportion of agreement
P_e = the expected proportion of agreement

To calculate this coefficient we must change the numbers in the cells to proportions as shown in table 7.5. In cell (a) 33 out of 50 pupils were classified as masters on both occasions and $33/50 = 0.66$, and so on for all cells and totals in the margin. The observed proportion of agreement (P_o) is, therefore, the sum of the proportions in cells (a) and (d), i.e. $0.66 + 0.16 = 0.82$.

Calculation of the Expected Proportion of Agreement

Since the proportion of masters on the first administration was 0.7 and on the second occasion 0.8 the proportion expected to be masters on both occasions is the product of the separate probabilities, i.e. $0.7 \times 0.8 = 0.56$.[5] By the same argument the expected proportion of non-masters on both administrations is 0.06. The sum of these probabilities (P_e) is, therefore, 0.62. Substituting in formula [7.3]

$$k = \frac{0.82 - 0.62}{1 - 0.62} = 0.53$$

We now have a single number which indicates the consistency with which a test classifies a group of children into masters and non-masters. This approach has been described as *decision-theoretic* approach to reliability. It provides a useful index of

---

[5] An analogy might help readers understand this point. The probability of any event is the ratio of the number of times it occurs and the number of times it could have occurred. As was shown in chapter 5 if one coin is tossed, two events could have occurred (H or T). Thus the probability of a head is half or 0.5. If two coins are tossed four events could occur (HH, HT, TH, T). Thus the probability that both are a head is now a quarter or 0.25. In other words the probability that both fall as heads is the product of their separate probabilities (i.e. $0.5 \times 0.5 = 0.25$).

Table 7.5 — Data of previous table as proportions (expected proportions in brackets).

1st administration \ 2nd administration	Masters	Non-masters	Total
Masters	0.66 (0.56)	0.04	0.70
Non-masters	0.14	0.16 (0.06)	0.30
Total	0.80	0.20	

the consistency of the test but it cannot be used to estimate the child's true score nor the standard error of the measurement.

By experience and use the teacher can gradually accumulate criterion-referenced items for a single objective which exhibit high consistency of classification. These can then constitute the test of that objective. If the degree of consistency is not examined there is a danger that the test items will be measuring different things and the resulting test will thus be an unreliable one.

IMPLICATIONS FOR TEACHERS OF THE STUDY OF RELIABILITY

This section attempts to draw together the importance of reliability for teachers' assessments of children.

(1) Assessment is both time-consuming and potentially dangerous (chapter 2). Assuming that it is undertaken to provide information which will be used to evaluate and make decisions about children, we need to know how much confidence can be placed in the results. Estimating the reliability of the test or essay used is one method of obtaining this information. If an assessment results in measurement (as in a test), in which pupils can be placed in rank order, or in a practice by which pupils are allocated to the next stage in learning, then the

means exist for estimating how well our methods accomplish these ends.

(2) A study of the reliability of an assessment alerts the teacher to its degree of consistency. Inconsistency (error) is inevitable: it results from many sources which teachers need to know if they are to interpret a result intelligently.

(3) When choosing a published test or considering its adoption, teachers are helped if they understand how to place confidence intervals around the score obtained by any child. This can only be accomplished using the standard error of measurement. All other things being equal the test with the highest reliability is the most useful.

(4) There are many ways of estimating reliability (table 6.1). Each permits a different conclusion. In reading test manuals the teacher is helped by knowledge of the features of the reliability quoted. (Tests produced by the National Foundation for Educational Research normally quote Kuder–Richardson coefficients.)

(5) The construction of tests is time consuming. There is little point using one whose scores contain a great deal of error. If the interpretation of those scores is to be used to make important decisions about children's learning a check on the test's internal consistency can easily be conducted and requires only one administration of the test. Reliable tests can be retained for later use, unreliable tests can be discarded.

(6) Estimation of the reliability of an assessment makes its degree of error explicit. Through a study of reliability greater accuracy of assessment can be achieved: this is an important aspect of professional accountability.

(7) Knowledge of the concept of reliability helps to assess the consistency with which markers carry out their task. Estimates of reliability of essay type tests show how the opinions of teachers differ and how the opinions of a single teacher about the same piece of work change over a period of time. Without knowledge of reliability no method of improving the consistency of an assessment can be adopted.

8

The Validity of an Assessment

Having constructed or obtained a reliable test one is now faced with a question crucial in deciding whether it should be used. The teacher may have concluded that if the test is a reliable one then it is a good one: but this is not so. One can obtain highly reliable assessments, yet these can quite easily remain of little or no use in the appraisal of children. Indeed, probably the most important problem in the use of assessment — and one which, unfortunately, teachers often have too little time to examine — is whether the test measures what it is supposed to measure. It really is of little significance if we can say of a test: 'it yields obtained scores which deviate only by a small amount from the corresponding true scores but I really haven't much idea what the test measures, and therefore, what I can infer about a child from the score obtained'.

Some examples may clarify this point. Whereas at one time it was widely agreed that intelligence test scores indicated a child's 'innate general cognitive ability' (Burt, 1955), today there is far less agreement as to what can be inferred from them. Vernon (1979) has presented a summary of recent changes in the interpretation of intelligence test scores. In clinical work and in child guidance, for example, intelligence tests (which are certainly reliable in the sense discussed in chapter 7) are often used in determination of brain damage or in the identification of children who seem to need remedial or special education. One could say that the tests are valid for these latter purposes, but not in the determination of the genetic potential for learning, though this was widely held to be the case 30 years ago (Cronbach, 1975) and is still apparently believed to be true by some (for example, Jensen, 1972). In similar fashion, the author was involved with a colleague some years ago in the use of a test designed to assess the child's style of thinking (Satterly and Brimer, 1971). It proved to have satisfactory reliability in distinguishing certain qualitative differences in approaches to a task, but subsequent work has failed to show that the test correlates with any criterion of behaviour or performance in school. This suggests that the test scores have failed to check against some other observation and that the test is, therefore, of little identifiable external merit. These two examples should serve to emphasize the most important aspect of test validation; namely, that one cannot meaningfully talk of an *assessment* or *test* being valid or invalid, but only its *interpretation* as valid or invalid for *some specified purpose.* In the general sense, however, we can think of the test measuring whatever causes, or enables, some individuals to get high but others low scores on that test.

The truth of Cronbach's (1971, 445) statement, 'validation of an instrument calls for an integration of many types of evidence' must already be apparent. It will become clear that no teachers are going to be able to conduct many of the studies that are relevant to the establishment of the validity of a given test: they are going to have to take on trust, or not, as the case may be, what is claimed by test publishers. A classroom teacher who constructs his or her own test or other instrument for assessment of the outcomes of a new course on, say, child care, may be prevented by lack of time from carrying out a systematic study of its properties. And yet it is invaluable for this teacher to know of the problems in validity if only to recognize the limitations of the assessment. But such knowledge is also necessary if teachers are going to exercise an intelligent judgment as to whether the evidence for validity presented by a test's publisher is adequate — or even downright unsatisfactory! In one sense, then, there is continuity in the twin concepts of reliability and validity. Although separated for convenience, they are both important in examining claims that any test or other method of assessment should be adopted and used.

TYPES OF VALIDITY

Assessments are made for a variety of purposes (chapter 1).

Table 8.1 — Types of validity and their purpose in education.

Type	Question asked	Purpose
(1) Content	Do the items and the observations they permit actually sample the domain of tasks the assessment is intended to measure?	To ensure that children are assessed by items which cover the objectives of teaching in proportion to the importance attached to them
(2) Criterion-related (a) predictive ability	Does the assessment predict the performance of children on an educationally meaningful criterion?	To decide if the assessment should be used to draw inferences about future performance in selection of pupils, or for placement in instructional alternatives according to the result
(b) concurrent validity	Does the result of the assessment agree with the present status of children on some independent external criterion?	To decide if the results of the assessment generalise to another made at the same time
(3) Construct	Does the test measure what it claims to measure? Is the psychological or educational theory behind the test sound?	To see if the inferences drawn from the results are in agreement with theory and other evidence

The study of validity is, therefore, the study of how well these purposes are fulfilled. Each type of purpose requires a different method of investigation. To simplify this problem, a threefold classification of validities is usually adopted:

(1) *content* validity;

(2) *criterion-related* validity;
(3) *construct* validity.

The teacher can investigate all these aspects, if necessary. Each type of validity poses a different question about the assessment as shown in table 8.1. In the sections which follow we shall provide examples of these types of validity and show, briefly, how teachers can obtain information on which to base decisions about the inferences that can be drawn from the results of the assessment.

Face or Faith Validity?

Before discussing the three types of validity listed above brief reference must be made to the concept of 'face validity'. Some writers fail to distinguish this type from content validity but they are not the same. Whereas claims for content validity are substantiated by evidence that the test measures what it claims to measure, face validity claims are unsubstantiated.

A fairly recent example of tests which gained widespread credibility amongst psychologists and educators on claims for face validity is provided by the so-called tests of creativity. These tests were devised to sample rather trivial but measurable components of the kind of thinking apparently characteristic of creative people. These included originality and novelty of response, fluency in suggesting new solutions to old problems and freedom from the restraints and inhibitions which characterize most (non-creative) people. Though these may well be global descriptions of what is involved in some types of creativity, the tests themselves (use of objects; making up titles for stories, etc.) have failed to correlate highly with one another, have not been shown to correlate substantially with external criteria of creativity, and have tended to trivialize the concept. The only claims for validity as tests of creativity, therefore, have come from the opinions of test constructors and users. For this reason Cattell has justifiably renamed the concept 'faith validity'.

Content Validity

A common use of classroom tests is to ascertain to what

extent the children have learned what they have been taught or expected to learn under guidance. This might be because the teacher or school wishes to evaluate a curriculum, because the teacher believes that the test provides a goal which motivates pupils or because the teacher is required to provide an order of merit for the class. In each case there is need to know how well the items or problems which make up the test match the objectives of the curriculum and the actual content of the teaching and learning experiences. Content validity is an especially important concept for achievement tests and requires that the teacher or test constructor builds into the test not only the topics which were covered but also items which demand the application of the skills and concepts in the manner in which they are presented and exercised during learning.

In chapter 4 we saw how, by the use of a specification grid, the teacher can map the objectives of the teaching and the contexts in which they were learned onto the content of the assessment. Drawing these up, it will be remembered, is principally to ensure that the test adequately represents the teaching and learning that have gone on. Here the teaching and testing are under the teachers' control. If an external test is used (one set either by an external testing agency, such as the examination boards or a standardized achievement test), it will have content validity only insofar as its contents represent the teaching goals of those teachers using it.

Quite obviously from the above, it is meaningful to think of a given test as having validity for the work and assessment by one classroom teacher but not for another. The problem facing test constructors and test publishers, therefore, is to try to develop a test which reflects the generally accepted aims of teaching over a wide area — a task notoriously difficult to achieve in view of the variations that exist in an educational system free from central control. This is one of the reasons why it is often difficult to compare the effectiveness of schools since no two schools teach to an identical syllabus nor accord equal status or time to the learning of skills and concepts. More will be said in chapter 10 about the methods adopted by the APU to draw up tests which can be used on a national basis. Although test constructors make sterling efforts to build tests of wide validity through the inspection of innovations in the curriculum (an extensive study of the text books most commonly used, knowledge of working parties of teachers such as those set up by the Schools Council and so on), the dangers inherent in allowing external tests to dominate the curricula have already been pointed out in the fifth objection in chapter 3. The arguments presented there encourage teachers to construct their own instruments for assessment if they wish to ensure a test's validity for their particular course of study. We conclude this section by summarizing the guidelines in the evaluation of the content validity of external tests:

(1) Look at the test manual or publisher's blurb to see if the content and sampling are described. For example, does a test of mathematics describe the items, the range of subject matter, the age group for which it is suitable and the relative balance between the mathematical operations and concepts it includes?

(2) Does the manual give details of who made the decision as to what is included in the test and how these decisions were made?

(3) If the test was designed to measure the objectives of a particular curriculum (say, the 'Science 5—13' curriculum) are its limitations (i.e. lack of generalizability for other curricula) expressly stated?

Courses of study, teaching methods and children's interests change. These changes may limit the lifespan of a test's appropriateness. (Note that one reading test constructed 30 years ago is still in widespread use in primary schools despite the change in the conception of reading from decoding or 'barking at print' to reading for meaning.)

The measurement of content validity

There is no way in which the content validity of a test can be measured. As Cronbach has pointed out, ensuring that the test contains homogeneous items (i.e. those which correlate highly with one another) does not ensure content validity. A test designed to contain items representing a relatively homogeneous set of teaching objectives or area of knowledge (such as knowledge of the symbols for the chemical elements) is sometimes known as a domain-referenced test. If, however, the domain (i.e. all the items that would have to be devised in order to test *all* the objectives) is itself heterogeneous, then high inter-item correlation would mean that the test did *not* represent it! Unlike criterion-related validity (see below) the correlation between the items and an outside criterion is of no help in establishing content validity. Cronbach gives, as an example, the fact that knowledge of the highway code does not correlate highly with a miles-without-accident criterion. This does not indicate that the test of knowledge of the code is invalid (Cronbach, 1971, 455).

Criterion-related Validity

(a) Predictive validity

All tests predict imperfectly and some teachers, mindful of the dangers inherent in the attempt to predict, may prefer to restrict their interpretations of an assessment to a description of a child's achievement at that point in time. Nevertheless, there are occasions on which teachers are concerned with the usefulness of predicting some *future* performance even if these occasions are kept to a minimum. For example, some comprehensive and middle schools use tests to 'band' pupils of similar ability to share a common teaching and learning environment. Though this purpose is ostensibly to produce relatively homogeneous groups it contains an implicit prediction about future performance — relatively high or low achievement in the subject at a later stage in school career. Some schools postpone such decisions as long as possible. Nevertheless tests and examinations are sometimes used to determine whether a pupil sits for O-level or CSE where the two syllabuses have sufficient in common to make this a practical alternative. In this case, a test taken now which predicts a later criterion effectively is said to have high predictive validity. All selection tests require this property.

There are obvious difficulties. In the first place, if we are looking for a test with high predictive validity for 'success in school' we need a criterion of that success. In the United

States, grade point average (GPA) has become an almost universal criterion despite its acknowledged deficiencies. In Britain some have employed a weighting system which uses the number and level of examination successes (five points for an A, four for a B, and so on: the assumptions here are too obvious to require enumeration). A firm which employs apprentices might be interested in the predictive validity of an aptitude test for achievement in engineering, or the staff of an assessment centre might value a measure of the personality of the offender as an index of suitability for alternative forms of treatment. These, too, are instances of the need for predictive validity. Unfortunately, however, if the assessment does not correlate very highly with the criterion we do not know which of three possibilities is the case. Either the assessment is a poor predictor of the criterion, or the measure of the criterion is unreliable, or both! Reliability and validity are required of both predictor and criterion, of course. In fact, although one can attach a number to the predictive validity of a test using the correlation between predictor (X) and criterion (Y), there is a mathematical limitation on the size of that correlation which is imposed by the reliabilities of both X and Y. Thus the correlation between predictor and criterion (r_{xy}) cannot be larger than the square root of the product of their separate reliabilities. Here and later in this chapter we use capital letters X, Y when referring to tests and lower case letters x, y when we mean the scores in tests X, Y respectively. As a formula:

$$r_{xy} \leqslant \sqrt{r_{xx}r_{yy}} \qquad [8.1]$$

where $\leqslant$ stands for 'is less than or equal to',

$$r_{xx} = \text{reliability of predictor}$$
$$r_{yy} = \text{reliability of criterion}$$

In this formula r_{xy} is sometimes known as the validity coefficient.

It is unlikely that many teachers are currently assessing the predictive validity of their assessments over a long period of time. In checking on the short-term predictive validity of a test, however, there is a possibility that a teacher's assessment of the criterion is distorted by memory of the score awarded to a child on the predictor. This would create a spurious impression of predictive validity. For this reason different teachers should be involved in the two assessments. A practical and simple method for determining criterion-related validity, but not as a coefficient, will be discussed following a brief consideration of concurrent validity since the method is applicable to both.

(b) *Concurrent validity*
Little need be said about this because the only operational difference between it and predictive validity is that the two measurements or assessments are made at or near the same time. For example, if the teacher wished to develop a questionnaire which measures 'boredom with school' the results ought, at the very least, to differentiate children who are independently rated as 'bored' or 'not bored' on everyday school behaviour. The extent to which it does so (the correlation between the two) is an index of its concurrent validity.

The measurement of criterion-related validity
One obvious way is to report the validity coefficient (the correlation) between predictor and criterion. Suppose a school uses a mathematics test (X) to help organize the sets or bands into which children are grouped, and reports the correlation of scores from this test with later success in O level or CSE mathematics (Y) as $r_{xy} = 0.45$. This indicates a moderate relationship between predictor and criterion. A more helpful interpretation is to find the coefficient of determination using the correlation, i.e. finding $(r_{xy})^2$. This would be interpreted as showing that 20.25% $((r_{xy})^2 = 0.2025)$ of the essential success in mathematics can be predicted from the scores in the school test.

Example
Suppose Peter scored 59% on our mathematics test in a group of children where the mean was 42% and standard deviation ten. If the predictive validity of the test is 0.45 what score

would he be expected to get in O level mathematics (the criterion) assuming a criterion mean of 38% and standard deviation of 12 points?

The equation used is:

$$\hat{y} = r_{xy} \left(\frac{\sigma_y}{\sigma_x} \right) (x_i - \bar{x}) + \bar{y} \qquad [8.2]$$

where

$\hat{y}$ = the predicted criterion score (O level)

r_{xy} = correlation between test and O level marks

σ_x = standard deviation of test scores

σ_y = standard deviation of O level scores

x_i = score test

$\bar{x}$ = mean of test scores

$\bar{y}$ = mean of O level scores

Hence for Peter:

$$\hat{y} = 0.45 \left(\frac{12}{10} \right) (59 - 42) + 38$$

$$= 47\%$$

If we wish to go further we can employ a procedure analogous to that of formula [6.14] by finding what is known as the standard error of the estimate (or prediction) on the criterion ($S_{\hat{y},x}$). Thus

$$S_{\hat{y},x} = \sigma_y \sqrt{1 - (r_{xy})^2} \qquad [8.3]$$

where

$S_{\hat{y},x}$ = the standard error of the estimated value for y from a given x

VALIDITY OF ASSESSMENT   233

Table 8.2 — Expectancy table to calculate the predictive validity of test scores for exam success.

Test scores	CSE grades						Total %
	Ungraded	5	4	3	2	1	
70–79				10	10	80	100
60–69			5	10	55	30	100
50–59		3	5	28	64		100
40–49		1	22	59	18		100
30–39	5	8	19	68			100
20–29	3	32	45	20			100

σ_y = standard deviation of the criterion
r_{xy} = validity coefficient

Applied to Peter's score:

$$S_{\hat{y},x} = 12\sqrt{1 - 0.45^2}$$
$$= 12 \times 0.893$$
$$= 10.72$$
$$\cong 11$$

This may then be interpreted as described in chapter 6. The odds are roughly two to one that Peter's score in O level mathematics would not exceed 58 (i.e. 47 + 11) nor fall below 36 (i.e. 47 – 11). The reason for this large margin of error, of course, is the low value for the correlation between predictor and criterion.

Normally, of course, teachers would not have knowledge of the actual external test scores by which to measure predictive validity in the way just described. In this case grades will be available and a very simple method — using an expectancy table — can be adopted (table 8.2). This is illustrated by the results of a school test in geography and CSE grades received but its use with any two tests (provided one is the predictor, the other the criterion) would be appropriate. In the left-hand column of table 8.2 are the school test scores (arranged in intervals of ten) and across the top the CSE grades. Entries in the table are the percentages within each grade. Thus 59%

of those who scored between 40 and 49 received grade three in the CSE exam, and so on. No statistical expertise is required to interpret this table. The test has predictive validity in that all highest scorers (over 70 on the test) achieved grade three or better, whereas 80% of the low scorers (under 29 on the test) achieved no better than a grade four. Obviously the predictive validity of the test varies at different points in its range. We can state that the probability that children who score over 70 in the school test will get a grade one is 0.8; the probability that they will get a grade two or higher is 0.9, and so on. The two principal disadvantages of the expectancy table, however, are that the number of cases from which percentages can be calculated is often small and one cannot derive a meaningful overall coefficient of validity other than the correlation from the data.

If an assessment is made and a criterion score available, then predictive or concurrent validity can be obtained by these methods. Remember, validity is not an all or none affair, and there is no fixed point at which a test becomes valid. But a validity coefficient which fails to attain significance at the 5% or 1% levels (see chapter 5) is not likely to be of much practical significance to a teacher.

'False positives' and 'false negatives' in prediction

There are probably few occasions on which irrevocable decisions about children are made on the basis of test score information. Nevertheless, in those areas of the country where 11+ selection persists, the decisions are inevitably subject to two kinds of error. We saw in chapter 3 that verbal reasoning tests taken at age 10–11 years do predict *some* of the variance in achievement at age 15–16 years although this can be explained in a variety of ways, including use of the self-fulfilling prophecy. Selection at 11 years, therefore, is made at the cost of predicting suitability for a 'grammar school education' when, in fact, the child turns out to be 'less suitable' than another not selected, and vice versa. In general, predicting 'success' when 'failure' results is known as a 'false negative' and predicting 'failure' when 'success' would have occurred, a 'false positive'.

No attempt is made here to examine the assumptions inherent in selection at 11 years, or at any other age for that matter. The point is that no assessment for selection is free from the two kinds of error. Menrens and Lehmann (1978, 124—5) present a useful discussion of the costs of faulty decisions. Some of these can be assessed. But the psychological effects of 'failure' seem incalculable. Clearly some tests can be shown to commit more errors in selection than others, but the use of a single test *alone* (however valid) in making a decision is indefensible.

Construct Validity

This is conceptually different from the other two types of validity. Whereas content validity is concerned with the correspondence between the objectives of teaching and what is assessed, and criterion-related validity with the relationship between the test and outside criteria, this type of validity is concerned with establishing the meaning of the scores or identifying the construct which is theoretically responsible for the difference between children on that test.

Psychological theory is structured around a system of constructs. For example, when, early in this century, Spearman found that the scores of groups of people on a number of mental tests tended to correlate positively he sought an explanation for this overlap in terms of the construct of 'g' or general intelligence. When constructors of personality questionnaires found that those people who experienced irrational fears also claimed to be easily swayed by their feelings they borrowed the construct of neuroticism to account for, or to summarize, this correlation. Psychological theory abounds with constructs: others with which the reader will be familiar are anxiety, extraversion, self-concept, achievement motivation, and many more. Some of these are used in education and in the everyday organization of experience. But whenever teachers ask what tests are *really* assessing or measuring they are asking for information of the validity of the construct.

The best discussions of construct validity to date are provided by Cronbach and Meehl (1966) and Cronbach (1971). The sections which follow are based upon them. At first sight it may appear to be obvious what a test measures (i.e. it may be 'face valid'). If an author claims that his test measures 'reading comprehension' and its format consists of a set of paragraphs or extracts followed by questions then, clearly, this is what it does indeed measure and further discussion is unnecessary. But if 'counter hypotheses' can be advanced and the test's author has not shown them to be false or less defensible alternatives, other names for the construct can be a distinct possibility. In the first place the test is probably subject to a time limit: then *speed* of reading may contribute to the variance in responding. If the author has not established by investigation the time limit necessary for all children to respond then he has not eliminated the possibility that speed, as well as comprehension, is being measured. (One well known test of reading, widely used in Britain, derives a measure of accuracy, speed and comprehension from the same set of paragraphs, so the example is not far fetched!) Secondly, the questions set may emphasize recall of factual information in the text. This places too much stress on memory, not enough on understanding, for it to be construed as assessing reading comprehension. Thirdly, the passages could well contain words of differential familiarity to the children. If so, is the test also measuring vocabulary? Finally, many of the passages appear to be 'cookedup' for the reading test and to have little or no literary merit or interest for the children in the age group. If so, are the passages so boring that readers, able to read the extracts, nevertheless lack motivation to do so? The important point here is not that a test can be a 'pure' measure of a single construct but that in a study of validity the competing claims for other explanations should be minimized. Indeed, all tests used in education will tap motivational components but it is part of a long process to establish just how much of test score variance is attributable to constructs other than the one the test ostensibly claims to measure.

Any performance by a child is determined by an unknowable combination of the characteristics of the test, the child, the test situation and so on. No one is more aware of this than the person who has tried to establish the construct validity of an instrument! Nevertheless, marketed tests are usually presented as if an interpretation of scores in terms of a single construct were intended. The processes of construct validation are the means whereby claims for a single interpretation are investigated.

Before we look at these processes one or two other words of caution are in order. Suppose one hypothetical test of comprehension contains information with which some respondents are already familiar. If they can answer the questions without careful reading of the passage than the test is not measuring *their* reading comprehension. In other words a test may be a valid measure of construct X for some pupils but not for others! Quite obviously, too, if the material of the test is familiar to pupils from one culture but not to those from another, the test may be valid for the children in one group but not for the other. This is one reason why statements about the differences between racial groups in mental test scores should be viewed with the greatest caution.

How, then, may construct validity be investigated? Basically, three methods have traditionally been adopted. Some will be beyond the scope of most teachers but all should be understood by teachers who aim to make an informed choice of tests, or to construct their own.

Correlation methods
Although this is established practice it is somewhat circular. The test constructed by the teacher (or the newly constructed published test) is correlated with tests with an established reputation for measuring the trait being examined. For example, if the new test were of reading comprehension, then construct validity would be claimed if it correlated substantially with an existing test of the same trait name. In the validation of group administered intelligence tests, the Stanford—Binet intelligence test has been used as the criterion for many years. Understandably, some critics have objected to the logic of this method. In the first place, it relies on the construct validity of the criterion itself and assumes that it measures what it claims to measure. Secondly, because construct validity is claimed for the new test if it does indeed correlate highly with the reference test, then the new test will yield almost the same information about

individual differences as the one against which it is being validated. If this is so, why bother to construct a new test? One answer to this question is, of course, that the 'new' test may be more convenient to use and to score and cheaper to produce than the criterion test. But it is small wonder that one critic has described this process of construct validation as 'finding out what we know already'. Given that the arbitrary specification of one test as *the* criterion for a construct suffers from these deficiencies it can be seen that test validation does not end with this type of demonstration. Other types of evidence will also be needed. Merely to show high correlations between the test under study and other tests is of comparatively little interest in itself.

Methods of factor analysis

These are mathematically quite sophisticated. Basically the techniques analyse the interrelationships among a *number* of tests (say a dozen at least) and try to account for them in terms of a smaller number of constructs. These underlying (or source) traits (or factors) are assumed to be responsible for the overlap in variance among the actual tests and can be used to show how much of the variance in each test can be explained by more than one construct. Each test receives a correlation (known as a 'loading') with the construct and those with the highest loadings are then assumed to be the best measures of that construct. In this way an investigator can gradually build up a picture of what a test measures. If it repeatedly receives a high loading along with other tests on a single factor, examination of the content of the tests should enable the investigator to identify what they have in common and hence name the construct. This account is too brief to give more than a rough idea of the procedure but interested readers could refer to a clear introduction to factor analysis by Child (1970). Unfortunately factor analysts invariably disagree as to which is the most appropriate technique amongst many and no teacher untrained in their use is likely to be in a position to re-examine one solution in the light of the alternative solutions from other techniques.

There are other difficulties in the factor analysis of educational tests. When scores obtained by children on a number of tests of achievement are factorized one typically finds that they can be accounted for by very few factors (Cronbach, 1971). This suggests that tests which have high 'face validity' (i.e. appear to be testing an easily definable attainment, separable from other attainments) nevertheless appear also to be measuring much the same thing as one another! To the teacher, this merely signifies that pupils best in one subject are also among the best in others, but it presents some difficulties for this method of construct validation.

In general, then, the results of factor analysis help to add one kind of information about what a test measures which must be considered alongside other information in a lengthy process of establishing test validity.

Deliberate attempts to alter test scores

These techniques are based on a simple rationale. If a test constructor claims to know what his tests measure he should be able to predict the effect upon them of a logically related treatment. Although this is unlikely to be a great deal of use in educational tests of cognitive outcomes it has been employed with psychological tests which are of interest to teachers. Karmel and Karmel (1978, 109) cite as an illustration the case of a test of anxiety. One would expect such a test to be susceptible to the influence of stress which, if the investigator did not have ethical objections, could then be experimentally administered, and its effects on scores examined. Jacobs (1966) has carried out a study which might serve as a model for investigations of this kind using educational tests. He studied the effects of coaching on test scores. Provided the coaching is in the use of those techniques which the test is designed to assess, a demonstration (with suitable experimental control) that scores are influenced by this coaching would strengthen the author's argument that the test does indeed measure what it claims. Given that *all* educational tests involve motivational components as well as those it is intended the tests should measure, it is possible to estimate the degree to which scores depend on motivation by experimental manipulation. This could be done using instructions and techniques to enhance the motivation of some groups of children drawn up at random but to depress it amongst others.

Which method?

Teachers are likely to find correlational techniques the easiest by which to check the validity of their tests. Factor analysis requires computing facilities and some mathematical expertise. Increase in test scores as the result of coaching in the relevant skills is corroborative evidence of validity, but only mildly so. But always remember to check the validity data presented by publishers when using standardized tests.

THE VALIDITY OF CRITERION-REFERENCED TESTS

In chapter 7 we looked at the special problems involved in estimating the reliability of criterion-referenced tests. These problems are a consequence of the different purposes of criterion-referenced assessment from those of norm-referenced assessment. Some difficulties are also encountered in the study of their validity. (Remember: do not confuse the validity of a criterion-referenced test with the criterion-referenced validity of a norm-referenced test!)

Criterion-referenced tests do not require variation in individual scores but they do demand that the content of the test samples the teaching a child has received towards the attainment of a specified objective. Thus what has been written about the content validity of norm-referenced tests applies also to criterion-referenced tests. In some respects it is easier to obtain high content validity for a criterion-referenced test because the objective tested is usually defined far more narrowly than in norm-referenced tests which are designed to cover a range of objectives. Because of this it is much easier to sample items which are representative of the achievement (see chapters 3 and 4).

There is no reason why a teacher should not make a check on the predictive validity of a criterion-referenced test using the methods already described. It would not, however, be very sensible to express the strength of the relationship between the test and a future criterion by calculating the validity coefficient. This is because there is only a small amount of variance in the criterion-referenced test because it yields only two values, 'mastery' or 'non-mastery', of the criterion. Nevertheless, we can easily show the extent to which the test predicts later levels of mastery by constructing an expectancy table (table 8.2). We could use this device to show that pupils allowed to proceed to the next unit of study or to a more difficult topic do better in the later work than pupils who score below the cut-off point. There may be ethical objections in allowing pupils to proceed to an exercise which they appear to lack the competence to learn. On the other hand, if teachers were to find that children below the cut-off score did as well as those above, they would have successfully invalidated the claim for the predictive validity of the item.

So far as the construct validity of the item is concerned, the difficulty may be more apparent than real. Remember that constructs are used in accounting for a range of performances. No construct — 'intelligence' or 'mathematical ability', for example — is defined by a single or small number of operations, but is an attempt to generalize the meaning of a number of related performances. In criterion-referenced tests the teacher's interest is in the mastery of a narrowly defined performance so it is difficult to see much point in naming an underlying factor responsible for many achievements. The criterion-referenced test builder may, therefore, claim that a test measures a performance in its own right and not as a representative of a wide-ranging construct. For example, in 'solving linear equations with two unknowns by the method of substitution' the performance is accounted for in those terms and not by 'mathematical ability' (the construct).

SUMMARY

The process of validating tests is a long and never-ending investigation of the behaviour of tests in a variety of contexts and for a variety of purposes. Information comes from judgments of how closely they match what has been taught, how well they correlate with a criterion in the present or future and how successfully they measure what they claim to measure. Teachers can contribute to this information, although establishing construct validity presents considerable philosophical as well as methodological problems. The teacher as teacher is unlikely to play an extensive part in the statistical analysis of a test's relationship with other tests, nor in the development of a theoretical network which helps to explain the inferences that may be permitted by a test's scores. Readers interested in this topic could refer to an excellent discussion of this aspect of validity ('nomological networks') by Cronbach (1971, 475–84).

The fact that a test has been used by teachers for a very long period of time and has come to be accepted by them as valid is, in itself, no particular recommendation. The longevity of a certain reading test, now 30 years old, whose validation studies were not impressive and which provides only limited inferences, testifies to the truth of this comment. Such is the inertia in school assessment that more recent and technically superior tests which measure a number of components in reading skill are slow to be adopted.

Although no universally acceptable answer to the question: 'What does this test measure?' is easily found it is, nevertheless, a question that every test user and everyone who makes use of a score as part of an assessment needs to ask constantly. We have described the sort of answers to look for so far as criterion-referenced and content validities are concerned. The teacher interested in the construct validity of a published test should set the following as a standard interrogation of the manual or publishers' claims (these are based on pp. 29–31, 46–8 of *Standards for Educational and Psychological Tests* 1974, published by the American Psychological Association):

(1) If the test is to measure a theoretical construct, it should *define* that construct in terms of the chief kinds of evidence that the test will provide. For example, if the test claims to be a test of the development of children's mathematical concepts, the concepts should be stated and the contexts in which they are to be tested described.

(2) The manual should summarize the evidence available to substantiate the above interpretation.

(3) Any evidence available concerning the relationship of the test scores to other established, conceptually linked, tests should be given.

(4) The age range for which the test is valid should be explicitly given. Any restrictions on its general use must be fully explained.

9

Setting Standards

The problems involved in setting and investigating standards are far more complex than most current educational and political discussion suggests. The chapter begins with a brief examination of what is probably the most heated issue in that discussion. This is done in order to identify some of the complexities involved and to show that the motivation of some of the erstwhile participants is not always entirely clear.

ARE STANDARDS FALLING?

One of the purposes of assessment is to ensure that educational standards are maintained. Although expenditure on education has increased, many claim that we have not received 'value for money' and that 'standards are falling'. This was the message of the *Black Papers* (Cox and Dyson, 1969a, 1969b, 1970, 1975, 1977), and is the moan of many contemporary employers. As readers will probably have suspected, the quality of the evidence adduced is not always commensurate with the conviction of the plaintiffs. Until quite recently, many believed that a convincing demonstration of a fall in educational standards had been provided by Burt who published an article to that effect in the *Irish Journal of Education* (Burt, 1969). The data, cited again in *Black Paper II*, purported to show a steady decline in standards of reading, spelling and in 'mechanical' and 'problem' arithmetic over the years from 1914 to 1965. Although neither report contained sufficient detail to permit a proper evaluation of this conclusion (there was no information on the methods of sampling employed nor even of the actual tests used) it now seems clear that over the last ten years of the period in question Burt had no access to schools as claimed, no funds to

prosecute the research and left no records in his otherwise
copiously-detailed diary of the work ever having taken place.
After a painstaking examination of the evidence, Hearnshaw
(1979, 259) wrote:

> The conclusion seems inescapable: the figures given in
> Burt's table in the *Irish Journal of Education* were, at
> least in part, fabricated . . . . The verdict must be, there-
> fore, that . . . Burt was guilty of deception.

Hearnshaw's conclusion should not be taken to suggest that
standards have *not* fallen. Indeed a more recent investigation
reported in the next section in this chapter is consistent with
the view that reading attainment may have 'levelled off'. But
there are several reasons why attempts to establish the relevant facts are unlikely to settle the issue. In the first place it
is easy to demonstrate that contemporary children are unable to do things that a different sample tested X years ago
were able to do. But it is obviously impossible to demonstrate the reverse. In fact, no cross-sectional study which
compares a vaguely specified sample of children in year N
with another in year $N + 10$, a second in year $N + 20$ and so
on can hope to answer the question 'are standards falling'?
Not only are samples non-comparable but curricular emphases
and allocations of time to different topics vary so much that
like is not being compared with like. Indeed, a contemporary
mathematics syllabus differs greatly in the extent of its
coverage from one in use, say, at the end of the Second
World War, and tests which adequately reflected the content
of teaching at one time do not necessarily do so at another.
Such an examination of syllabuses may well show that children today are taught some topics considered far too difficult for children 20 or so years ago and vice versa. That they
were taught these topics does not mean that their learning
has been successful, of course!

Critics might argue that basic objectives in teaching of
reading (and English) have remained sufficiently stable for
meaningful comparisons over time to be made. But, even
here, the language of the culture is not static so that children are conceivably exposed to words and phrases which

vary in their frequency of occurrence over time. Given that children are more likely to be able to pronounce words with which they are orally familiar than those which they have never heard, one would expect average ability in word recognition to reflect these changes, independent of any changes in the underlying attribute (reading ability) ostensibly 'being compared'. Moreover, the frequency with which testing itself takes place changes with time, and the decline of the 11+ examination most certainly implies that schools spend rather less time on 'teaching for test-taking' than was at one time the case. For these and many other reasons attempts to compare standards in the absence of controls over all other factors known to affect performance are unlikely to be particularly rewarding — whatever their potential in ideological and political warfare!

An alternative approach to the measurement of performance on the same tests over the years is to examine changes in the numbers of children who attain pass standards in the various public examinations. This type of count would undoubtedly reinforce the claims of those who believe standards are rising. Certainly a greater proportion of children achieve passes in O level examinations (or their CSE equivalents) today than was the case 30 years ago and many more stay on to A level although these increases have tended to level off over the last few years (DES, 1977). Similarly, many more young people obtain university degrees in this country than ever before. Such evidence that standards are rising is easily countered by the 'more means worse' argument of course. The most constructive interpretation that teachers can make of this controversy, however, is that contained within the Bullock Report (DES, 1975): standards are never high enough, but teachers and pupils must constantly strive to raise them.

STANDARD OR LEVELS OF ATTAINMENT?

We have managed to get this far in our discussion without saying what we mean by 'standards'. In fact a good deal of the argument seems to have failed to distinguish *standards* in

education from *levels of attainment.* One dictionary definition of a standard is that it is an accepted or approved
example of something against which others are judged or
measured. In this sense, a standard would be a model of
attainment or performance used for comparison or measurement, or as a target held up to learners as a basis for their
aspirations. Such an approved example may be specified
without reference to any particular person. For example, a
height of five feet six inches would be a reasonable standard
for 14 year old high jumpers to clear. Similarly, the correct
solution of eight pairs of simultaneous equations out of a
total of ten would be an appropriate standard in school
mathematics, provided the number of unknowns was stated.
Here the standard originates in a prior specification by the
teacher of an acceptable aim possibly to dub the pupil as
'master' of a given objective or as 'ready' to proceed to the
next task in a hierarchy of learning, for example.

At other times, however, the standard may only be specified with reference to a level of excellence attained by a
performer who, in the eyes of experts, exhibits exceptional
talent in the performance in question. Here the standard is
not so much 'what is acceptable' as 'what has become possible'. In both cases, however, setting appropriate standards
involves stating the criteria of acceptability which are appropriate for the learners in question. Although the standard of
excellence may serve as a model or goal for the learner in the
long term (witness the upsurge in interest in women's gym-
nastics following the televised appearances of stars from
Eastern Europe) it can clearly be a hopelessly inappropriate
basis against which to measure the faltering steps (and vaults)
of a beginner.

Now if we conclude that standards (whether their origin is
exemplified in the 'excellent performer' or more abstractly
described in terms of the performance itself) serve as targets
for effort and bases for judgment, there seems no evidence
for the claim that standards in education have declined over
the years. There are, it is true, instances (relatively trivial)
where this might be the case; for example in the standards of
neatness for its own sake set for pupils' work. But the content of contemporary curricula implies the existence of a far

greater range and diversity of standards than their historical counterparts. Rightly or wrongly children are expected to attempt to demonstrate competence in far more areas than hitherto. And even if it were feasible to demonstrate that teachers have 'lowered' the levels of their approved examples or model performances this could just as easily be taken as evidence of intelligent modification of demands in the direction of the possible as of sloppiness. After all, setting a high level of acceptability which no learner can hope to reproduce has no particular utility in the motivation of the immature, whatever its effect on the expert.

It seems clear then that much of the contemporary anxiety about standards in education concerns what children actually achieve rather than what is presented to them as exemplars or models against which their own efforts are subsequently to be judged. It is, of course, a characteristic of many members of 'older generations' to deprecate and to disparage the achievements of the young. Space does not permit an explanation of this phenomenon but it is by no means established that memories of past performances are infallibly accurate. But unless the same tasks are presented year after year to genuinely comparable and representative samples of pupils we simply lack the data by which to conclude that levels of performance have changed in a particular direction.

In one sense, the standardized test constitutes an educational standard, through its repeated use. But assessment practices and tests used in schools are so very varied that the making of direct comparisons is a hazardous occupation. So far as reading is concerned, for example, Goodacre (1971) found that more than half the LEAs which replied to her survey left the decisions to the head teacher, but that the most common instrument (a graded word test now 30 years old) failed to match the objectives of modern teachers of reading. One year later a report by Start and Wells (1972) suggested that reading comprehension of 11 and 14 year olds had levelled off or even declined. Chapter 2 of the Bullock Report (DES, 1975) presents a good summary of the evidence and of a further relevant report by Horton (1973). The chapter rightly criticizes the two tests used for their narrow conception of the reading process. Many other difficulties in interpretation — particularly the 'ceiling effect' of the test which would, by definition, inhibit a demonstration of any upward movement of scores — are also identified. A test is said to have a ceiling effect if many of those taking it achieve near the maximum score. Nevertheless, the report did acknowledge the possibility of a slight downwards movement in the level among 11 year olds over the years 1964—70 in one of the tests but little significant shift was detected at age 15 over the years 1960—71. The conclusion of the report seems a sane one: changes in level of reading (narrowly conceived) are not disturbing but they offer no room for complacency. In advocating the need for a more thorough monitoring of standards, the report anticipated the funding of the APU (see chapter 10).

Because there is an urgent need to establish alternative ways by which slow learners in our schools may be helped, there seems little or no justification for a massive research expenditure merely to determine whether or not 'standards are falling'. Levels of attainment do, indeed, frequently disappoint among very many pupils despite the honest endeavours of most teachers. But to attribute these failings to the setting of low standards is to force a simple explanation on a complex phenomenon. Raising levels of acceptability is of itself unlikely to result in improved performance, especially among those already failing to 'reach the standard'.

HOW CAN STANDARDS BE SET?

One of the objections to assessment advanced in chapter 2 was that tests can become the objectives of teaching. Standardized tests are, of course, chiefly used in norm-referenced assessment and are designed to maximize the variance within a representative group of respondents. This is achieved by the deliberate construction of tests composed of items of known and, usually,increasing levels of difficulty. Although the items are carefully constructed by writers who, from experience, have a reasoned expectation of their suitability for the children in the relevant age range, the inclusion of such an item as part of a test is based upon an empirical study of its characteristics. Although tests may become standards over time, no particular questions of standards are raised during their construction and development since any item which discriminates among its respondents is potentially useful. Criterion-referenced assessment, on the other hand, raises serious problems of standard setting, in particular the specification of the criterion or cut-off score.

Readers will recall that criterion-referenced assessment is designed to describe an individual's performance in relation to a standard held to indicate mastery of the objective. In general it is not necessary for a pupil to achieve a 100% correct score on an objective for him or her to be classified as a master of that objective. Instead a score of, say, 80 or 90% is held to be appropriate. If the objective is one which forms part of a hierarchy where later objectives are logically dependent upon earlier pre-requisites then the problem of specifying a minimal acceptable level of performance arises. Critics of this process have argued that specification of the criterion score is inescapably arbitrary and that because of error of measurement and the unpredictable nature of future performance no assessor can know with confidence the score which is necessary for success or readiness for the next objective. So great is this problem that an entire issue of the *Journal of Educational Measurement* has recently been devoted to the issue of standards and criteria (Volume 15, Winter, 1978).

Glass (1978) has identified six techniques by which criterion scores have been determined. They are presented in the following section.

Techniques for Determining Criterion Scores

Study of the performance of a large group of comparable children

This is an extension from norm-referenced testing. In order to determine what is a reasonable level of expectation for a group the *median* score for pupils of the same type (who had the best teaching available) is taken as the most appropriate single reference point for establishing the criterion score.

Counting backwards from 100%
Mastery does not indicate perfection. Teachers and other experts in the relevant subject area try to reach agreement and decide how far a master shall be allowed to fall short of perfection. This decision is, obviously, arbitrary and the criterion score will depend upon how tough or lenient the 'experts' are prepared to be.

Study of the performance of established masters
In this method a study is undertaken of the performance of established masters on the items which test the attainment of the objective. Their performance is then taken as the criterion score. Glass calls this 'bootstrapping on other criterion scores'.

Judging minimal competence
This is the method recommended by Ebel (1972). Experts (teachers) study a test or an item and then declare that a child with minimal competence should be able to achieve such and such a score. The basis for the expert's judgment may well have been acquired from knowledge of the results of the first three methods, of course.

Two kinds of objection can be offered to this method. In the first place, empirical studies have shown surprisingly large disagreements between experts. One example that can be cited is from the field of medical education where, one hopes, clinical teachers will have clear ideas as to what are the minimal levels required for the successful practice of medicine! Nevertheless, Meskauskas and Webster (1975) found that one group of experts specified 68% competence on a set of items as indicative of minimal competence, whereas another placed the level at only 49%. The second objection to this method is that it implies a degree of knowledge on the part of the experts of the dependency of the whole performance on mastery of the elements. The nature of this difficulty may be clarified by use of an analogy. It is possible to analyse the act of playing an off-drive in cricket into a number of logically related structural elements having a natural order: gripping the bat is a pre-requisite of back-lift, back-lift is a pre-requisite of a pendulum-like movement, a pendulum-like movement is necessary to impart momentum to the ball using the full face of the bat and so on. And yet slow-motion photographic analysis of the greatest batsmen in action invariably reveals lack of mastery of some of these elements. Thus, although many intellectual tasks also yield themselves to this kind of analysis and instructional psychology has benefited greatly from Gagné's work on the structure of task hierarchies (Stones, 1979), psychological studies have provided no grounds for the belief that experts can specify minimal competence with any dependability.

Decision theoretic approaches

These were touched upon when the problems of reliability and validity of criterion-referenced tests were discussed in earlier chapters. They are potentially time-consuming because they involve the determination of scores on an external criterion of mastery as well as on the criterion-referenced test itself.

Quite obviously, a criterion-referenced score which separates masters from non-masters ('sets the standard') should differentiate levels of competence in the performances on other tasks it is designed to predict. It is often easier to find an example from other branches of education and training than schools. One would expect one apprentice who has achieved a criterion score which classifies him as a master to outperform another who has not yet been dubbed master, in a range of other engineering tasks. If the criterion scores so used are plotted against an objective assessment of performance on these tasks for a group of apprentices, as shown in table 9.1, the problem of setting the standard is simply that of adjusting the criterion score to *maximize* the value of the expression:

$$f(c) = (P_A + P_D) / (P_B + P_C)$$

where c is the criterion-referenced score, P_A the number of apprentices who are masters on the criterion-referenced test and high performers on the external tasks and P_D the number who are non-masters and low performers. The rationale for this approach is obvious: the higher $(P_A + P_D)$ relative to

Table 9.1 — The relationship of criterion-referenced test scores to performance on an external criterion.

Criterion-referenced test scores \ External criterion	High performance	Low performance
Masters	P_A	P_B
Non-masters	P_C	P_D

$(P_B + P_C)$ the more effective is the prediction using the criterion score.

So far as the writer can judge there are few, if any, studies in schools which seek to determine a minimal acceptable standard (i.e. the value for the criterion score) necessary for later success although there are, in principle, no reasons why they should not be undertaken.

Operations research methods
Glass (1978) cites the work of Block (1972) as an example of this approach. Minimal standards are determined by dividing a population of learners at random into equivalent groups and teaching them until they achieve pre-determined levels of proficiency on a criterion-referenced test, say 10, 15, 20% and so on. Given that an external measure (that which one is trying to predict) is available, a graph which relates level of mastery on the criterion-referenced test to performance on the external criterion is plotted. Inspection of the graph provides a guide to the identification of the criterion-referenced score above which little or no increment in performance on the outside criterion is obtained. The hypothetical curve relating criterion-referenced score to the external criterion is shown in figure 9.1. This method then determines the point along the horizontal (x) axis beyond which the curve of performance on the external criterion 'flattens out'. This is then established as c. Although there might well be small rises after c, it would be a matter for the professional judgment of teachers whether the time and effort needed to increase the value for c were worthwhile in the light of improvements in performance on the external criterion.

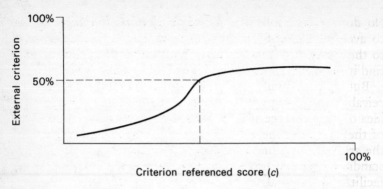

Figure 9.1   Hypothetical curve: criterion-referenced test scores and scores on external criterion.

A practical, if global, application of this technique would be where a teacher attempts to determine the cut-off or criterion score on a reliable school examination to identify minimal competence for progress to the next examinations, say in deciding whether O level or CSE presents the most appropriate 'next step', or in the normal use of criterion-referenced testing within the sequence of instruction designed to ensure the attainment of hierarchically organized objectives.

NEED STANDARDS BE ARBITRARY?

One of the difficulties inherent in the type of standard setting which involves labelling children as masters/non-masters if of course the imposition of two categories on achievements which actually vary from 'no-performance' to 'perfect performance' (or 'near-perfect performance'). Labelling theorists would insist on the dangers inherent in the practice. Though writing about 'deviance' as a label the words of Erikson (1962) could just as easily apply to the use of the label 'master':

> Deviance is not a property *inherent* in certain forms of behaviour: it is a property *conferred upon* these forms by audiences which directly witness them.

No doubt the implication of this statement (for mastery) is to avoid the use of the term altogether or to turn attention to the assumptions which underlie the practice of those who find it necessary to use this term.

But it is difficult to see how accountability could conceivably work in practice without some dependency on the idea of performance standards, at least implicitly. The essence of the argument therefore, seems to be not how can we take the arbitrariness out of standards altogether, but how can our standards (though to a certain extent arbitrary) be useful and facilitate individual and group learning, rather than remaining a dead hand on educational development.

Recent events in the United States — where by March 1978, 33 states had taken action to mandate the setting of minimum standards of competency in elementary and secondary schools (Pipho, 1978) — and to a lesser extent in Britain seem to suggest that some form of standard setting is politically acceptable. The problems in the two countries are to a certain extent different, of course, in that there are no nationwide examinations in the US. But it would be far too simple-minded to believe that the very existence of a number of examination boards ensures that standards are maintained or remain comparable from year to year in Britain. In any case, schools are seeking to accomplish far more than is conceivably 'graded' by O and A level exams!

One fashionable view of how to avoid arbitrary standard setting is embodied in the concepts of 'functional skills' (Burton, 1978). This argues for the identification of minimal levels of functioning in everyday skills and concerted efforts to ensure that all children attain these levels. The approach can be attacked on the grounds that it sometimes embodies a very insulting model of the future lives of children. One frequently hears views of the kind: 'All these children need to be able to do is to fill in football pools, read the *Sun*, handle their wage packets and know how much change to expect when shopping.' Granted that there are notional levels of competence on, say, reading and writing, needed to enable pupils to go further, no-one in his or her right mind would be likely to specify the potential limits of a pupil's future exercise of these skills. And this view, that the purpose of schooling is to transmit the minimal levels of skill and knowledge to prepare the child for adulthood, is predicated on agreement as to what sort of adult functioning is appropriate. In a wry comment on this way of conceptualizing the child's survival skills, Bowles and Gintis (1976) point out that survival in a capitalist society is more likely to be ensured by mastery of subservience to authority, a submission to motivation by extrinsic rewards and through exceptional toleration of routine and repetitive tasks. Given that all these seem to be required, would schools be correct in regarding them as competences? Much earlier, Dewey questioned the moral basis for the belief that schools should prepare pupils to live in a corrupt society.

It seems very unlikely, therefore, that standard setting through the identification of minimal competency for adult functioning will give a clear guide to schools. (Folklore is rich in stories of scrap metal millionaires who can neither read nor write.) Nevertheless, a high level of performance in basic skills enlarges the choice that children can eventually make in adult society but those who hold conceptions of minimal requirements (employers, for example) constitute only one set of participants in the standards debate.

Another possible source of standards will obviously be the cumulative experiences of teachers as to what can 'reasonably be expected' of pupils at various ages and stages of development. The Department of Education and Science has only very recently released check lists of what children ought to be able to do in basic mathematics, whatever the syllabus they have followed. One could, of course, adopt a purely empirical method of ascertaining what these 'reasonable expectations' for children are. This was essentially what Binet and the other pioneers of intelligence testing did to grade items in order of increasing difficulty and in the development of the concept of 'mental age' which corresponded with given scores. This commonsense view has its drawbacks. Unless the samples of children studied are representative of their age groups, the standards set by the principle of reasonable expectation will lack generalizability and could be dominated by local norms. A given level of performance is only provisional; that is it results from the teaching that has been provided. Different methods and emphases in teaching can easily modify these levels of achievement and the realization by teachers that similar children elsewhere have attained higher levels of performance can act as a powerful stimulus to improved teaching towards the attainment of higher standards.

Standard setting seems likely to be a continuous process of revision as curricula, norms and the expectations and requirements held by different audiences change with time. Although schools cannot afford to be insensitive to concepts of the 'country's needs' they are unlikely to gain clear guidance for standard setting from those who have such conceptions. Institutions like schools have a tendency to enshrine the technologies of yesterday and present them as cultures for today. The teaching of Latin for the proper conduct of church services (technology), only later became a mental discipline of intrinsic value (the culture). This is a case in point. It may be a cause for some regret that shop assistants of today are unable to add up long columns of figures and reach a correct answer for the shopping bill but modern electronic technology renders such skills largely redundant in that context. (There are better reasons for an understanding of numbers than the conduct of commercial life, of course!). Similarly, although it is widely claimed that growth in a modern industrial society depends upon its educational system, this remains an untested assumption of popular political platforms.

CONCLUSIONS

In summary, we have seen that a distinction can be drawn between standards (the characteristics of the performances held up as models against which judgments are to be made) and levels of performance (that is, what pupils actually achieve). We have argued that there are three chief approaches to standard setting:

(1) the pragmatic approach — trying to lay down minimal levels of competence which a child needs to achieve in order to 'function effectively' in adult society;

(2)   the scientific approach — the systematic examination of adult competences and the setting of performance standards because they have been shown to have high predictive validity (chapter 7); and

(3)   the norm-referenced approach — an examination of the levels of attainment of large representative groups of pupils to find out what can reasonably be expected of those at various positions of the normal curve of attainment in that subject.

Each poses problems and has serious disadvantages. In all cases, however, the methods seem applicable only to those problems that have a small definable set of possible solutions. 'Laying down basic standards', though an intuitively appealing notion, will have to take far more factors into account than are apparent in the public pronouncement of those who have vested interests in the maintenance of the structure of society, or in its complete upheaval. From the point of view of the individual learner, however, standards serve as goals without which learning activities cannot be organized and learning potential be harnessed (Gagné, 1974). From this perspective many standards will be relative to the child's competence and current status as a learner. Meanwhile, a standard which is too low for a given child can encourage boredom or complacency, one which is far too high defeatism and low self-esteem. With these potentially deleterious psychological effects in mind, the setting of standards which act as appropriate goals for the individual learner must be approached with a subtlety and ingenuity absent from the appraisal by those whose chief interest in educational standards is politically motivated.

10

The Work of the Assessment of Performance Unit

BACKGROUND AND CONTROVERSY

Not since the heirs of Matthew Arnold (the inspectors of schools) actually inspected schools and examined pupil performance in basic subjects has government displayed a systematic interest in the formal examination of educational standards. However, as teachers in Arnold's time were well aware, they, not their pupils, were the primary objects of the assessment. More importantly, their salaries depended upon the children's results. This system ('payment by results') was not finally abolished until the end of the 19th century despite Arnold's unflagging opposition to it (he died in 1888). Since then, teachers have seen changes in the roles of HMI from the conduct of general inspections to a less obtrusive function as advisers and as organizers of courses and conferences.

More recently a more active role for some of the inspectorate has been proposed. Under the overall control of the Department of Education and Science, HMI and others are now actively involved in the first ever nationwide attempts to assess and to monitor performance standards using sampling techniques involving regions, schools within regions and pupils within schools. A justification for the setting up of the Assessment of Performance Unit (APU) in 1975, was set out in the pamphlet *Assessment: Why, What and How* published by the Department of Education and Science and the Central Office of Information (1976). It points to the great variation which currently exists between schools and LEAs in assessment practices, the consequent lack of a 'national picture' of performance and the near-total ignorance of the effectiveness of schools in serving the requirements of pupils and the demands that society makes upon them.

The original terms of reference of the APU were fourfold (Dennison, 1978):

(1) to identify and appraise existing measuring instruments and methods of assessment;
(2) to sponsor the creation of new instruments and assessment methods;
(3) to promote with teachers and LEAs the conduct of experiments;
(4) to identify significant differences in achievement, particularly underachievement, and relate to the circumstances of learning, making the information available to those who allocate resources in the DES, schools and LEAs.

Insofar as the aim of the APU is to make parents, employers and others concerned better informed about the achievements of schools, these terms of reference — if a trifle imprecise — seem unobjectionable. Yet the peculiarly British insistence on local- and teacher-control inevitably means that the work of the APU will remain controversial.

Since the establishment of the APU, a number of disagreements have emerged and at least one prominent educationist has 'walked out' of a steering committee! In the first place, because schools and teachers have been called upon to fulfil more roles than ever before, there has been an unavoidable dispute as to which aspects of the broad contemporary curricula should be assessed. The resulting decision has been to adopt a *cross-curricular approach.* The decision has inevitably been seen as an arbitrary, not to say capricious, one. The three most obvious candidates *language,* (reading, writing, spoken English and the study of foreign languages), *mathematics* (communication through numbers, graphs, models and diagrams) and *science* were selected along with three other, more controversial, areas. These are: *personal and social development, aesthetic development* and *physical development.* Progress appears to have been most rapid in mathematics and, to a lesser extent, in language. But of the three non-cognitive areas agreement as to what, exactly, should be assessed has, apparently, not yet been reached. It is, of course, difficult enough to reach a consensus as to what is a basic requirement for all pupils of a given age group in mathematics and language. But it is all the more problematic to identify, let alone to assess, the essence of aesthetic development and of the moral aspects of 'personal and social growth'. Nor is every teacher happy at the prospect of this kind of information appearing 'on file' (see chapter 12). The most likely outcome of difficulties of this kind seems to be that the APU will concentrate on the first three areas of development with only token reference to the remaining cross-curricular viewpoint. As Dennison (1978) implies, one wonders whether the inclusion of the last three areas for assessment was any more than a sop to those who deplore the narrow-minded conception of assessing a school's effectiveness by concentrating on the measurable aspects of basic attainment.

A second area of controversy concerns the fears of teachers of the possible abuse of the procedures and results of the assessment. Since the APU is dominated by HMI who are themselves direct employees of a government department, some teachers fear removal of their historical autonomy over the content of the curriculum and the possible influence of a potentially malevolent government hostile to individual non-conformity. Even if some of these views are exaggerated — even paranoid — it is difficult to escape the conclusion that definitions of the curriculum implied by the choice of what to assess will have at least some effect on the emphasis of teaching in schools. For some observers, of course, such an influence is seen as wholly beneficial!

A third objection to the work of the APU seems to be largely unfounded, at least to date. Some feared that an inordinate amount of time would be spent in very many schools in helping the unit's testing programmes. Initially three age groups (11, 13 and 15 year olds) have been selected for study and samples of about 12 500 chosen at random from schools of different types in England and Wales. To obviate the need for lengthy periods of time in testing, matrix sampling techniques (see chapter 4) are being used.

Thus no child has to take all tests or even items, so the fears expressed of loss of teaching time have been somewhat allayed. Progress in mathematics seems to have been most rapid, based as it is on the pre-existing 'tests of attainment in mathematics in schools' (TAMS) already developed by the National Foundation for Educational Research which has a substantial investment in the continuous monitoring of performance.

Of considerable interest to statisticians and theoreticians of assessment, however, is the controversy concerning the choice of the method for the measurement of performance, and in particular, for the monitoring of changes in attainment over time. The method adopted is described more fully in the appendix to this chapter which should be read as an optional extra by those dissatisfied with the brief treatment to be given here. Before this contentious issue in the projected work of the APU is discussed, however, we shall briefly describe the procedures to be followed in the assessment of mathematics as an example of the unit's techniques since it is in this area that the methodology seems to have been most clearly worked out.

Mathematics is conceived by the APU as involving key activities or processes to be exercised in major content areas. The content of the subject is broadly divided into areas such as number, geometry, algebra, measures and fractions (DES, 1978). Each will be assessed using items which test *skills* (learnt mathematical routines), *concepts* (new tasks which test the pupil's ability to transfer what he or she has learnt in one context to its exercise in a second context) and *application* (that is, the ability to use mathematical knowledge in situations with 'real-life flavour'). In addition to these three major categories of process the mathematics monitoring team intends to assess the child's ability to use the knowledge he has acquired in an investigation or by demonstrating an awareness of the potential of the techniques he has mastered. This is obviously a much wider conception of the subject than that held by old-fashioned 'number crunchers' who so often publicly deplore low mathematical attainments among today's children. The APU team is also attempting to assess the ability of children to derive a mathematical formulation of a problem presented in a different medium (e.g. verbally). Readers who are interested in studying some specimen items which fulfil these objectives may find them in DES (1978). Some practical tests in mathematics are also envisaged (Sumner, 1975) in the interests of obtaining as broad a picture as possible of mathematical attainment. Affective responses to the subject are also being assessed, especially attitudes. Although the final form that the reports are to take has not yet been decided it is likely that variations in performance between types of school, regions and sex will be presented both in overall performance and in respect of the various separable aspects of mathematics assessed.

MONITORING AND OBJECTIVE MEASUREMENT

The comparison of levels of performance over time presents serious difficulties as has already been discussed in chapter 9. As we saw there, the fact that today's children are unable to perform on items as well as their counterparts of 30 years ago — as some have claimed — need not necessarily reflect any changes in the effectiveness of teaching nor in the underlying abilities of children. Rather, differences in the amount of time and attention devoted to the topic may well be reflected in lower (or higher) levels of achievement. Thus it could easily appear that a topic or test item which was once relatively 'easy' for children aged 11 (indicated by the proportion of children who correctly answered the item) is much more difficult for today's children of the same age. Facility indexes for long division items would almost certainly illustrate this principle, for example. Thus, if the difficulty of an item is assessed using a facility index or if standardized scores are used on the same test over a long period, the measures of difficulty or relative levels of performance depend upon the nature of the sample of children tested. An item which is 'easy' for one sample can be 'difficult' for another simply because the samples are not truly comparable in their composition or because the objective assessed by the item has not received an equivalent amount of teaching time or emphasis. Items in mathematics are particularly susceptible to this latter kind of influence, unlike items which assess basic communicative competence in language where specific teaching effects are less apparent.

Faced with difficulties of this kind the APU has adopted the Rasch method of objective measurement. The remainder of this chapter will describe some of the principal features of the method in a non-technical way. The appendix will illustrate the workings of one simplified version of the technique on a small sample of scores. Because the method is likely to be the prime source of the monitoring data and to provide the raw data for an 'are standards falling?' debate it is hoped that teachers will read the appendix and not be too deterred by the mysterious ways of the statistician. Although classroom teachers are unlikely to carry out the method on their own scores — for one reason their sample sizes are not large enough — it seems important for teachers to have some understanding of the assumptions, strengths and weaknesses of the technique since it would obviously be highly undesirable if they were to remain mystified by an arcane yet influential technique.

An Outline of the Technique of 'Objective Measurement'

If a person reports his or her height as 5 feet 7½ inches we do not normally stop to ask the name of the measuring instrument used: we also normally assume that the words 'in stockinged feet' are implied (even though men do not ordinarily wear stockings). But if we are told that a child's standardized score on a reading test is, say, 120, we do need to make enquiries about the instrument used to interpret that report and, in particular, whether the standardization sample (the group used to calculate the norms for interpretation) is an appropriate one or not. As we saw in chapter 5, the meaning of a score on a standardized test depends upon the items which make up the test (we can easily alter scores by putting in a few very easy or difficult items), the ability of the child and the ability of the children which made up the standardization sample. If a child's performance (indicated by his raw score) places him at the 85th percentile for ten year olds, the same raw score may place him at only the 75th percentile for

11 year olds but at the 95th percentile for nine year old children. In this sense his score depends on the company he keeps! (Wright, 1968). This restriction of interpretation is, of course, a constraint on all types of score on interval scales of measurement (chapter 5) which lack a true zero point to indicate complete absence of the attribute being measured.

Attempts have been made sporadically over the last 20 years to develop measures of human ability and performance analogous to measures of physical characteristics on ratio scales. In mental and performance testing these properties have been equated with objective measures. The idea is to obtain a measurement of the difficulty of an item independently of the sample on which it is tried out, to accumulate items of varied but known difficulties in an item bank and then to assemble a test of items through which an individual child's ability or attainment may be estimated.

The properties of such a method can best be understood by comparing the method with the traditionally simple measures of item difficulty described in chapter 4. There it was shown how the easiness (or difficulty) of an item could be measured by finding out how many children in a sample succeeded on that item and expressing the result as a proportion (if 16 children out of 50 succeeded on an item, the facility index is 0.32). The ability of an item to discriminate high and low ability was studied either by seeing how well the item differentiated the top 27% from the bottom 27% of children where the sample was large enough, or top and bottom halves for classroom size groups. Quite obviously, an item's difficulty is 'sample bound': our mathematics item with facility index of 0.32 for 11 year old children would (or should) have a facility index at or near 1.0 for pupils preparing for the A level examination in mathematics.

To overcome this difficulty the Rasch method of objective measurement is based upon two staggeringly simple assumptions (far more simple than may be met in practice, as we shall see later). Whereas in our chapter on reliability (chapter 6) we saw that there are many reasons why performances vary, the so-called objective method assumes that only two factors come into play when a child encounters a test item. These are:

(1)   the ability of the child;
(2)   the difficulty of the item.

The more able the child the more likely he (or she) is to succeed; the easier the item, the most likely all children are to succeed. Nothing else influences the outcome of a child's attempts to solve the item.

The mathematics is more fully explained in the appendix to the chapter but, basically, the method first derives a mathematical statement for the probability of a given child getting the item correct (his 'chances of being correct'). Quite obviously if a child has no ability then no matter how hard he (or she) tries his (or her) chances of being correct must be zero. Similarly, if an item's easiness is zero then no matter how able children are, no child can actually answer it. Now if only pupil ability and item difficulty influence the outcome of an attempt to answer the item, all pupils who get the same score are estimated to have the ability associated with that score. Thus it is necessary to obtain only one estimate of ability for all children who obtain the same score.

Table 10.1 — Responses (1 = 'right', 0 = 'wrong') of twelve children to a five-item test.

Child	Items					Total
	1	2	3	4	5	
1	1	1	1	1	0	4
2	1	1	0	1	0	3
3	1	1	1	1	0	4
4	1	0	1	1	1	4
5	1	0	1	0	0	2
6	1	1	1	0	0	3
7	1	1	1	1	1	5
8	0	0	1	1	1	3
9	1	1	0	0	0	2
10	1	0	0	0	0	1
11	1	0	1	0	1	3
12	0	1	0	0	0	1

These ideas may seem a little strange at first but they can easily be grasped by considering the following set of data. These data show the scores of 12 children on a five-item test where 1 stands for a 'right' answer and 0 for a 'wrong' answer (table 10.1). The data have been compiled purely for purposes of illustration of the method.

As a first step in working out the values for item difficulty and for the ability estimate associated with each of the raw scores it is helpful to recast the data of table 10.1 into order of total score; this has been done in table 10.2. Now on a test of five items there are six possible scores (0, 1, 2, 3, 4, 5). But a score of nought by any child can be taken to mean that all items were equally difficult for him or her (an unlikely assumption in practice, but convenient for the mathematics involved). Similarly, a score of five can be taken to mean that all items were equally easy. Therefore, in any test composed of k items scores of nought or k provide no differential information about an item's difficulty and are excluded from further examination. By the same argument any item which is answered correctly or incorrectly by all children (there are

Table 10.2 – Rearrangement of data in table 10.1.

	Items					
Child	1	2	3	4	5	Total
10	1	0	0	0	0	1
12	0	1	0	0	0	1
5	1	0	1	0	0	2
9	1	1	0	0	0	2
2	1	1	0	1	0	3
6	1	1	1	0	0	3
8	0	0	1	1	1	3
11	1	0	1	0	1	3
1	1	1	1	1	0	4
3	1	1	1	1	0	4
4	1	0	1	1	1	4

Table 10.3 — A score-group matrix (matrix A).

Items Score-groups	1	2	3	4	5
1	$a_{11} = 1$	$a_{12} = 1$	$a_{13} = 0$	$a_{14} = 0$	$a_{15} = 0$
2	$a_{21} = 2$	$a_{22} = 1$	$a_{23} = 1$	$a_{24} = 0$	$a_{25} = 0$
3	$a_{31} = 3$	$a_{32} = 2$	$a_{33} = 3$	$a_{34} = 2$	$a_{35} = 2$
4	$a_{41} = 3$	$a_{42} = 2$	$a_{43} = 3$	$a_{44} = 3$	$a_{45} = 1$

not any in our example) provides no differential information about the ability of the children being tested: it, too, is excluded from the analysis. Only one child (number seven in table 10.1) achieved full marks and was, therefore, excluded from table 10.2 which is based on the scores of the remaining 11 children.

All the information obtained from table 10.2 is now collapsed into a score-group matrix (matrix A) where the elements (a_{ji}) represent the number of children in score-group j with a correct response to item i. Collapsing table 10.2, where the lines have been drawn to separate the score-groups, yields matrix A (table 10.3). It is easy to see how the values in matrix A are obtained. Each is the number of children with a score of j who get item i correct. Thus $a_{23} = 1$ comes from the fact that of the children who scored a total of two, one got item three correct. Similarly, $a_{44} = 3$ shows that of the three children who scored four on the test all got item four correct.

To continue the method one further matrix is needed. It consists of only one column and is implicit in tables 10.2 and 10.3. Called matrix R, its elements (r_j values) are simply the number of children with a score of j. Thus there were two children with a score of one, two children with a score of two, and so on. The complete matrix is shown in table 10.4. From these values and those in table 10.3 difficulty indices for each item and ability measures for each score-group can be calculated. The method is described more fully in the appendix to this chapter but it is sufficient here to say that

Table 10.4 — Matrix R: numbers of children in useful score-groups.

Score-groups	Elements
1	$r_1 = 2$
2	$r_2 = 2$
3	$r_3 = 4$
4	$r_4 = 3$

the difficulty of an item is simply the average of the odds of success in that item. Difficulty values are placed on a scale ranging from positive (easiest items) to negative (hardest items). The mathematics of the log method[6] for doing this may be examined in the appendix to the chapter and the reader who wishes to understand the application of the technique to the above illustrative data may inspect it there.

The consequences of the method will probably be of greater interest to most readers than its mechanics. If the scores of two groups of children of different average attainment are studied by plotting raw test scores against percentiles as in a conventional item analysis one finds that the ogives, though similar in shape, are some distance apart. The ogive for the high scoring group is displaced to the right relative to the ogive for the low scoring group. (Refer back to table 5.5 and figure 5.2 to remind yourself how to construct an ogive.) In figure 10.1 we see an ogive drawn for a group of high scoring children and another for a group of low scoring children.

Notice that in the lower scoring group, a score of 28 places the child at the 50th percentile whereas a score of 36 is required in the higher scoring group to achieve the same percentile ranking. Similarly, whereas 8% of the lower scoring group have scores equal to or higher than 31, a score of 39 in the higher scoring group is needed to mark a similar percentage cut-off. It is very clear from this figure that different values for item difficulty would be obtained if two groups

---

[6] Log is short for logarithmic.

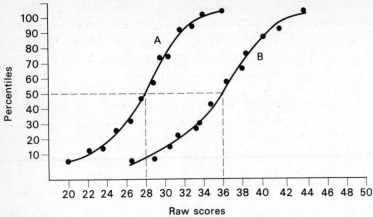

Figure 10.1   Ogives for low (A) and high (B) scoring groups on a test.

differing in attainment to this extent were used for item calibration.

Now study figure 10.2. It shows the same two groups as before (remember, their means differ by about seven points) on the same test whose maximum score was 56 marks only this time the Rasch method has been used. In figure 10.2 the raw scores are once again plotted along the horizontal axis whilst the estimates of ability (known as logabilities) are plotted up the vertical axis. To distinguish the curves the open circles denote the lower scoring group and the closed denote the higher scoring group. They coincide almost exactly. No matter that the two groups differ in average attainment, we have remarkably similar ability measurements for each score-group using our new objective measurement. If you actually come across data from a Rasch analysis it will probably take the form of such a conversion curve. All you have to do to find the ability measure which corresponds to a given raw score is to locate the raw score (the 'score-group') along the horizontal axis, look up vertically to the curve and across to the corresponding ability estimate. Since the scale is a logarithmic one, however, the intervals are not equal. To place the ability estimate on a ratio scale simply find the anti-logarithm of the log score. Thus, in figure 10.2, a raw score of 20 on the test corresponds with a log (ability) measure of

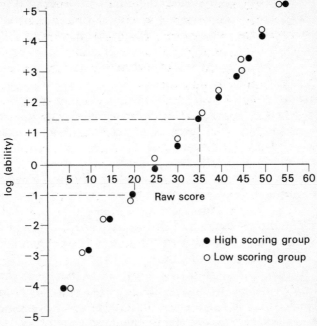

Figure 10.2   Curves showing raw scores against log (ability) for the two groups shown in figure 10.1.

−1.0 and the antilogarithm is 0.3679. (*Natural* logarithms and antilogarithms are used not the common logarithm to the base ten with which some readers may be more familiar.) You can do this easily using log tables or a calculating machine whose relevant key is marked 'ln' by convention. A score of 35 on the test, however, corresponds with logability of +1.3, the antilog of which is 3.6692. Now the values are on a ratio scale (see chapter 5) such that a raw score of 35 indicates roughly ten times 'more ability' than a score of 20 on the objective measurement scale (that is, 3.6692 is roughly 10 x 0.3679).

Assumptions of the Method

Remember that the method (more correctly the mathematical model on which the method is based) assumes that the child's performance on encountering a test item is determined only by the child's ability and the item's difficulty. Thus the model assumes that the difficulty of a given item remains constant across all children, so that if their actual performances differ it is because of differences in their ability. Therefore, no room is left in the model for the possibility that the difficulty may vary because of differences in teaching method.

Mathematics items are, as we have already said, particularly susceptible to differences in teaching. A good example is provided by Goldstein and Blinkhorn (1977) in their critical appraisal of the Rasch method. They point out that an item in 'binary arithmetic' would probably be easier for children taught 'new' than 'traditional' mathematics. On the other hand, 'rote multiplication' or long division might be easier for those taught traditional mathematics. In these circumstances the Log (difficulty) values for the item might well differ from group to group.

A further assumption of the model is that there are no 'spill-over' effects from one item to the next. That is, no allowance is made for the possibility that the competence required for success in one item is involved in another. This is attributable to an assumption called 'local independence' in which performance on item 'a' is held to be independent of performance on item 'b'. In no way, then, can the method accommodate the 'real life' occurrence in which responses to early items can have an effect (positive or negative) on later responses (Goldstein and Blinkhorn, 1977). The assumption (local independence) is obviously not met in tests where several questions are posed of a single stimulus — say a passage of prose, a poem, a map or a graph, which are common in teacher-made tests. Thus we see that items which conceivably test meaningful educational objectives may have to be eliminated from consideration because they do not fit the model. This is a somewhat limiting feature: if the item does not behave as it is *assumed* to behave, discard it! Whereas we have set out the *content* requirements of 'good' and 'poor' items in conventional item analysis, the operational definition of 'good' and 'poor' items in the Rasch technique is those that do and do not conform to the assumptions of the model, respectively.

We have talked a good deal about the idea of an item 'fitting' or 'not fitting' the model. We conclude this introductory section by trying to indicate what is meant by this concept. Basically the technique adopted is to use the estimates of ability and item difficulty (symbolized b^* and d^* in the appendix) to calculate the expected values for a_{ji} in matrix A (table 10.3) (that is, the number of children who would be expected to get the answer right in each score-group from knowledge of the ability of children in that group and the difficulty of the items). This expected value is the number one would get if the model 'fitted perfectly'. Actually the Rasch method obtains a value analogous to the z-score we examined in chapter 5. This standard deviate (symbolized y_{ji}) is formed as follows:

$$y_{ji} = \frac{\text{difference between value for } a_{ji} \text{ and expected value for } a_{ji}}{\text{variance of the expected values of } a_{ji}}$$

(Remember a_{ji} is the element in matrix A (table 10.3). Compare the formula for y_{ji} above with that for z (formula [5.10].)

The statistic used to compare actual values with expected values (or rather, to evaluate the size of the discrepancy) is known as χ^2 'chi square'. It is described in all basic statistics text books. When its value is larger than would be obtained by chance five times or more in 100, then the difference is said to be 'statistically significant'. When this comparison is made for a single item summed over all score-groups, a larger than chance value for χ^2 indicates that the item's behaviour cannot be accounted for in terms of the ability of the children and the difficulty of the item. An item which does not fit the model (i.e. receives a larger than chance value for χ^2) may not do so for a variety of reasons. It may be badly constructed (the principles described in chapter 4 for the construction of items apply equally to Rasch methods, of course) or incorrectly scored. Sometimes an item with a very different discrimination index from the others will not fit for that very reason. Equally, if an item is measuring a different underlying ability from that measured by all the others it, too, might provide a poor fit to the model. Unfortunately, teaching effects might also have a similar result on the fit of an individual item. In fact, far more research needs to be undertaken before the reasons for any one item's poor fit are fully understood. The advice given by Wright and Panchapakesan (1969) is to examine all items having poor fit for their possible deletion or revision.

Quite clearly, *if* a reasonably reliable and objective index of an item's difficulty (which is also constant across all samples taking that item) can be obtained by the Rasch method, it should be possible to monitor the performance of children over time in response to that known level of difficulty. This would enable the APU team to report changes in levels of attainment in a more objective manner than has so far been possible. A second consequence is that banks of items calibrated for difficulty level can be assembled. This enables directly comparable tests to be assembled as well as items which match the levels of attainment of candidates to be selected. Willmott and Fowles (1974) have provided some suggestions for applications of the method and have envisaged its use by individual teachers having a need to use a test which is both adapted to personal requirements and yet rooted in external standards of performance. They also report their view that the model provides a guarantee that examination standards have been maintained. The reader should, however, bear in mind the caution that has been expressed elsewhere in this chapter and the comments by Goldstein and Blinkhorn (1977) that, in its present state of development, the method is best reserved for research purposes only.

REPORTING THE RESULTS OF OBJECTIVE MEASUREMENT

Chapter 12 is given over entirely to some of the issues in the reporting of results and in the communication of their meaning to parents and others with legitimate interest in them. The problems in reporting Rasch indexes of ability are qualitatively different, however, and are reported here.

The appendix to this chapter outlines the method and presents an approximation to the method which is more commonly used when a computer is available. The remainder of this section suggests ways in which Rasch scores can be interpreted to those whose motivation to understand the mathematical rationale is limited.

In table 10.1 responses by 12 children to five items were presented. These have been used in the appendix to illustrate the method and ability estimates for score-groups one to four inclusive obtained and set out there (the b^* values). It was not possible to obtain estimates for children who scored nought or full marks, but this would not be a disadvantage in a test containing a large number of items of appropriate difficulty since these two scores would not be expected to occur. From the values it can be seen that all children who scored one received an ability estimate of -1.407 and those who scored four an estimate of $+1.575$. Although teachers may gradually come to interpret negative ability scores they are, in the words of Willmott and Fowles (1974, 51), 'difficult to adopt with any enthusiasm'. We might add, too, that parents are unlikely to enthuse over their offsprings' ability if this is expressed as a negative quantity!

The WITS Scale

In the description of the technique earlier in the chapter, Wright's suggestion that we find the antilogarithm of the log (ability) scale was mentioned. This has the advantage of providing measures on a scale whose zero point actually means 'no ability'. The results of analysing the scores which were presented in figure 10.1 appear in table 10.5 but, since computers are available for all meaningful practical applications of the method, log (ability) measures are improved upon by what is known as maximum likelihood estimates where the antilogarithm method is not suitable. Accordingly statisticians have sought to determine alternative methods of reporting the meaning of the scores.

Using the log (ability) method, however, values for item difficulty range from positive (easiest) to negative (hardest)

Table 10.5 — Log (item difficulties) for high and low scoring groups in figure 10.1.

Item number	Low scoring group	High scoring group
4	–4.468	–4.458
6	–4.169	–4.419
16	–1.766	–1.140
26	–1.361	–1.140
42	–0.874	–0.598
46	0.909	1.066
52	2.002	1.854
56	3.106	2.920
58	3.674	3.954
59	5.581	5.474

and are in the opposite direction from the ability values (positive: most able, negative: least able). However, the direction of sign is arbitrary and in practice the sign of the item difficulty values is changed so that the most difficult items receive positive and the easiest negative values.

In order to show the construction of the WITS scale we shall use some of the data on which figure 10.1 is based. The test consisted of 60 items but in order to simplify matters and save space we have quoted the values for only ten items selected to represent the range of difficulty from easiest (now negative in sign) to hardest (now positive in sign). Notice that with this number of items estimates range from roughly –5 to +5. Estimates of item difficulty for the low scoring and the high scoring group are given to indicate how close they can become even though the average ability of the two groups differed considerably. They are shown in table 10.5.

The scale which has been proposed places item difficulty values on what has been called the WITS scale. It uses a very simple transformation:

$$D = 50 + 4.551d$$

where

D = the new difficulty value on the WITS scale

Table 10.6 — The WITS scale for reporting attainment. From: *The objective interpretation of test performance* by A. S. Willmott and D. E. Fowles, NFER, 1974, page 52.

WITS score	Difference between WITS score and item of difficulty 50	Odds of correct response to item of difficulty 50	Probability[a] of correct response to item of difficulty 50
30	–20	1:81	0.01
35	–15	1:27	0.04
40	–10	1:9	0.10
45	–5	1:3	0.25
50	0	1:1	0.50
55	5	3:1	0.75
60	10	9:1	0.90
65	15	27:1	0.96
70	20	81:1	0.99

[a]Probability to two decimal places.

d = the solution based on the maximum likelihood method

Thus for item 42 (assuming they were maximum likelihood values)

$$D = \begin{cases} 50 + 4.551\,(-0.874) = 46 & \text{low scoring group} \\ 50 + 4.551\,(-0.598) = 47 & \text{high scoring group} \end{cases}$$

Since items of average difficulty receive values of zero the new scale obviously has a mean of 50 ($50 + 4.551 \times 0 = 50$). A helpful way of reporting such results and bringing out their meaning has been provided by Willmott and Fowles (1974). Table 10.6 has been reproduced from that book by kind permission. Suppose an item has a WITS difficulty of 50 (average difficulty) and WITS attainment measures are provided for each score group at intervals of five points along the scale. The second column in table 10.6 shows the difference between each WITS attainment score and the item of WITS difficulty 50. The third column shows the probability of success on this item for each score-group. Thus children in score-group 30 have only about a one in 100 chance of getting the item right whereas children in score-group 50 have a 50% chance of being correct. Children whose WITS ability exceeds the item's difficulty by 20 points (i.e. those in score-group 70) have a 99 in 100 chance of getting the item of average difficulty correct.

Suppose John has a WITS ability score of 60 and Peter has a WITS score of 50. We can compare their respective performances by saying that John has a 40% better chance of a correct response to the item of difficulty value 50 than Peter (i.e. 90% minus 50%). This method of reporting Rasch scores has obvious advantages for those able to cope with the concept of probability. It provides both a statement about a child's chances of success in meeting items of varying difficulty as well as a basis for comparisons between two or more children. Thus it serves both criterion- and norm-referenced purposes.

If a pool of items is drawn to represent the domain of knowledge a teacher wishes to assess, WITS scores for each pupil then indicate the child's attainment in relation to the area of knowledge defined by those items. If each pool of items contributes a relatively discrete objective, then a WITS score for each child on that objective can be obtained. Work is currently being undertaken to extend Rasch methods to essay type questions. If successful it should then be possible to estimate and compare the performance of pupils even though no two of them choose to answer the same questions from a pool of items on a single paper.

APPENDIX

In this appendix the mathematical model and the log method are applied to the illustrative data presented in table 10.1. The presentation of the argument here is taken from Wright and Panchapakesan (1969, 24) but presented in slightly modified form. Remember that only two factors are assumed to come into play when a child encounters a test item: the ability of the child and the difficulty of the item. Three symbols are basic to the argument:

a_{ni} = the score of the nth child on the ith item

It can take only two values: 'right' ($a_{ni} = 1$) or 'wrong' ($a_{ni} = 0$)

$$Z_n = \text{the child's ability}$$
$$E_i = \text{the easiness of the item}$$

The argument begins with the assumption that the probability, P, of a child getting an item correct ($a_{ni} = 1$) is as follows:

$$P(a_{ni} = 1) = Z_n E_i \,/\, (1 + Z_n E_i) \qquad [10.1]$$

i.e. the product of his ability and the easiness of the item divided by one plus this product. It follows that if a child has no ability ($Z_n = 0$) then no matter how hard he tries his chances of being correct remain at zero. So, too, if the item has zero easiness ($E_i = 0$) then no matter how able no child can answer it. Now if formula [10.1] gives us the probability of being 'right' (and only two outcomes are possible) the probability of being 'wrong' must be one minus the probability of being correct, that is:

$$1 - P(a_{ni} = 1)$$

Hence

$$P(a_{ni} = 0) = 1 - P(a_{ni} = 1) \qquad [10.2a]$$
$$= 1 \,/\, (1 + Z_n E_i) \qquad [10.2b]$$

Thus, in words, the probability of a child getting the answer wrong is one divided by one plus the product of the child's ability and the easiness of the item.

Because $a_{ni} = 1$ means 'right' and $a_{ni} = 0$ means 'wrong', formulae [10.1] and [10.2b] can be combined to give:

$$P(a_{ni}) = (Z_n E_i) a_{ni} /(1 + Z_n E_i) \qquad [10.3]$$

Notice that the first term on the right-hand side now contains a power (a_{ni}). This is known as an exponential equation which can be solved by using logarithms. So formula [10.3] can be rewritten using logarithms as follows:

$$P(a_{ni}) = \exp\left[a_{ni}\left(\log Z_n + \log E_i\right)\right] / \left[1 + \exp\left(\log Z_n + \log E_i\right)\right]$$
[10.4]

Now if the ability of a child is estimated by the number of correct answers $(\Sigma(a_{ni} = 1))$ to a given set of items, then it is only necessary to obtain one ability estimate for all children who obtain the same score. In other words, any child who gets a certain score is estimated to have the ability associated with that score and all children with the same score receive the same ability estimate. Since we are now regarding all pupils within a single score-group as having the same ability, formula [10.4] can be rewritten in terms of score-groups:

$$P(a_{ni}) = \exp\left[a_{ni}\left(\log Z_j + \log E_i\right)\right] / \left[1 + \exp\left(\log Z_j + \log E_i\right)\right]$$
[10.5]

where j is the score obtained by the nth child and all children with this score of j are estimated to have the same probability governing their responses to item i.

Let us see now how this method works out on the highly simplified test data presented in table 10.1. No person in his or her right mind would actually estimate item difficulty on such a small data base but this has been done here purely for illustrative purposes. A sample size of at least 100 is required to make application of the method worthwhile: the APU uses samples very much larger than this, of course. Our illustrative data, shown in table 10.1, were obtained from 12 children who took a five-item achievement test. Table 10.3 shows matrix A, a score groups x items matrix containing elements a_{ji}, and table 10.4 shows matrix R which is actually a column vector (a matrix with only one column) containing elements r_j. These are simply the number of children in each of the $k - 1$ score-groups.

Two methods of estimating item difficulty are described by Wright and Panchapakesan (1969). The maximum likeli-

Table 10.7 — Item difficulty for each score-group.

		1	2	3	4	5	Total	Mean
Score-	1	0	0	-2.485	-2.485	-2.485	-7.455	-1.491
group	2	2.485	-0.693	-2.485	-2.485	-2.485	-3.871	-0.774
	3	1.099	0	1.099	0	0	2.198	0.440
	4	2.485	0.693	2.485	2.485	-0.693	7.455	1.491
Total		6.069	0	0.406	-2.485	-5.664	-1.673	
Mean		1.517	0	0.102	-0.621	-1.416		-0.084

hood method is to be preferred on mathematical grounds and, although Cohen (1979) has presented a relatively quick method, it usually involves obtaining repeated approximations to item difficulties which can be tedious and require a computer. The other method, the log method, is illustrated on the data.

Having obtained the simple matrix already described one further table is required. The data in matrix A and matrix R (tables 10.3 and 10.4) are now transformed into another matrix (matrix T, table 10.7) where the elements t_{ji} are given by

$$t_{ji} = \log[(a_{ji}) / (r_j - a_{ji})] \qquad [10.6]$$

In this formula a_{ji} and r_j have already appeared in tables 10.3 and 10.4 respectively. Quite obviously the value for t_{ji} is the logarithm of the odds of a correct answer being obtained to that item for children in a given score-group. For example, take item one for score-group one in matrix A (table 10.3). Here $a_{11} = 1$ and $r_1 = 2$ (table 10.4). The value for t_{11} therefore is $1/(2 - 1)$ or $1/1$ (i.e. one child 'right' to one child 'wrong'). Since the natural logarithm of $1/1$ is 0 this is the value for t_{11} placed in matrix T (table 10.7). Exactly the same value is obtained for t_{12}, for the same reason. In other words, an item of difficulty value 0 is one for which the odds of success are 50%.

Unfortunately in this method, problems are encountered where $a_{ji} = 0$ or where $a_{ji} = r$ because here t_{ji} will be infinite as can easily be seen from formula [10.6]. Where this occurs the elements in T are modified using a constant w. Here $w = r_j/N$ (i.e. the number of children in the score-group divided by the number of children who figure in the analysis, 11 in our example). The modified t_{ji} in these cases become

$$t_{ji} = \log[(a_{ji} + w) / (r - a_{ji} + w)] \qquad [10.7]$$

Applying this to our example where $a_{ji} = 0$ (e.g. $a_{24} = 0$) we get

$$t_{24} = \log\left(\frac{0 + 2/11}{2 + 2/11}\right)$$

$$= \log\left(\frac{2/11}{24/11}\right)$$

$$= -2.485$$

The complete matrix of t_{ji} values is presented as matrix T in table 10.7. Totals and means of rows and columns are also shown.

Calculation of Item Difficulty Value

The formula for the difficulty value d^* of each item is

$$d_i^* = \bar{t}_i - \bar{t} \qquad [10.8]$$

where

$\bar{t}_i$ = the mean of the values for each item (the column mean)
$\bar{t}$ = the mean of all items

In words, the difficulty of the item is the difference between the average value of t for that item across all score groups and the overall average of t for all items across all score groups. Thus for our five items:

$$d_1^* = 1.517 - (-0.084) = 1.601 \text{ (easiest)}$$
$$d_2^* = 0.000 - (-0.084) = 0.084$$

$$d_3{}^* = \quad 0.102 - (-0.084) = \quad 0.186$$
$$d_4{}^* = -0.621 - (-0.084) = -0.537$$
$$d_5{}^* = -1.416 - (-0.084) = -1.332 \text{ (hardest)}$$

As a check on the values their sum should equal zero within
the limits of rounding error.

Calculation of Estimated Ability

To calculate the estimated ability associated with each score-
group we proceed as follows. All children in a given score-
group receive the same ability estimate, $b_j{}^*$. The relevant
formula is

$$b_j{}^* = \bar{t}_j - \bar{t} \qquad [10.9]$$

where

$\quad \bar{t}_j$ = the mean of the k values for each score group

For the four score-groups:

$$b_1{}^* = -1.491 - (-0.084) = -1.407$$
$$b_2{}^* = -0.774 - (-0.084) = -0.690$$
$$b_3{}^* = \quad 0.440 - (-0.084) = \quad 0.524$$
$$b_4{}^* = \quad 1.491 - (-0.084) = \quad 1.575$$

A simple ogive (figure 10.3) helps translate raw scores into
log(ability) estimates (compare figure 10.2). Thus any child
whose log(ability) score is nought has a probability of a
correct response to an item of difficulty value nought which
is roughly equal to 0.5; that is the odds of a correct response
are one to one (see table 10.6).

Although the log(ability) method yields only approximate
results its advantage is that the values, as has been shown, can
quite easily be obtained by a teacher with a calculator and a
little motivation. As an example of how close they can
become compare results obtained by the log(ability) method
with those by the maximum likelihood (maxlike) method:

	Log	Maxlike
$b_1{}^*$	−1.407	−1.694
$b_2{}^*$	−0.690	−0.494
$b_3{}^*$	0.524	0.519
$b_4{}^*$	1.575	1.669

In fact, the discrepancies are far smaller than the standard errors of the maximum likelihood values.

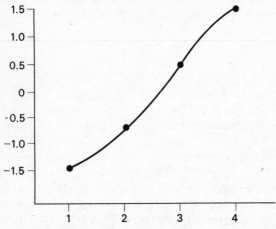

Figure 10.3   Simple ogive to translate raw scores in log (ability) estimates for the example used in appendix.

11

Diagnostic Assessment

FORMAL AND INFORMAL DIAGNOSIS

The chief purpose of diagnostic assessment is, of course, the identification of underlying learning problems or difficulties (often called 'learning disabilities') from the features of a child's performance. Generally speaking there are two main approaches:

(1) to locate the relative weaknesses or 'malfunctioning' of the child's perceptual or intellectual processes; and
(2) to infer the nature of intellectual processes hidden from view to the outside observer.

At first sight there may appear to be little difference between these approaches but the distinction can be illustrated with reference to the diagnosis of reading disability. One test which has been extensively used for this purpose is the Illinois test of psycholinguistic abilities (ITPA). The rationale of this test is to 'dissect' language ability into a number of 'subskills' or pre-requisites and to present subtests which correspond to them. The 'subskills' evaluated include:

(1) auditory reception (the ability to comprehend the spoken word);
(2) auditory closure (the ability to complete a whole word when only part of it is heard);
(3) auditory sequential memory (the ability to reproduce a sequence of auditory symbols); and
(4) sound blending (the ability to synthesize separate phonemes and to integrate them into a whole word).

In all, twelve such subskills are investigated.

Readers will appreciate that this test is a sophisticated one; despite this Newcomer and Hammill (1975) reviewed a number of studies but were unable to conclude that its validity for diagnosis had been satisfactorily demonstrated. The important point for our purposes, however, is to note that the test embodies a *formal analysis* of the target ability (reading) and thereby directs the search for specific strengths and weaknesses. Scoring helps the user depict these by means of a profile and enables the teacher to prescribe a set of remedial activities appropriate to the deficits identified.

The second type of diagnosis is less formal but leaves more scope for the teacher's ability to intuit the nature of the underlying problem. In it, no particularly structured analysis of what is involved in the target activity is used. Instead, close observation of the child's performance on the actual task (reading) is undertaken and his or her attempts examined, through which the kinds of processes 'going on' are then inferred. This approach is exemplified by the work of Goodman (1970) who studied the errors (or 'miscues') made by children in oral reading and tried to suggest the processes that operate when the syntactical and semantic information extracted from the passage interacts with what the child already knows. As a result, Goodman conceived of reading as being a 'psycholinguistic guessing game' in which the child guesses from the context, and from what he or she already knows, the words he or she is finding difficulty in reading. This conception has led Goodman to argue that miscues are worthy of the teacher's serious attention only when the meaning of what is written is altered. Unlike the ITPA, the diagnostic information provided by this approach is not a set of scores on component skills in reading but a qualitative and quantitative analysis of the miscues themselves. To this end, *Reading miscues inventory* (Goodman and Burke, 1972) has been published.

These two approaches to diagnosis — illustrated by reference to reading ability — are not, of course, mutually exclusive but complementary. Whereas the former depends on a formal structural analysis of the task itself, the latter relies on naturalistic observations, i.e. those occurring during the performance itself. We shall refer to these as *formal-structural diagnosis* and *informal-heuristic diagnosis* respectively. ('Heuristic', by the way, means discovering by one's own efforts.) As is obvious, the latter can subsequently lead to the later development of a formal-structural model of the learning task.

STAGES IN THE PROCESSES OF DIAGNOSIS AND REMEDIATION

Classroom teachers are chiefly interested in diagnostic assessment insofar as the information acquired can lead to the development of remedial programmes, or indicate where further teaching is required. Criterion-referenced assessment is capable of identifying what the child has and has not learned, of course, but diagnostic assessment is concerned with a closer examination of failure in an attempt to find reasons for it. The purpose of diagnostic assessment is, therefore, different from criterion-referenced assessment but the latter often constitutes the 'warning signs' that more extensive diagnostic assessment is required.

Although there will be variations in approach to diagnosis according to the time and facilities available in schools the sequence shown in figure 11.1 represents a very common type of model.

We are not suggesting that classroom teachers will have a great deal of time in which to conduct diagnostic assessment separately from their normal classroom activities. Nor will it be possible to cope effectively with the most intractable problems of educational or mental deficiency. In extreme cases, referral to the educational psychologist may be the only course of action left open. The most serious learning deficiencies are likely to be 'picked up' quite early in schooling and children who are clearly unable to cope with normal classrooms identified for possible treatment in special schools. Even so, a large number of pupils in ordinary schools were judged by the Warnock Report (DES, 1978) to be in need of special help, and psychologists in the Schools Psychological Services are overwhelmed with 'cases' referred for their attention.

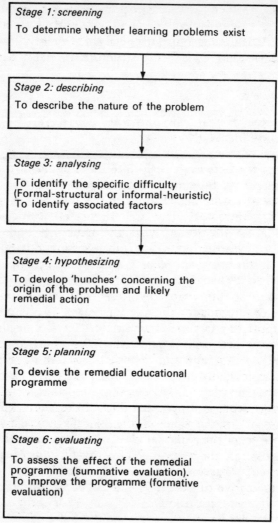

Figure 11.1   Stages in diagnostic—remedial assessment.

Very many books are now available on the diagnosis of a wide range of disabilities and it is clearly beyond the scope of a chapter of this kind to examine how all specific abilities can be studied. Instead, the general principles of the stages in figure 11.1 will be described and brief summaries of the methods by which performance in basic skills may be studied will be discussed. This, it is hoped, will encourage classroom teachers to develop assessment procedures suited to their own environment and needs, derived from a few basic principles.

Stage 1: Screening

Using standardized or published tests

Screening can be accomplished in a number of curriculum areas by use of group-administered standardized tests. These enable teachers to identify those children whose level of functioning is 'well below' the mean. In any large group of children teachers may expect to find a number of children whose performance is poor. On the assumption of a normal distribution of the ability or performance examined, one expects to find roughly 16% of children whose scores on the day are lower than one standard deviation below the mean. Just where the 'line is to be drawn' for a child to be deemed in need of diagnostic assessment will probably depend as much upon the facilities available as on the needs of the child. If the test used is one which, for example, expresses the child's performance in terms of a reading age, rules of thumb for labelling those in need of diagnosis have tended to be used. Moseley (1976) has suggested that a child whose reading age score is lower than 80% of the score expected of a boy or girl of the same chronological age is described as 'backward' and, presumably, may be helped if teachers have time to diagnose the nature of the problem faced. In practice, many teachers have adopted a criterion of one year's retardation as indicative of backwardness in reading, but this seems far too stringent a criterion. (A pupil of 15 who is reading at the level of a 13 year old is certainly functional in reading.) Since reading deficit tends to be cumulative more children in secondary than in junior school will be classified as 'backward' by this method. It does not mean that their actual reading skills are 'getting worse', of course. Similarly, the Department of Education and Science has provided guidelines for the cut-off score on intelligence tests below which children are described as 'subnormal'. Very low performance on an intelligence test has traditionally been regarded as indicative of low all-round learning potential although many have criticised the wisdom of this interpretation. The difference between classifying children as 'backward' using the reading age criterion from that using a standardized score is obviously that the latter yields a predictable proportion of backward pupils, which is likely to remain consistent over time, whereas the former cannot accomplish this. For this reason it is probably advisable for teachers to use a standardized test as an initial screening device where possible. Tests which claim to provide 'arithmetic ages' have never been as popular as those which supply a summary 'reading age'. Although teachers may believe that the 'age' is more easily understood than a standardized score, the former does present quite considerable difficulties and may even be misleading. If reading ability is the object of the screening then several group-administered tests yielding standardized scores are now available. (The books by Vincent and Cresswell (1976) and Pumfrey (1977) provide extremely valuable sources of tests for all ages and stages in reading.)

We have already implied a distinction between the types of disability identified by the use of an intelligence test on the one hand from tests of specific abilities (reading, mathematics, etc.) on the other. Low scores on the former are often held to indicate children who are in need of special educational treatment 'across the curriculum', as it were. Low scores on the latter are taken to show poor progress in a specific area of educational attainment. Sometimes a diagnosis is attempted using both types of test. The most frequently encountered instances of this practice concern backward readers who may have to take an intelligence test when a reading score has been found to be low. This is often done to distinguish between two types of children which make up the group whose poor reading proficiency is giving cause for concern. Typically, some psychologists have claimed that this method separates 'underachievers' from 'slow learners'. The concept of 'underachiever' is applied to children whose reading is below average but whose intelligence test score is average or even higher. Basic to this labelling is the assumption that the intelligence test measures the child's potential for learning, the achievement test the actual level of functioning. Thus a child who has a high or average IQ but whose level of reading is below average is assumed to be able to do better and an explanation often sought in terms of social, cultural and emotional factors (Vincent and Cresswell, 1976). The idea of the underachiever accords with common sense but, in fact, the concept is a confused one (Thorndike, 1967). For although some children inevitably have an IQ which is higher than their standardized reading score there are others for whom the reverse is true. These, presumably, are 'overachievers'; those who are doing better than they ought to! One might have expected that the existence of these pupils would lead to a widespread mistrust of the intelligence test as a measure of potential, but the labelling continues. Nevertheless, although the concept is confused, knowledge that a child has an average or high IQ in spite of low achievement can be useful in alerting the teacher to look for possible causal factors in the child's environment.

It is probably better for a child in school to be thought of as an underachiever than as a 'slow learner', however! These latter are those children whose standardized test scores in school subjects are low and whose intelligence test scores are also below average. These are children who are thought of as 'doing as well as can be expected'. They may well be screened as in need of diagnostic assessment but there is a clear implication that no matter how skilled the remedial teaching high expectations are unrealistic. Now this will indeed be the case for those whose IQ is very low (say less than 70–75) but above this no such inference is warranted. The correlations between intelligence test scores and school progress are far too low to posit a straightforward inference of the above type for any given child.

Although screening may appear to be a comparatively simple task some of the difficulties involved have been described. As we said in the chapter on reliability (chapter 6), however, even the best tests are less than perfect and children's scores vary from day to day. The use of a single test on a single occasion by which to decide whether diagnostic assessment is required is, therefore, indefensible in theory and practice. It seems desirable that a variety of sources of information including test scores, and if possible, the opinions of more than one teacher who has taught a pupil, be integrated into the decision making process.

At least two more sources of information may be available: the results of 'readiness tests' and the teachers' own observations.

Using 'readiness tests'
These are familiar to teachers of young children in the assessment of 'readiness for reading'. They are chiefly formal-structural in intention. Such tests attempt to diagnose the competence of children in those intellectual and perceptual skills held by psychological and educational theory to be determinants of subsequent success, in particular to judge whether the child possesses those attributes on which the skill to be taught seems to depend. Unfortunately, the concept, though a common sense one, is fraught with problems. Readers interested in the concept can find a useful discussion in Downing and Thackray (1971). Although use of such tests may be able to identify those children who are 'more ready' than others, no precise cut-off point can ever be determined. Moreover, pupils have been known to read before they have been adjudged 'ready' to do so! (Vincent and Cresswell, 1976) and Ausubel's advice (1958) to teach first and then to infer readiness from those who do profit from the teaching seems sensible, if somewhat circular.

Although tests and check lists have been published by which, it is claimed, young children's readiness for reading can be assessed, their use as a screening device is probably only to be recommended with individual children as they are too time-consuming to be adopted on a large scale and are probably more correctly thought of as part of an attempt to prevent later failure than as a help in 'curing' a disability. Intelligence tests are of little use for this purpose with young children but tests which include aspects of visual and verbal functioning have achieved some success in the prediction of the ability to profit from reading teaching once this has been taking place for about a year (Feshbach et al., 1974). By and large, however, once schooling has well and truly begun (in middle and secondary schools) the best predictors of ability to profit from the next stage of teaching and learning are performances in earlier stages (Ausubel et al., 1978).

Using teachers' observations

Understandably, the bulk of tests useful for screening purposes has been composed of tests in basic subjects of the curriculum. Those for reading skills probably predominate. But the more formal-structural approach that such tests represent by no means exhausts the methods available. Indeed, in secondary schools (except perhaps in the first year in reading skills) very little formal screening occurs. In other areas of the curriculum and with older age groups, observations of children learning whatever it is they are being taught are the chief source of screening information. Generally speaking, as specialization occurs, no teacher worries overmuch if a pupil's performance is poor in particular subjects

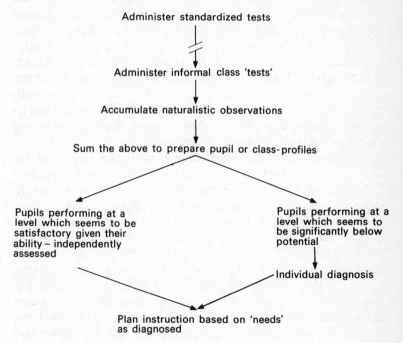

Figure 11.2   A model of screening and diagnosis. Adapted from Ripley and Blair (1979, 94).

other than those which are basic. Only where the pupil is low in attainment on account of a non-specific learning disability or because he or she has failed to master the basic subjects to a level where he or she can profit from teaching is diagnosis indicated. Possibly the administration of a published test provides the context in which teachers form their own judgments as to a child's need for diagnostic assessment with the score a mere by-product of little interest. (Vincent and Cresswell (1976) suggest that this is probably the only justification for the longevity of the Schonell graded word reading test; one which they rightly describe as 'antiquated'.)

In conclusion, the processes involved in screening and later diagnosis are as shown in figure 11.2.

Stages 2 and 3: Describing and Analysing the Problem

These stages shade into one another and are differentiated by the amount of detail they incorporate. In order to discuss this section we shall assume that severely learning-disabled children have been screened for and are receiving special attention. The problems described, therefore, are those encountered among children considered able to profit from normal schooling. Whereas the screening may have employed standardized tests to identify those pupils whose performances are below average, interest in comparisons among children stops at the stage of diagnosis and is replaced by as detailed a study of the individual child as time and facilities allow. This attempt to understand the learning problems of the individual in his/her own situation unencumbered by comparisons, is known as 'idiographic' assessment.

It is extremely unlikely that much time will be set aside in a busy school day for diagnostic testing using instruments specially designed and marketed for that purpose. Instead much diagnosis will take place during normal learning and teaching. This is, in fact, an advantage since the diagnosis will then be of the child's actual performance in the skill itself rather than in some artificial test item or situation. In general terms, the purpose of the diagnosis will be to find out the relatively broad area of the curriculum where learning difficulties occur and the type of skill in which the child is judged to be less than satisfactory (description), followed by a much closer study of the child's behaviour in order to determine the precise nature of the difficulty experienced (analysis). There is no particular mystery about the process: informal but systematic observation can go a long way in diagnosis. Such observation can take one of a mixture of three main forms:

(1)   the use of check lists based on task analysis;
(2)   skill analysis during the performance; and
(3)   case-study analysis.

We shall attempt to describe each of these in turn in relation to skills other than reading since extremely valuable sets of procedures for the diagnosis of reading disability have been described in numerous publications; chapter 8 in Vincent and Cresswell (1976) is a particularly helpful one in this connection.

Task analysis
This is probably the most formal of these informal procedures! Here a specific task is broken down into its successively smaller components. In other words, it is a formal analysis of the final performance in terms of subskills which are incorporated into it and which are assumed to be prerequisite to overall satisfactory performance. To accomplish this quite difficult task the 'task analyser' begins with a description of the final performance and 'works downwards' to the most elementary skills involved. Each of these is then made an item in a check list and the child's performance assessed on each. This device is then assumed to indicate precisely at what element or combination of elements the child's overall performance is 'breaking down'.

As an example of a learning hierarchy, consider figure 11.3 which shows one model of the structure of the task: 'The pupil will be able to determine the work done when lifting a physical object through a specified height.'

The teacher who wishes to diagnose the learning problem presented by this task can prepare a quick check list as follows:

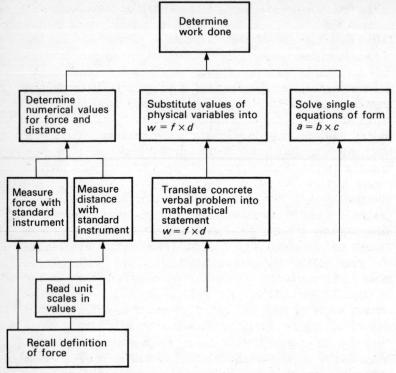

Figure 11.3   Learning hierarchy for work problem. Adapted by arrangement with Holt, Rinehart and Winston – New York, from *The conditions of learning*, 2nd ed. by R. M. Gagné, 1970.

(1) Can read unit scales.
(2) Can recall that weight is the vertical force on a mass resulting from effects of gravitation.
(3) Can measure force (wt) using a standard instrument.
(4) Can measure distance using a standard instrument.
(5) Can use standard instruments to determine 'error-free' values for f and d.
(6) Can recall formula $w = f \times d$.
(7) Can substitute values obtained from (5) into formula $w = f \times d$.
(8) Can multiply real numbers to obtain product.

(9)   Can solve linear equations of the general form $a = b \times c$.
(10) Can solve for the specific values of f and d.
(11) Can name units for the answer.

Now it is conceivable that the pupil may fail to obtain an answer to the physical work problems presented because of errors at one or a combination of 'positions' in the hierarchy. Indeed, failure may even occur in an element which the teacher has not included in the check list because it is even lower in the hierarchy than the level where it was assumed all pupils had the requisite competence. Recognition of the numerals nought to nine is a pre-requisite for the task, but a failure at this level would suggest that the topic was wholly inappropriate for the pupil in question! In other words, although the task could be successively analysed into smaller and more elementary components, a teacher will have to make certain assumptions as to how much competence can be taken for granted before a topic is begun. Quite obviously, certain kinds of task are very much easier to analyse in this way than others. For this reason one finds many more examples in mathematics and science than in arts subjects. Nevertheless, attempting to write a task analysis (or learning hierarchy) and thereby identifying pre-requisites is salutary for the teachers of all subjects and an invaluable aid to diagnosis. This method can, therefore, be classified as a formal structural method.

Skill analysis (an example of an informal-heuristic approach)
Teachers are likely to find skill analysis much easier to perform than task analysis since it is not necessary to build a model of structure to carry it out. It is really little more than a systematic analysis of a homogeneous set of performance items (e.g. a number of similar arithmetic roblems; several written paragraphs; a set of comprehension exercises) in order to detect errors. Those which occur frequently are held to be more relevant to the diagnosis than those which seem to be 'careless slips'. As an example, consider the performance on an informal test of subtraction administered to a

group of seven year olds. The teacher has marked all those items where a particular pupil has made mistakes and has concluded, after study of the performance and questioning, that the child has been confused by the presence of noughts. In particular he seems to have multiplied by nought in some cases (figure 11.4). Similarly, at a more advanced level, an older pupil has reached a wrong answer when simplifying an algebraic expression which involves factors and fractions (figure 11.5). Here the teacher observes that an error has been made when factorizing the expression $a^2 + bc + d$. If this type of error were to be repeated in similar items a clear diagnosis with implied remediation would be made. At this stage, source of difficulty rather than interpretation of the problem is the goal of the analysis.

Skill analysis can be carried out most easily in school subjects where criteria of 'correct/incorrect' can be applied or where the performance varies along a continuum of 'good to poor'. Too often, teachers have little time to go beyond the correction of errors in children's work and, if the work has then to be covered in red ink (or its equivalent) this can be

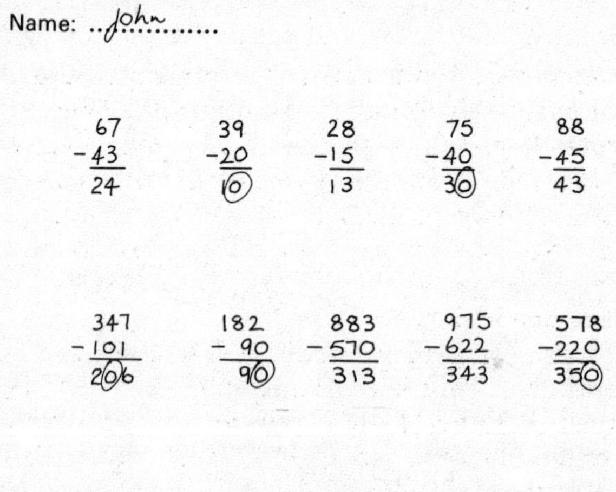

Name: ..John.......

$$
\begin{array}{ccccc}
67 & 39 & 28 & 75 & 88 \\
-43 & -20 & -15 & -40 & -45 \\
\hline
24 & (0) & 13 & 3(0) & 43
\end{array}
$$

$$
\begin{array}{ccccc}
347 & 182 & 883 & 975 & 578 \\
-101 & -90 & -570 & -622 & -220 \\
\hline
2(0)6 & 9(0) & 313 & 343 & 35(0)
\end{array}
$$

$$
\begin{array}{ccccc}
513 & 654 & 845 & 497 & 260 \\
-206 & -352 & -203 & -82 & -109 \\
\hline
307 & 2(0)2 & 6(0)2 & 415 & 1(00)
\end{array}
$$

'Careless slips'

Figure 11.4   Skill analysis of subtraction performance.

$$\frac{2}{x+4} - \frac{x-5}{x^2 \boxed{+7x} + 12}$$

$$= \frac{2}{x+4} - \frac{x-5}{(x-4)(x-3)} \qquad \text{LCM} = (x-4)(x-3)$$

Incorrect Signs

$$= \frac{2(x-3)-(x-5)}{(x-4)(x-3)}$$

$$= \frac{2x-6-x-5}{(x-4)(x-3)}$$

$$= \frac{x-11}{(x-4)(x-3)}$$

Figure 11.5   Skill analysis of simplifying task.

very depressing. Nevertheless, the principal purpose of this kind of analysis is to discover learning problems followed by constructive attempts to remediate performance, not to 'grind the pupil down'. So there is no real need to cover the pupil's work with actual 'corrections' to fulfil the aim of the analysis. Notice that it is not the purpose at this stage to offer explanation of the learning problems nor to suggest possible remediation.

Note also, in passing, that criterion-referenced assessment is a form of diagnostic assessment when it is used to examine performance rather than to classify as master/non-master. Thus criterion-referenced assessment can serve the functions both of assessing progress and diagnosing learning failure, if not learning disability.

Case-study analysis
Much of the teachers' informal diagnostic assessment will be of the skill analysis type, but occasionally it will be necessary

for several members of staff who teach a pupil to pool their knowledge in a detailed study of his or her performance and general school adjustment. Case studies are an attempt to integrate information from all possible sources in trying to evaluate and understand the problem faced by a child which transcends his or her learning of the specific subject or skill. The types of assessment which are relevant will go beyond the kinds of information with which this book has been principally concerned, to include classroom observations, performance data, general data about school adjustment and, perhaps, health and home records (used with caution!). Remedial teachers in schools will be particularly anxious to understand as many facets of the child's adjustment to school as can be evaluated by whatever assessments have been made, in the (correct) belief that the more intractable learning problems are influenced in a complex way by many overlapping factors. But this is an extremely time-consuming task, and case-study analysis will probably be undertaken only where children who exhibit the most severe learning difficulties in the normal school are identified.

The following guidelines may be helpful in standardizing the case-study report which can then be discussed with parents. The full report cannot be written until stages 4, 5 and 6 shown in figure 11.1 have been conducted, of course:

(1) Include only that information which is likely to be of value in working with pupils.

(2) Distinguish impression judgments, opinions and objective information.

(3) List specific performance data (test scores, grades) making sure that the name of the test is included where relevant.

(4) List the specific basic skills where the child is judged to require remedial teaching.

(5) List specific remedial teaching — if tried — and evaluate outcome in terms of pupil progress (stages 4 and 5).

(6) Make specific suggestions for further remediation (stage 4).

(7) Include possible causal interpretations but avoid the types of explanation which 'blame' parents. These latter

are unlikely to be conducive to the establishment of productive home/school relationships.

Stages 4 and 5: Hypothesizing and Planning

We shall deal only very briefly with this since the task of diagnosing the underlying causes of learning disability is a complex one and conclusions are, at best, extremely tentative even when conducted by experts. Therefore the purpose of the hypothesis is not so much to construct a theory of ex- explanation of the phenomena as it is to erect hunches as to the most appropriate educational actions to take.

It is assumed that by this stage the teacher or teachers in- volved will have identified in fairly precise terms the target weaknesses in performance. If teachers other than those who made the diagnosis are to be involved, the weaknesses will have to be spelt over with some precision if time is not to be wasted nor effort duplicated. Generally speaking, no matter what the performance to be 'remediated' three chief kinds of factors must be assessed (and action designed in stage 5). These factors are (Ripley and Blair, 1979):

(1) *learner-style* variables;
(2) *task* variables; and
(3) *resource* variables.

Decisions may be made by considering some important ques- tions.

Learner-style variables
(a) Has the child shown any marked preference for working alone or in groups and how much anxiety or need for re- assurance has he/she shown in previous work? Is a syste- matic attempt to improve the child's self-concept indicated as a pre-requisite for or concomitant of remedial work (for example, through counselling)?
(b) Is the child able to work at a single activity for a stretch of time or is he/she able, at present, only to concentrate for short periods?
(c) In what type of structure does the child work most

effectively? For example, is it to be strictly controlled or loosely disciplined: structured formally around tight objectives or largely informal with emphasis on a discovery approach?

(d)   Do attempts need to be made to change the attitudes of the child to work as a pre-requisite for remedial teaching?

(e)   If the child has reacted to failure defensively or by withdrawal, what steps can be taken to change this approach?

(f)   What kind of reward structure seems likely to provide the most appropriate incentives to effort? For example, does the child respond best to praise, to the intrinsic satisfaction of success or may it even be necessary to employ sanctions in the event of 'inadequate' motivation? Is it necessary to work out a systematic reward schedule for the pupil?

(g)   What are the existing *strengths* in the child's approach to tasks which can be built upon in the remedial work (for example, special ability at drawing; comparative efficiency in dealing with practical problems)?

Task variables

(a)   Given that the child has been diagnosed on account of performances which have failed to match certain basic objectives, which instructional objectives will be retained for the child, unmodified or modified? There is no particular justification for maintaining an objective for a pupil who, in spite of the best teaching available, has failed to learn it. A tactical withdrawal to an objective at a lower level of performance may be indicated. Alternatively, a new objective may be set following negotiations with the learner.

(b)   How can the task be presented so as to minimize the probability of a child's continued failure?

(c)   How far can tasks taken from the child's everyday experience be utilized to provide a context for the remedial work? For example, can advantage be taken of the child's spontaneous interests as raw material for the development of the deficient skill?

(d)   Can the remedial requirements be incorporated into the existing class organization or to what extent will modifications have to be made to accommodate the difficulties? For example, is it desirable or possible to withdraw the child into a separate group if small group teaching is indicated? (Small group teaching would be considered a 'task' rather than a 'resource' variable if it was designed to permit certain forms of interaction among learners having similar difficulties.)

(e) Is remediation of the skill required to be confined within a subject, or can opportunities be taken or provided across the curriculum? If, for example, the remedial work is required in a rather specific topic in mathematics, opportunities in other subjects are likely to be limited. If the language behaviour of the child is in question then all subjects are potentially capable of providing remedial contexts or tasks. Teacher cooperation is a pre-requisite for this type of task setting, of course.

(f) Are existing structured remedial programmes suited to the learner's requirements? None of the published remedial schemes is a panacea, of course. Nevertheless, it is worthwhile consulting specific books on remedial teaching, liaising with other teachers who have faced similar problems, etc., to see whether existing tasks and processes serve the needs of the child and teacher. The best examples are found in reading remediation, notably American. Ripley and Blair (1979) for example, list a number of commercially available programmes for remediating basic skills in reading. Local Authority advisers in remedial work are usually able to help teachers find materials which may save considerable time and effort in devising remedial tasks.

Resource variables

It would be silly to construct a remedial programme which demands resources far in excess of the possible. So the question of resource allocation is designed to match the conclusions reached from assessments of learner-style and those relating to task analysis. Indirectly this serves as an assessment of the extent to which the school or teacher is able to meet remedial needs, with possible corrective effect. The most crucial questions concern the allocation of resources of time and effort:

(a) If the remedial task demands substantial individual teaching, how can this be accomplished without detriment to the progress of the average and most able members of the class? Are self-teaching devices available which minimize the dependency of the slow-learner on the types of immediate or personalized enforcement which can only be supplied by the teacher?

(b) Can a more efficient use of time and effort be achieved by grouping pupils with similar problems?

(c) What instructional materials (filmstrips etc.,) and approaches (remedial 'games') are already available? Can any be constructed to meet specific needs?

(d) Does the teacher have the skills necessary to promote the kind of improvement in performance that are required? Does the local teachers' centre, university school of education or similar institution provide courses which are of value in strengthening the teachers competence?

No doubt, practising teachers will be able to supply many more questions than the above. Nevertheless, posing such problems will, it is hoped, enable teachers to hypothesize the forms of educational intervention which offer a reasoned basis for planning remedial work outside the context of the specialized remedial centres. The advice has been intended to generalize no matter what area of intellectual functioning is held to be deficient. It has, of course, excluded reference to the subnormal whose problems are generally too severe to be accommodated within normal schooling, at least given our present state of medical and psychological knowledge.

Stage 6: Assessing and Evaluating the Effectiveness

We shall concentrate chiefly on how progress in the skill remediated can be assessed although there may be many other aspects by which remedial teaching can be justified, even where little or no measurable progress can be demonstrated. (For example, caring for the individual learner and demonstrating concern for his or her problems may in indirect ways have even more profound effect on children's learning than moral exhortation to behave well towards others.) Similarly, progress in the skill may be minimal but be accompanied, nevertheless, by progress in the development of attitudes or other affective components of learning (for example, increased enjoyment or interest).

There is an important difference between finding out whether the pupil has made progress *following* remedial teaching and finding out whether that progress (if made) is the *result of* remedial teaching. The former — though not without its difficulties — is relatively straightforward in theory, the latter much more difficult to carry out in practice.

It will simplify matters if we deal with these issues separately although both are subject to common but major difficulties which must be discussed. No matter how carefully the measurement is conducted there will always be a difference between the scores obtained on two occasions (i.e. before remedial teaching and after remedial teaching) even if there is no difference in the underlying ability being assessed, because of the presence of measurement error in the scores. This concept was dealt with quite fully in chapter 6 where reliability was discussed. The effect of the presence of measurement error is neatly and clearly described by Vincent and Cresswell (1976, appendix A). Briefly, if we assume a normal distribution of scores of a group of children on the first occasion the differences between the scores on the two occasions will themselves be normally distributed but with a standard deviation which is equal to the product of the standard error of the test and the square root of two (i.e. $SD_{diff} = SE_x \sqrt{2}$). Thus any group of pupils assessed on two occasions using a test with a standard error of six will yield 'gains' or 'losses' of about 17 points (that is, 2 x 8.48) to 5% of pupils whilst 68% of pupils will receive 'gains' or 'losses' within 8.5 points of the mean of the new distribution. This fact enables the statistically-minded reader to compare the actual difference in score (second testing occasion minus first testing occasion) obtained, with what is to be expected from the known unreliability of the test, as indicated by the size of the standard error.

A second difficulty relates very closely to this. When the scores on two test occasions are imperfectly correlated (i.e. always!) the errors which cause test scores to vary are most 'influential' amongst the highest and lowest score bands in the group. Because of this, the average scores of pupils who are 'high' or 'low' on the first occasion are less extreme on the second. This phenomenon is called 'regression to the mean' and is a statistical artefact. Its importance for the assessment of remedial teaching is clear: some of the apparent change in remedial pupils (those who by definition scored substantially lower than average on the first test) is attributable to the regression of the scores rather than to improvement. Nevertheless, if the results of the standardized testings have been used to measure progress over a long period of time, and are backed up by criterion-referenced evidence of qualitative improvement in the actual features of the performance itself, the ubiquitous effects of regression may be assumed to be comparatively negligible, thus strengthening the belief that progress has been made.

There is one further source of potential error when interpreting difference scores (second testing minus first testing) as indexes of progress. Some of the improvements may well result from practice on the test items themselves with no improvement in the underlying ability being assessed. This is especially likely to happen where the same test is used on a number of occasions and can be overcome to a limited extent if parallel forms of the test (chapter 6) are used.

This has necessarily been a brief and inadequate account of some fairly tricky statistical problems in the interpretation of 'progress' (gain or loss) scores. The dangers are worth reiterating. When using a test on two occasions to assess progress remember:

(1) Part of the differences between scores will be attributable to the presence of measurement error. Actual differences between scores, therefore, should be compared with those expected from measurement error to see if progress has been made.

(2) Any group of children who are relatively extreme on the first testing occasion (for example, pupils given remedial help because of low scores on a standardized test) will tend to receive a mean score on the second occasion which is nearer to the overall mean of the second testing. Thus results from two testings will be subject to regression to the mean which confuses the interpretation of progress. As Vincent and Cresswell (1976, 88) remark: 'the pupil who does really badly on a test could hardly do worse on a second occasion'. The reverse applies to a pupil or groups of pupils who are outstandingly good on the first occasion, of course. Teachers must be aware of claiming 'progress' using measurement of this kind.

(3) Test scores can also 'improve' because of the practice effects where the same or parallel forms of a test are taken on more than one occasion.

(4) Indexes of progress derived from the difference between scores on tests taken on two occasions should always be interpreted with great caution because some change in score is inevitable. Where possible, progress should be assessed using a combination of evidence, such as where the results of standardized tests can be supplemented by qualitative assessment of changes in actual performance as are obtained from the administration of criterion-referenced tests or provided by the processes of skill analysis described in this chapter.

(5) In subjects or areas of skill or knowledge where no standardized tests exist, progress is best assessed by an examination of actual performance. Many teachers might, in view of the difficulties described above, prefer to emphasize the qualitative aspects of progress rather than risk the difficult interpretation of test scores. In any event, if progress is to be reported, more information is potentially contained in a skill analysis than in a standardized score.

We have seen some of the problems in an attempt to assess progress following remedial teaching. It is very unlikely that teachers will have the time or resources to research whether the progress is *attributable* to the remedial programme, but it is useful to be aware of some of the difficulties. It has already been shown how changes in scores will result whether or not there has been 'real' progress. The problem of demonstrating that it is the remedial programme which is responsible for the changes and not the multitude of other factors known to affect performance requires, at very least, a comparison between two groups, 'identical' at the start of the enquiry, but only one of which receives the remedial teaching. This, of course, is the classic two-group (one-control) design which is itself barely adequate even though difficult to carry out in the practical setting of schools. Many complex experimental designs exist by which to tease out what is known as the 'treatment effects' and the reader interested in them could consult the book by Campbell and Stanley (1966). Without some sort of check provided by the control group progress could well be erroneously attributed to the remedial work when it belongs properly to the normal maturational effects or even to some extraneous external influence such as a relevant television programme! Ethical difficulties also arise, of course. Is a teacher justified in the deliberate withholding of a programme which it is hoped and believed will have beneficial effects in order to set up a control group?

In order to justify the remedial programme, then, teachers may assemble a variety of supporting evidence. They may point to the improved 'work-tone' of the class, to clear acquisitions of skill brought into view by qualitative descriptions of performance and to improved adjustment and attitudes on the part of individuals. Teachers are certainly not going to be able to show beyond doubt that these attributes would not have come about had remedial teaching not taken place (a roundabout way of arguing that remedial teaching 'works'!). Nevertheless, continuous monitoring and the use of a number of test scores and other types of evidence will provide some of the feedback necessary if the remedial teachers are to sustain their own motivation.

Because of an increase in awareness of the principle of accountability coupled with the impositions of increasing limitations on expenditure, one might anticipate the cost-effectiveness of remedial teaching to come under a good deal greater scrutiny than has been the case to date. Perhaps the

most useful type of evidence that teachers can offer in support of their work is qualitative descriptions of the features
of improved performance where criterion-referenced assessment has been practised. If standardized tests are used (either
the same test over time or parallel forms with an interval
between) a rule of thumb can be given (Vincent and Cresswell,
1976). Those gains in score which are more than twice as
large as the standard error of the test may reasonably be used
to claim that the improvement has been a 'real' one as distinct from one that could have arisen easily by chance. In
case the reader's grasp of chapter 6 has proved somewhat
tenuous, a reminder of the procedure may be in order. If the
reliability, r_{tt}, of the test whose standard deviation, σ_x, is 15
is 0.96, then the standard error of the measurement is given
(formula [6.14]) by

$$
\begin{aligned}
SE_m &= \sigma_x \sqrt{1 - r_{tt}} \\
&= 15\sqrt{1 - 0.96} \\
&= 3
\end{aligned}
$$

Any increase in score which is greater than six points on the
standardized test, then, probably indicates a real improvement.

12

Reporting and Communicating the Results of Assessment

Although some teachers record marks as misers hoard money most would probably wish to keep results only insofar as they inform decisions about learning and teaching or can be useful in accounting to parents and other interested parties. Recently, several local education authorities have attempted to standardize records and the presentation of results, so that a common set of information is available about children at any stage of their educational career. This has often involved the setting up of working parties through which teachers have tried to decide which assessments should be recorded and in what form, in order both to 'spell out' and to 'sum up' children's progress. This obviously involves the making of many value judgments and agreement is often hard won. But, by and large, the methods of communicating results and the amount of detail incorporated are very variable even between schools within a given local authority.

Many views exist amongst teachers on the ethics of recording and reporting. Some take the stand that since the results of an assessment can be so easily misunderstood or even misused they should remain confidential to the teacher and the school. For example, the results of intelligence testing are never released for wide consumption. In the event of an individualized testing — say for diagnosis by the educational psychologist — the numerical score is seldom supplied even to the parent of the child referred. Instead a verbal description couched in terms of ability relative to the norms is given. ('Peter's score shows him to be intellectually superior/of average ability.') Because of the mystique which has surrounded the IQ, its overvaluation by some as predictive index of future performance and a still widespread belief in its unalterability, many have considered the information too dangerous to divulge. The morbid curiosity engendered in some has ensured the commercial success of books containing tests with standardized scores, particularly amongst the middle class. Fortunately, there are signs that the dependency on intelligence test scores as a valid index of 'intellectual capacity' is waning (Gilham, 1978). The usefulness of these tests has been dealt a series of body blows in recent years, culminating perhaps, in the revelation of what appears to have been dishonest use of scores by the late Sir Cyril Burt, one of the strongest proponents of intelligence testing in this country (Hearnshaw, 1979). Nevertheless, the possible reintroduction of extensive testing at age 11 consequent on recent political developments in the UK may lead to a resurgence of that dependency. Even in areas where secondary education is non-selective, however, it is common for the results of an intelligence or verbal reasoning test taken in the primary school to be available in comprehensive schools, where they are used to ensure a 'mixed ability' structure of first year classes.

Our introduction has served in an indirect way to draw readers' attention to three quite crucial questions concerning the communication of results. They are:

(1) Who is to receive the results?
(2) What contents of the reports are they to receive?
(3) In what form shall the results be reported?

The essential task in answering the first question is to decide who has a legitimate interest in the results: this is tantamount to identifying those who are to make, or to help children to make, decisions about their learning (formative and summative) and about how to invest their future efforts. It is immediately obvious that no overall answer can be given for it will have to be modified in the light of the age of the child and the stage of education reached. Although prospective employers may be held by some to have a legitimate interest in the results of a school's assessment of a child towards the end of his or her secondary career, these parties are in no way involved in decision making at an earlier stage. Quite obviously, too, the other questions must be answered having regard to the nature of the decision to be taken. A particular decision may depend on data of a general kind concerning a pupil's attitudes and 'reliability' whilst another may rely upon far more specific information, for example the learner's skill in craftwork or with the English language. The form in which the information is to be communicated will also depend upon many factors, not the least of which will be the ability of the recipient to comprehend the information contained in the report. With difficulties of this kind in mind we shall examine the alternatives open to teachers in answering the three central questions. In so doing recommendations will be implied by which current methods of reporting and communicating results may be improved whilst we remain conscious of the fact that teachers' time available for extensive record keeping is severely limited by the dynamics of everyday classroom life.

WHO RECEIVES THE REPORTS?

Children

There may be occasions on which teachers will seek to justify the withholding of assessment results from children but, by and large, the information -- whether from spontaneous and informal appraisal or from more systematic and formal methods -- is a potentially valuable source of feedback to children. This feedback provides *knowledge of results* from daily interaction with the teacher and informs the learner's appraisal and decision making. Children require this indication to reinforce their successful attempts to learn, to indicate their adequacies and inadequacies in pursuit of an objective (criterion-referenced evaluation), to guide them in their future efforts in the short term and to aid them in their long-term career planning. Young children probably benefit most from the kinds of informal feedback during learning which are part and parcel of ordinary classroom interaction. The decision as to how frequently this is to be provided cannot be the subject of rules. However, studies of interaction have repeatedly shown the uneven distribution of this type of feedback in typical classrooms. Teachers are often unaware of the unconscious differentiations made between pupils of varying levels of attainment. Individual differences in the need for reassurance reveal themselves very early in children's school career. It is a matter for the teachers' professional judgment to make decisions as to how often to communicate an assessment. It would be hopelessly unrealistic to claim that all children receive such communication as and when it is required! Often teachers may find themselves able only to apply an encouragement to 'carry on the good work' or to alert the child to the futility of the course of action adopted in problem solving. Occasionally teachers may set aside the time to summarize the child's attainment relative to an agreed objective where such a 'landmark' can be determined. An opportunity for this kind of assessment is provided where a relatively formal evaluation of the child's attainment in basic skill is undertaken (for example, when hearing him or her read, or testing for a 'reading age'). Everyday communication will be largely formative. Some form of summative assessment is required where children are to change schools, to move to other teachers or for purposes of the school report or 'parents' evenings'. Here difficulties are experienced by teachers in combining and integrating the information obtained from spontaneous formative and planned summative assessment perhaps using standardized tests. In general, results of all such assessments are evaluated by teachers for their corrective or confirmatory feedback. Where such information can be communicated to children consistent with the principle of respect for their efforts there seems no ground for withholding it from them.

The second major reason for communicating your assessment to children is that it has an effect on the motivation of pupils. This, admittedly, is double-edged. Few children escape at least some incidents of insensitive criticism where effort has been made and the results of ill-conceived assessments may serve to depress as well as to enhance motivational levels. It is a matter of some regret to those who hold progressive ideologies of teaching that many children apparently see little point in hard work unless their products are to be assessed. Sometimes teachers do not assess as a matter of deliberate policy, at others they simply do not find time to mark the work. Although theories of competence motivation have pointed to the degree of internal satisfaction consequent upon the attainment of mastery, a curiosity satisfied or an obstinate problem solved, many learners require outside assistance to obtain an overall assessment of 'how well they are doing'. Although schools can never 'overassess' in the senses described in this chapter (that is, assessing to inform decision about the effectiveness of past learning and the content and direction of future effort) they can easily run the risk of overassessing for other purposes (grading children, sifting and sorting them, for example).

Quite obviously communicating an assessment to children will have different consequences according to the age and stage of education reached. In the infant and junior schools children are largely discovering their abilities. Teachers of these age groups know the importance of postponing any assessments which influence children to conclude that they are 'no good' at learning and never will be. Later in a school career there may be some grounds for arguing that pupils should be helped to reach a realistic appraisal of their status after several years of study in a particular academic discipline. It may be a principle of effective motivation for pupils to be given the results of an assessment to help them decide which parts of the curriculum are relevant to their personal needs and aspirations. An example of this principle is seen where careers guidance is undertaken and results of aptitude tests, examination successes, assessments of personality and personal interests are used to reach an intelligent 'guess' as to the appropriateness of the next stage in a young person's development. The point at which pupils are adjudged to be 'ready' for such decisions has, of course, vexed teachers and parents for very many years.

Regardless of teachers' views on how often and in what form children should be assessed, two overriding principles remain. The reports are to be as accurate as possible but stated within the known limitations of the methods employed (the reliability of standardized tests: the subjective opinions of other methods) and their communication is to be as honest as possible consistent with the respect of teacher for pupil. There may be occasions when complete honesty may be judged as damaging: we are not advocating that teachers abdicate their function as moral beings! Unfortunately teachers sometimes distort the evidence even to the point of providing spurious praise for shoddy work. Pupils are quick to see through the cowardice of such a stance.

Parents

Few would dispute the legitimacy of parents' claims to receive the results of the assessment. The purposes of communicating to parents are probably threefold: to fulfil the demands of professional accountability; to inform parents of pupils' progress; and finally, indirectly to influence learning by a positive effect on home–school relationships. Few parents are in direct daily contact with schools and can be informed only indirectly of the results of informal formative assessments which constitute much of day-to-day teacher–pupil interaction, except insofar as teachers' comments in exercise books may be seen. Although many schools claim to be open to parental enquiry or visit, many parents do not avail themselves of the opportunities even of attending the ritual 'parents' evening'. Because of this the nature and quality of the formal termly or yearly report assume great importance. A great deal of time is spent in writing school reports which are very varied in nature. Although it is popularly believed that the aims and curricula of schools have changed beyond recognition to many parents, surprisingly few changes have taken place in the terminology of the school report, which is usually a mixture of evaluation of attainment followed by a comment on effort and attitude. Rarely, however, are parents informed of the objectives of the teaching or of how closely a child's performance approaches these objectives. Because of this, parents often receive a general impression of how well the child performs in relation to some usually ill-defined group but seldom do they receive any indication of what pupils can actually do, their strengths and their relatively weak areas. A second consequence is that parents are only vaguely aware of the objectives of a school and its underlying philosophy: they are likely to interpret what goes on as 'too much play' or as 'educational frills' in the absence of more positive explanations. The chief point here is not that it is reasonable or even feasible for schools to provide a blow-by-blow account and justification of all their practices but, rather, that it is difficult even for the parent who is interested to find out what is happening. The child's own daily reports are often notoriously unreliable for this purpose! It is undeniably the case that many parents are apt to evaluate school curricula and the children's progress in terms of somewhat roseate memories of their own school days and attainment. But, equally, it is bewildering for them to gain a picture of attainment in the absence of any statement from the school as to what is being assessed, how and why. In recognizing that if some of the processes of assessment described in this book are adopted changes in reporting will be required, the means of communication to parents will be described in later sections where answers to our second and third questions will be attempted.

Teacher: Self and Other

Teachers need, as it were, to receive their own reports since they provide an indispensable guide to many aspects central to teaching. Not only do the results of assessment provide knowledge of the effectiveness of the teaching and of the curriculum but they also inform decisions for placement, the need for extra teaching, the diagnosis of learning failure and as a record on which future communication with parents will be based. Moreover, teachers are, in an important sense, learners and require feedback. The consequences of the results of assessment for the motivation of pupils apply equally to teachers. There is no need to labour these points.

Reports of the assessment can, however, also be of great value to other teachers. Examples of occasions on which they are useful are when taking over a class for a period in the absence of a teacher to avoid unnecessary replication of work, or when receiving children into another class or school. There are, of course, dangers in this aspect of reporting. Given the subjective nature of a great deal of assessment, especially where it is evaluative rather than descriptive, many teachers prefer to 'find out for themselves' rather than accept the appraisal of other teachers. This is particularly important where classroom conduct is involved. Nevertheless, children may often find themselves at a disadvantage when transferring from school to school unless an assessment of competence and performance in relation to basic objectives is also available. Wildly inaccurate and dishonest assessment is worse than useless, of course. Similarly, when one teacher takes responsibility for a class taught for a while by another teacher a record of 'work done' and at what level seems a minimal requirement if anything approaching continuity is to be achieved. (I have recently seen an exercise book which contained two sets of identical notes on 'soils'. Upon enquiry I was told that these notes were given by Miss A, those by Mr B when he took over after Christmas. If such simple records cannot be kept and transferred there seems little hope that assessment records can be passed on unless the school standardizes the report form and requires regular completion.)

Employers

Whereas what has been written so far seems scarcely controversial, there is widespread disagreement about the extent to which schools should supply assessment information which may be regarded as private between the pupil, the home and school. Many employers rely upon their own selection procedures though they often limit the pool from which prospective employees are drawn by using school assessments or the results of external examinations. There is no standard practice. Sometimes employers send lengthy questionnaires which require assessment of the pupil in many aspects, both academic and personal. At other times open-ended requests for references are required which leave it to the respondent to decide which assessments to include. Whilst recognizing some responsibility to prepare pupils for a career or for 'life after school' many teachers believe the interests of employers (hiring 'productive units') to be incompatible with the aims of education and, therefore, with the features of children they think most important to assess.

In practice, of course, the dilemma does not apply to teachers in primary or middle schools. Although many teachers feel uneasy at reporting assessments to prospective employers, most teachers probably recognize that to refuse information would be to jeopardize a pupil's chance of a job. Given that information is provided, there seems some obligation that it should be interpretable. Most certainly schools should resist any suggestion that their practices of teaching and assessing should in any way be modified to suit prospective employers. The latter, for the most part, look for general educational attainments rather than for specific skills which, they believe, they are themselves often in a better position to teach. Meanwhile schools can probably restrict their reports of assessment to exclude *specific* details of attainment and to eschew comparisons amongst pupils.

Higher Education Admissions Officers

This is probably the final group which can lay any sort of claim to receive reports of individual children's progress. Many admissions officers place reliance on examination performance supplemented by head teachers' assessment of the applicant's suitability for the course of study. Colleges in our older universities have maintained close links with certain schools, others look chiefly to examination results. Once minimal educational qualifications have been met admissions tutors are free to apply almost any criteria of their own choosing. There seem no grounds for arguing that college demands place any specific assessment obligations upon schools.

The 'General Public'

This amorphous body expresses its interest in the results of schooling through a variety of agencies, pressure groups, etc. Press release of examination results used to be a common feature: today it is recognized that the quality of schools cannot be determined in this way since few schools are strictly comparable in respect of all the factors known to influence attainment. Nevertheless, parental choice of schools is written into the 1944 Education Act, and a junior minister in government has recently (1979) recommended that results are published to assist parents in the choice of secondary schooling. Choice is, of course, constrained by the existing limited provision and can be exercised only by a few.

WHAT ASSESSMENTS SHALL WE REPORT?

During a child's school life a great deal of information about his or her background and progress may well accumulate. Some of this consists of formal written material which may be confidential or open whilst some remains a matter of oral report. By and large, teachers are not going to have a great deal of time to prepare and maintain written material although many local authorities have introduced standard record cards to ensure that minimal information is retained. The headings on such cards are frequently a mixture of formal assessment, teacher judgment and teacher opinion, and range from scores and comments on standardized tests of attainment to behavioural ratings and items of information considered relevant to an understanding of the child's educational progress.

It is not always apparent, however, just what *use* schools and teachers are able to make of such information. 'Getting to know the child' must mean more than storing information about him, but decisions as to what it is worth recording are more complex than would appear at first sight. Answers to the question will vary with the age of the child, the stage of education reached, the objectives of the school as well as with decisions as to what it would be proper to release to the recipients of the report, as discussed in the previous section.

Assessment of the child in the infant school is certain to be largely informal, the teachers having postponed the need to make comparative (i.e. norm-referenced) judgments at that stage. It will probably be backed up by more formal recording of landmarks reached in basic subjects — especially in reading, language work and in the development of number concepts — and may include a teacher's subjective assessment of a pupil's adjustment to school. Few would be likely to disagree with this content of school records: the information is not contentious nor does it represent an invasion of privacy.

But so widespread is the view that a child's school progress can only be fully understood in the context of home and family background that many teachers believe that assessments of such factors should also be made — and reported orally if not actually recorded. It is widely supposed that factors such as 'language in the home', the 'social class' of the family, the family structure (whether a one-parent family), material standards and so forth exert a considerable effect on a child's dispositions to learn. There is now a considerable body of evidence to show that school differences account for far less of the variance in achievement than features of the family or home (Rutter and Madge, 1976). Unfortunately, some have concluded from this that 'schools make no difference' and that knowledge of a child's eventual progress can be predicted from knowledge of home and family factors, perhaps improved by knowledge of his IQ.

Space does not permit an examination of the assumptions of this approach since our principal concern is with whether teachers are advised to spend time in the acquisition of such information about their pupils. Although it is the case that a social class index can be obtained quickly and easily and, having done so, that it can differentiate children's progress (working class children tending to do less well than middle class children) this is not very helpful to teachers especially since there is a very large variation within each of these social classes. Similarly, most teachers have probably heard of Bernstein's work on 'restricted' and 'elaborated' codes. This represents a useful way of conceptualizing language differences and of postulating links between these and forms of thought. But, against the wishes of the theorists themselves, the differences have too readily been seen as causal. So we find the following causal beliefs: working class → restricted use of language → simple, concrete ways of thinking → poor school progress, especially as the work becomes more academic and abstract, on the one hand; and middle class children → elaborated use of language → complex abstract thought → good school progress on the other. This is part of the way in which teachers set different patterns of expectation for pupils from different 'kinds of home'. The way these can fulfil themselves has already been discussed in chapter 3. Although children do bring large differences with them when they start school no particularly satisfactory causal chain linking home and family factors with educational progress has been postulated that will be true of any one pupil.

For these reasons, then, it seems that assessments of home and family provide little systematic information which would enable teachers to understand children or to teach them. This conclusion, of course, runs counter to the testimony of many teachers. When questioned as to the value of this assessment, however, the stock reply is that it makes teachers more fully aware of learning-relevant features in the child's home background. The adaptive value of such awareness comes from its potential for translation into courses of action, and here it is not at all clear that teachers teach more effectively as a result of it. If the content of the awareness is of a background believed by the teacher to be unconducive to progress it can just as easily depress levels of expectation as enhance them.

Obviously, from time to time there will be personal details which may permit the teacher to show greater empathy or sympathy with a child's difficulties and rightly these may figure prominently in an assessment. Such factors include bereavement, separation, parental illness or absence. The same can be said of a child's state of health, either permanent or temporary. We are not arguing that the teacher should (or even could) deny the relevance of this information in assessing children but that its use demands the greatest circumspection and confidentiality.

There is, then, a large class of incidental assessments which form part of a teacher's appraisal of the child. By 'incidental' is meant that the teacher has no control over its origin and no direct responsibility for its change. The bulk of the answer to 'what assessments shall we report?' will then refer to those features of the cognitive development of pupils for which schools are directly responsible, conducted, so far as is possible, with objectivity and without prejudice.

Teachers report, for all age ranges, the extent to which their pupils have obtained the objectives of schooling (criterion-referenced assessment) but this seems far less extensive than the more familiar norm-referencing. Although criterion-referencing is potentially more informative of the content of children's accomplishments, parents have become accustomed to expect statements about the child's capability in relation to an imprecise conception of 'average progress'. One way of overcoming this would be to specify in advance a number of distinct levels of capability (the objectives) and systematically to work through the resulting check list. This would result in the production of a report not unlike that presented to the car owner following the MOT test. In that test objective criteria — say of braking efficiency — are prescribed and the car assessed in relation to them. Such check lists are quite feasible in basic subjects especially in the early years of schooling. Several objections can be offered, of course. The prescription *can* become a straightjacket and blind the teacher to evidence of learning other than that for which he or she is looking. True, it is difficult to decide in advance what to assess and to report without at the same time setting some constraints (categories) as to what will be regarded as 'admissible evidence'. Having *no* prior list of attributes or criteria to report, however, also has its dangers. Some writers, notably Marshall (1968), have argued that the most valuable and informative type of report is that which records whatever it is that 'floats to the top' of a teacher's recollection of a pupil's salient characteristics (the 'flotation technique'). No doubt this, if fearlessly adhered to, could result in some interesting — even bizarre — reports which would come as a pleasant alternative to the 'could do better' type of report. Nevertheless, this recipe for reporting smacks of 'stream of consciousness' writing which usually reveals more about the reporter than the reported, and seems to have little to recommend it.

The central problem then is this: teachers are unable to assess without having at least some idea of what they are looking for (the idea that an appraisal by a value-free observer can be made is no longer acceptable to philosophers of science) yet they run the risk of overlooking the unexpected evidence of learning if they adhere exclusively to their prior check lists. To leave open the question of what to report can lead to assessments which are an idosyncratic mixture of ability and social constructs (Wood and Napthali, 1975); to close them entirely is to imply that one knows in advance *all* the possible outcomes which can be held as meaningful indices of children's learning and development.

Where the goals of learning and teaching can be unambiguously described and objective criteria of their attainment set up, the child's performance in relation to them can be reported. Where the teacher is required to make an overall summary this report can take the form of a global evaluation of a child's learning which should clearly separate the cognitive (knowledge and capabilities) components from the various affective (attitudes and motivations) comments. Norm-referenced reports where used are valueless unless the characteristics of the group with which the child is being compared are described. Reports thus demand the prior specification of levels of competence and preparation of criteria and some form of check list representing the chief objectives of the teaching. *Post hoc* comparisons of children which result from norm-referenced assessment of whatever it is that happens to have been taught seem less informative unless the purpose of the report is to choose a quota (as in selection). Room can also be found in the report for any specific feature of the child which, in the expert judgment of the teacher, is relevant to his or her ability to learn — such as the child's particular flair or special learning disability. Similarly, the achievements in unexpected areas or in individual work may require comment outside the specific evaluation criteria.

The overriding consideration, however, is that teachers distinguish those aspects of children for which they have primary responsibility and expertise in their assessment from those in which they are lay people. If the report is to be open to those groups identified in the first section of this chapter the content should be limited to that which the teacher is prepared to defend, should distinguish fact from opinion and should be stated with its margin of error, where this is known. The content of the report will also be influenced by knowledge of the recipients' ability to understand and interpret the information it contains. Yet to include details to one interested group, say employers, which are withheld from the assessed and the parents, unless this confidentiality has been agreed, is to invite charges of cowardice and to forfeit the trust of the learner whose interests are the teacher's primary responsibility.

Before leaving this section two other questions about what to report remain. Teachers differ in the extent to which they believe 'effort' or level of achievement should be reported. There is something pretty depressing about a report along the following lines: 'John has worked to the best of his ability but his standard of work is low'. This may, in fact, be true of many pupils but it raises the problem of whether or not this kind of report is useful for certain pupils. Faced with the difficulty, teachers have been known to give a bonus of a few marks to compensate such children. It is already difficult enough to determine the precise meaning attached by teachers to marks they assign but to muddy the waters still further seems very poor practice. It is preferable, therefore, to record and report 'effort' and achievement separately.

Finally, teachers who are uneasy at norm-referenced assessment but who have not developed a criterion-referenced system sometimes claim that their marks are allocated according to the 'personal growth' of the pupil. They argue that a given attainment which is well within the grasp of one pupil represents all that can be expected of another. This has intuitive appeal as a basis for assessment but it introduces yet another subjective element into the assessment and further obfuscates the meaning of the marks. Comparing the growth of pupils on the basis of an increase or decrease in the marks awarded over a period of time is also a hazardous procedure. It is clear that an improvement of, say, x marks by two pupils, one at the tenth the other at the 90th percentile, is not directly comparable. (Understanding the reason for this is helped by an analogy: John who runs the mile in eight minutes may, after training, reduce his time to six minutes but Bill, whose time is five minutes at the start of training, may attain only one quarter of this improvement in time by running the distance in four minutes thirty seconds.) Unless the reporting and marking are completely individualized teachers are advised to avoid *measures* of change as being most unreliable and reserve such reporting to the verbal comments which accompany the marks or grades awarded.

IN WHAT FORM?

We have so far discussed the merits of the claims by various parties to have access to the results of an assessment and, in general terms, the kinds of contents the reports might contain. Our third major issue concerns the form that reports take. The principal consideration, quite obviously, is that they should be interpretable by those who receive them and that their intention should be understood. Traditional methods of school reporting tend not to be particularly informative. 'Nigel's main problem lies in essay questions', 'Nigel has a great deal to learn', 'Nigel needs to take more care with written work', 'Nigel tends to be inaccurate' are typical of the comments received on the termly report by one boy recently. This is not to say that these remarks are not true but commenting on weaknesses in general disposition tells the recipient nothing about the particular features of a child's attainment. Nevertheless this type of written report together with marks or grades seems to constitute the most common form in which the results of an assessment are communicated to parents.

No doubt practices in reporting vary widely in British schools, both in the records kept within them and the forms of communication to parents and others. The production of school reports for external consumption is more widespread in middle and secondary schools than in those for younger pupils. These latter prefer to communicate their assessments informally through parents' evenings or by letter. In the former the issue of reports usually precedes the parent—teacher conference. The secondary school report traditionally communicates the assessment in broad subject fields in which the pupil receives a single mark or grade and a comment which compares the pupil with an abstract standard or with other children in the same class. Sometimes there is a separation of cognitive from motivational and attitudinal comments, at other times the teacher is free to construct general remarks which consist of a mixture of these two. As often as not, the same report form is used for the entire school and, understandably perhaps, makes little or no use of modern techniques in graphics or typographical design.

It is extremely unlikely — some would say undesirable — that a standard report form would be developed for use in all schools of a given type, for pupils of a given age range. Nevertheless, if the recommendations for assessment implied in this book were adopted, reports of an assessment — wherever carried out — would contain a minimum set of characteristics. In place of the naming of a broad subject field (history, geography, mathematics, child care, or whatever) there would be a list in terms of actual pupil performance of the activities which make up the objectives of the curriculum, and the pupil's level of mastery of them described. This level could be as a dichotomy (master/non-master) but only where the criterion score (chapter 5) can be defended as non-arbitrary: that is where a minimal level of competence can be shown to be required before a child can move on to the next objective with a reasonable probability of success. The level can also be shown by the actual score obtained out of the number of items set per objective or, if a visual representation is required, as a simple graph which accumulates to give a profile of a child's performance on the objectives which make up the specific area of the curriculum being assessed. This last method is becoming increasingly common in the use of criterion-referenced tests in basic subjects, as the following example illustrates. It shows an extract from a criterion-referenced test in mathematics appropriate for use with level three (eight to nine year old children).

Such record cards provide a clearer and more detailed picture of the results of cumulative assessment than is permitted by the more global appraisal of the traditional report. They are also invaluable in diagnosis of learning and teaching effectiveness.

The preparation of a report form specifically constructed to each level of schooling and area of the curriculum is required by this method of course. The statements of objective are, as we have repeatedly reminded readers, more easily prepared in some school subjects than in others. The fact that not all teaching and learning goals can be stated behaviourally is no argument for not doing so where the subject matter and its organization lends itself to this type of analysis.

The practice of stating goals is of obvious advantage in the

Objective	No. right	Graph					Teacher's comments
301 To identify numbers up to 1000 expressed as compact numerals or in words	3	░	░	░			*Has Problems with words*
302 To identify numbers up to 300 expressed as compact or expanded numerals	5	░	░	░	░	░	
303 To add two numbers with sums up to ten: equation and vertical forms	2	░	░				*Finds equation*
304 To subtract from numbers up to ten: equation and vertical forms	2	░	░				*form difficult.*

Figure 12.1   Reporting the results of criterion-referenced assessment. From pupil's record card. *Yardstick criterion-referenced test in mathematics.* Thomas Nelson & Sons Ltd. Reproduced by kind permission.

motivation of pupils. The goal cards also enhance communication between teachers who share or take over responsibility for a particular group of children and facilitate meaningful and specific discussion with parents.

The goal cards imply absolute standards of marking but they can easily be transformed into norm-referenced statements if required. For example, suppose the mean mark obtained by a given class of children on objective 302 is 3.5. Then it is easy to state the child's performance in relation to that mean. If the objectives are relatively homogeneous within a given domain of learning overall scores and means for the domain can be added. There is no reason, except perhaps shortage of time, why teachers could not elaborate on this treatment by describing the scores obtained in terms of their positions relative to the median (this is easily understood as being in the 'top' or 'bottom' half of the marks for the class/ year group by parents) or other quantiles (chapter 5) if a more analytic placement of the child in the group is required.

The teacher who has understood how marks can be translated into standard scores should find little difficulty in calculating T-scores, for example. This seems warranted only where the group is large enough to yield a distribution of scores which is not too asymmetrical (non-normal). However, in all cases where norm-referenced description is adopted the characteristics of the normative group should be described.

For some reason, elementary statistical treatment of school marks is considered to be incomprehensible to the majority of recipients and, therefore, unwarranted. Yet the author has found little difficulty in communicating simply the concepts of normative group and standardized score to parents and children. For example, when discussing progress in basic mathematics with the parents of 11 year old children the results of standardized tests were available: Mary had received a score of 120 on a test with mean 100 and standard deviation 15. Parents were helped by being told that this means Mary was being compared with a large group of children of all abilities where the average score was 100. Her score indicates that she scored higher than about 90% of those children. (Recall from chapter 5 that the score of 120 is 1.33 standard deviations above the mean and (from the appendix) that the area of the normal curve between the mean and this score is 0.4082. Therefore the 50% of scores below the mean and 40.82% above make the 90% of scores below Mary's.) With little difficulty one can go even further. Where reliability coefficients and standard errors of measurement are reported margins of error can be quoted. Again, to Mary's parents:

As you know, Mr and Mrs Smith, our marks are never completely accurate or reliable. But we can say of this test that although Mary's score could vary from day to day the chances are that her true score lies somewhere between 120 and six points on either side. So we can be confident that her score is somewhere between 114 and 126.

No great feat of intelligence is required to explain this to parents, yet schools persist in quoting percentages with no information whatever as to the difficulty of the test nor of the performances of other children in the group. One supposes that parents gradually acquire a hazy notion of the frame of reference which a teacher adopts, such that over 70% is acceptable but anything much under 50% is held to be unsatisfactory. In fact, a score of 40% on a really difficult test may be very creditable indeed. The present situation in which schools fail to specify the basis on which marks are assigned and their resulting meaning is little short of chaotic, however. Perhaps the low expectations of parents have contributed to the gulf that exists between modern methods of measurement and reporting and schools' actual practices.

Letters or Numbers?

Prompted by deep suspicion of numbers and their statistical manipulation (many believe the statistician begins with raw scores and ends up with cooked ones) many teachers prefer a letter system as an index of learning and performance. This system — used by GCE examining boards, for example — typically uses the symbols A to E. Perhaps many teachers believe that the letter system has a clear meaning and is understood by most people. Certainly they do not convey an air that measurement has taken place and are more correctly thought of as an evaluation. Where literal grades are accompanied by a verbal definition of their characteristics these are not always terribly informative, however. Sometimes they are little more than tautological! One local examinations syndicate (Cambridge) announcing the meaning of its GCE A and O level results states:

> [The grade] indicates the standard reached in the subject, grade A being the highest and grade E the lowest.

Of course it is precisely the nature of the standard which is *not* indicated by such a bland statement. One obvious disadvantage of literal grades is that they cannot be summed or averaged unless converted to numbers. In practice there is little difference between the interpretations of grades A to E and one to five (the latter capable of being averaged) and personal preference seems to turn on whether or not one believes that the number system implies a greater degree of precision in meaning than the actual data justify.

This difficulty may assume greater proportions than a matter of preference, however, where a teacher is required to provide an overall summary of a pupil's achievements in a course or over a period of one year. Suppose the objectives of the course are in conceptually separable sets of outcomes, what meaning will be attached to the composite? Assuming that teachers are prepared to argue that separate marks can be combined to give a composite and the resultant can be attributed to an underlying variable called 'achievement in the course' (mathematics, English or whatever) then the practice seems justifiable. In criterion-referenced assessment, however, where the object of reporting is not to reach an overall summary mark there seems little point in finding a composite.

Teachers are not always free to decide whether or not to combine marks and they may often be required to do so despite doubts as to the meaningfulness of this action. In combining marks teachers should, however, be aware of a few basic principles:

(1) When combining scores, the different types of learning outcome represented by the separate scores are obscured by the composite.

(2) The resulting composite score will be distorted if the variations (standard deviations) for each component are different from one another. Thus, if a teacher adds two sets of scores whose standard deviations are 16 and eight respectively, the former score will contribute twice as much to the composite as the latter. Since different standard distributions are likely to arise because of marker idiosyncracies, the practice can be a risky one to undertake.

(3) Equal weighting within a composite score can be obtained if raw scores are first transformed to z-scores as described in chapter 5. If this method seems too time consuming teachers might consider using an even simpler method which will yield exactly the same rank

order of children. It consists of a straightforward adjustment to the raw scores made by dividing each score by the standard deviation of the distribution. The method, therefore, adjusts each raw score for the variation in the total distribution such that any composite is composed of directly comparable components. If composite scores are to be reported, however, they should be accompanied by a statement which explains how they have been derived.

SUMMARY

A number of principles of reporting can be abstracted from the foregoing discussion. They imply recommendations as follows:

(1) The purposes of reporting results should be clarified and their form be made appropriate for that purpose. The overriding aims are to inform learners, teachers and parents of the progress made, to aid decisions as to placement within an instructional programme, to provide knowledge of results to enhance motivation and to provide data for the assessment of teaching effectiveness.

(2) A number of interested parties can lay some claim to receive results. Although there are occasions on which information can be made available to outside bodies (such as employers and higher education admissions officers) priority of access is for children, parents and teachers.

(3) Assessment and the recording of results can be interpreted as an invasion of privacy. Only those assessments which are strictly relevant to cognitive learning should be communicated.

(4) Records which are descriptive of the qualitative features of learning (such as those obtained by criterion-referenced assessment) are of greater value in making decisions about individuals than assessments which draw comparisons between children, save in the rare

instances where selection is required.

(5) Assessments accompanied by notes which interpret the meaning of results in a form suited to the level of understanding by the various recipients are of value. There is little or no justification for reporting results which are meaningless or which the teacher is unable to defend.

(6) Reports should clearly distinguish those assessments based on teachers' opinions from those obtained from objective measurement. Where objective measurement has been applied and the reliability of tests known, confidence intervals for the true scores should be supplied (chapter 6).

(7) It is preferable to separate comments which refer to achievement from those relating to the child's 'effort' and behaviour.

(8) Goal cards, listing the objectives of teaching, can be an effective method for children to record their individual progress.

(9) Adoption of a uniform method of marking and reporting within classes and schools aids interpretation and minimizes variance attributable to teacher idiosyncracies.

(10) Most marks lack meaning unless they are stated in terms of norms, group summaries (the mean or median) or objectives mastered.

(11) If a composite mark is to be derived from a number of relatively discrete tests or examinations, the latter should be made directly comparable either by transformation to z-scores or by dividing each score by the respective standard deviation before summation.

(12) Where the complete distribution of scores is reduced to a limited set of literal categories (A, B, C, etc.) brief descriptions of the meaning of the categories should accompany the report.

Guide to Further Reading

Readers will appreciate that the references in this book can only provide an introduction to what is by now a vast field of study. In anticipation that some readers will wish to follow up some of the more important implications of the study of assessment for schools and teachers, a limited guide to the field is offered here. Full details are given only when a work does not appear in the reference list below.

Those who wish to make a fuller study of the technical aspects of test design, construction and validation are recommended to consult the excellent source on these topics edited by Robert L. Thorndike (1971). If you wish to examine test items of a high standard of construction in most areas of the curriculum refer to the handbook by Benjamin Bloom, J. Thomas Hastings and George Madaus (1971).

For a sociological critique of the often covert effects of assessment on children and society read Patricia Broadfoot (1979). Many of the problems and dilemmas in assessment practices, especially with older pupils, are frankly discussed by Derek Rowntree (1977), and for an extreme attack on its worst effects look at Hoffman (1962). If, after this, you are convinced that assessment is indefensible and would like to see what teaching in an assessment-free environment might be like, study the work of Marshall (1968).

Readers who would like an introductory survey of psychological tests might start with Lee Cronbach (1961). A reasonably up-to-date critique of intelligence testing is provided by Kamin (1974) and, as an example of the kinds of re-appraisal currently going on in the area of the psychological assessment of children (especially if you are knowledgeable of the work of the schools' psychological services), the book edited by Bill Gilham (1978) is a provocative starting point. Finally, if you have a head for formulae and wish to study the theory of mental measurement try Frederick Lord and Melvin Novak (1968). For up-to-date developments two journals — *Journal of Educational Measurement* and *Educational and Psychological Measurement* — are worth consulting if you can get near the library of a university school of education, or other reference library.

Readers may also wish to obtain catalogues of published tests to see what exists in their special field of interest. Among those publishing or distributing tests in this country are:

NFER Publishing Company
Thomas Nelson
Hodder and Stoughton
University of London Press
Oliver and Boyd
Macmillan
George Harrap
Chatto and Windus

A word of warning here, however. Because a test has been published it doesn't follow that it's a good one. Check, especially, the details of standardization, reliability and validity presented in the relevant manual and, if you can get hold of a copy in a reference library, see if there's a critical appraisal of the test you're interested in in the *Mental Measurements Yearbook* by O. K. Buros, published by the Gryphon Press. Test prices are rocketing, too!

Each year sees a rise in the number of articles on assessment, reflecting current interest in these controversial topics. Keep an eye out for periodic reports on the work of the APU published by the *Department of Education and Science.* Note, too, some of the criticism. Desmond Nuttall has continued the debate with his article 'Will the APU rule the curriculum?' published in the June 1980 issue of *Education* vol. 155, no. 21. Similarly, Schools Council Publications issue reports of special interest to teachers of particular subjects; for example, the report on problems in assessment of CSE history issued recently. More detailed study of the results of recent research into assessment at CSE and GCE level has been provided by B. A. Bloomfield, J. L. Dobby and L.

Kendall (1979) *Ability and examinations at 16+* published by Macmillan. Teachers who have particular interest in the assessment of children with special learning difficulties could make a good start with D. A. Sabatino and T. L. Miller (1979) *Describing learner characteristics of handicapped children and youth* (Grune and Stratton), and for a comprehensive survey of changes in assessments and school evaluation read the book edited by Robert Glaser (1978) *Research development and school change* (Wiley), especially the chapter by Ben Bloom.

References

Alkin, M. 1970: Evaluating net cost-effectiveness of instructional programs. In M. C. Wittrock and D. E. Wiley (eds) *The Evaluation of instruction: issues and problems.* New York: Holt, Rinehart and Winston.

Anderson, S. B., Ball, S. and Murphy, R. T 1975: *Encylopaedia of Educational Evaluation.* San Francisco: Jossey-Bass.

Ausubel, D. P. 1958: *Theory and problems of child development.* New York: Grune and Stratton.

Ausubel, D. P., Novak, J. D., Hanesian, H 1978: *Educational psychology: a cognitive view.* New York: Holt, Rinehart and Winston.

Bar-Tal, D. 1978: Attributional analysis of achievement-related behaviour. *Review of Educational Research,* 48, 259–71.

Black, H. 1962: *They shall not pass.* New York: William Morrow.

Block, J. H. (ed) 1971: *Mastery learning: theory and practice.* New York: Holt, Rinehart and Winston.

Block, J. H. 1972: Student evaluation: toward the setting of mastery performance standards. Paper presented at annual meeting of American Educational Research Association, April 1972. Chicago.

Block, N. J. and Dworkin, G. 1976: *The IQ controversy.* New York: Pantheon.

Bloom, B. S., Engelhart, M. A., Furst, E. J., Hill, W. H. and Krathwohl, D. R. 1956: *Taxonomy of educational objectives.* Handbook I: *Cognitive domain.* London: Longman.

Bloom, B. S., Hastings, J. T. and Madaus, G. F. 1971: *Handbook on formative and summative evaluation of student learning.* New York: McGraw Hill.

Bonavia, D. 1978: Clock turned back to improve standards. *Times Educational Supplement,* 19 May 1978.

Bowles, S. and Gintis, H. 1976: *Schooling in capitalist America.* London: Routledge and Kegan Paul.

Broadfoot, P. 1979: *Assessment, schools and society.* London: Methuen.

Browder, L. H. 1971: *Emerging patterns of administrative accountability.* Berkeley: McCutchan.

Bruner, J. S., Jolly, A. and Sylva, K. 1976: *Play: its role in development and evolution.* Harmondsworth: Penguin.

Buber, M. 1958: *I and thou.* New York: Charles Scribner.

Burt, C. 1955: The evidence for the concept of intelligence. *British Journal of Educational Psychology,* 25, 158—77.

Burt, C. 1969: Intelligence and heredity: some common misconceptions. *Irish Journal of Education,* III, 75—94.

Burton, N. W. 1978: Societal standards. *Journal of Educational Measurement,* 15, 263—71.

Campbell, D. T. and Stanley, J. C. 1966: *Experimental and quasi-experimental designs for research.* American Educational Research Association.

Cast, B. M. P. 1940: The efficiency of different methods of marking English compositions. *British Journal of Educational Psychology,* 10, 49—60.

Cattell, R. B. 1973: *Personality and mood by questionnaire.* New York: Jossey-Bass.

Child, D. 1970: *The essentials of factor analysis.* London: Holt, Rinehart and Winston.

Child, D. 1977: *Psychology and the teacher,* 2nd edn. London: Holt, Rinehart and Winston.

Cleary, T. A., Humphreys, L. G., Kendrick, S. A. and Wesman, A. 1975: Educational use of tests with disadvantaged students. *American Psychologist,* 30, 15—41.

Cohen, L. 1979: Approximate expressions for parameter estimates in the Rasch model. *British Journal of Mathematical and Statistical Psychology,* 32, 113—20.

Cox, C. B. and Dyson, A. E. (eds) 1969a: *Fight for education (Black Paper I).* London: The Critical Quarterly Society.

Cox, C. B. and Dyson, A. E. (eds) 1969b: *The crisis in education (Black Paper II).* London: The Critical Quarterly Society.

Cox, C. B. and Dyson, A. E. (eds) 1970: *Goodbye Mr Short (Black Paper III).* London: The Critical Quarterly Society.

Cox, C. B. and Dyson, A. E. (eds) 1975: *The fight for education (Black Paper IV).* London: Dent.

Cox, C. B. and Dyson, A. E. 1977: *Black Paper V.* London: Temple Smith.

Cronbach, L. J. 1961: *Essentials of psychological testing,* 2nd edn. New York: Harper and Row.

Cronbach, L. J. 1971: Test validation. In R. L. Thorndike (ed) *Educational Measurement,* 2nd edn. Washington: American Council on Education.

Cronbach, L. J. 1975: Five decades of public controversy over mental testing. *American Psychologist,* 30, 1—14.

Cronbach, L. J., Gleser, G. C., Nanda, H. and Rajaratnam, N. 1972: *The dependability of behavioral measurements.* New York: Wiley.

Cronbach, L. J. and Meehl, P. E. 1966: Construct validity in psychological tests. In C. I. Chase and H. L. Ludlow (eds) *Readings in educational and psychological measurement.* Boston: Houghton Mifflin.

Cureton, E. E. 1966: Kuder—Richardson reliabilities of classroom tests. *Educational and Psychological Measurement,* 26, 13—14.

Dearden, R. 1968: *The philosophy of primary education.* London: Routledge and Kegan Paul.

Dennison, W. F. 1978: Research report: the assessment of performance unit — where is it leading? *Durham and Newcastle Research Review,* 40, 31—6.

Department of Education and Science 1975: A language for life. (The Bullock Report) London: HMSO.

Department of Education and Science 1977: School leavers CSE and GCE. *Statistics of Education,* Vol. 2. London: HMSO.

Department of Education and Science 1978: Report of the Committee of Enquiry into the education of handicapped children and young persons (The Warnock Report). London: HMSO.

Department of Education and Science 1978: *Monitoring mathematics.* London: DES.

Donaldson, M. 1978: *Childrens' minds.* Glasgow: Fontana.

Downing, J. and Thackray, D. 1971: *Reading readiness.* London: University of London Press.

Dunstan, M. 1959: Examining in English at the matriculation level. *Unpublished M.Ed. Thesis.* University of Sydney.

Ebel, R. L. 1972: *Essentials of Educational Measurement.* Englewood Cliffs, N.J.: Prentice Hall.

Erikson, K. T. 1962: Notes on the sociology of deviance. *Social Problems,* 9, 307—14.

Feschbach, S., Adelman, H. and Fuller, W. W. 1974: Early identification of children with high risk of reading failure. *Journal of Learning Disabilities,* 7, 639—44.

Finlayson, D. S. 1951: The reliability of the marking of essays. *British Journal of Educational Psychology,* 21, 216—34.

Flanagan, J. C. 1955: The development of an index of examinee motivation. *Educational and Psychological Measurement,* 15, 144—51.

Flanders, N. A. 1970: *Analyzing teacher behavior.* New York: Addison-Wesley.

Foster, J. 1972: *Recording individual progress.* London: Macmillan.

Fraenkel, J. R. 1969: Value education in the social studies. *Phi Delta Kappan,* 50, 457—61.

Gagné, R. M. 1970: *The conditions of learning,* 2nd edn. London: Holt, Rinehart and Winston.

Gagné, R. M. 1974: *Essentials of learning for instruction.* Hinsdale, Ill.: Dryden Press.

Gaudry, E. and Spielberger, C. D. 1974: *Anxiety and educational achievement.* New York: Wiley.

Gerberich, J. R. 1956: *Specimen objective test items: A guide to achievement test construction.* New York: Longmans.

Gilham, B. (ed) 1978: *Reconstructing educational psychology.* London: Croom Helm.

Glaser, R. 1968: Adapting the elementary school curriculum to individual performance. *Proceedings of the 1967 Conference on Testing Problems.* Princeton, J.J.: Educational Testing Service.

Glass, G. V. 1978: Standards and criteria. *Journal of Educational Measurement,* 15, 237–61.

Goldman, L. 1971: *Using tests in counseling,* 2nd edn. Calif.: Goodyear.

Goldstein, H. and Blinkhorn, S. 1977: Monitoring educational standards: an inappropriate model. *Bulletin of British Psychological Society,* 30, 309–11.

Goodacre, E. 1971: *Children and learning to read.* London: Routledge and Kegan Paul.

Goodman, K. S. 1970: Reading: a psycholinguistic guessing game. In H. Singer and R. Ruddell (eds) *Theoretical models and processes of reading.* Newark, Del.: International Reading Association.

Goodman, Y. and Burke, C. 1972: *Reading miscues inventory.* New York: Macmillan.

Gosling, G. W. H. 1966: *Marking English compositions.* Australian Council for Educational Research.

Green, B. F. 1970: Comments on tailored testing. In I. Holtzman (ed) *Computer assisted instruction, testing and guidance.* New York: Harper and Row.

Gronlund, N. E. 1971: *Measurement and evaluation in teaching,* 2nd edn. New York: Macmillan.

Guilford, J. P. and Fruchter, B. 1973: *Fundamental statistics in psychology and education,* 5th edn. Tokyo: McGraw Hill.

Hargreaves, D. H. 1967: *Social relations in a secondary school.* London: Routledge and Kegan Paul.

Hartog, P. 1941: *The marking of English essays.* London: Macmillan.

Hartog, P. and Rhodes, E. C. 1936: *The marks of examiners.* London: Macmillan.

Head, J. J. 1966: Multiple marking of an essay item in experimental O-level Nuffield biology examination. *Educational Research,* 19, 65–71.

Hearnshaw, L. S. 1979: *Cyril Burt psychologist.* London: Hodder and Stoughton.

Henrysson, S. 1971: Gathering, analyzing and using data on test items. In R. L. Thorndike (ed) *Educational Measurement.* Washington, D.C.: American Council on Education.

Hoffman, B. 1962: *The tyranny of testing.* New York: Crowell-Collier Press.

Horton, T. R. 1973: *The reading standards of children in Wales.* Windsor: NFER Publishing Co. Ltd.

Hunter, I. M. L. 1962: An exceptional talent for calculative thinking. *British Journal of Psychology*, 53, 243–58.

Ingenkamp, K. 1977: *Educational assessment.* Windsor: NFER Publishing Co. Ltd.

Jacobs, P. I. 1966: Effects of coaching on the college-board English composition test. *Educational and Psychological Measurement*, 26, 55–67.

Jencks, C. et al. 1973: *Inequality: a reassessment of the effect of family and schooling in America.* London: Allen Lane.

Jensen, A. R. 1972: *Genetics and education.* New York: Harper and Row.

Jewett, A. and Bish, C. E. (eds) 1965: *Improving English composition.* Washington: National Educational Association.

Kamin, L. J. 1974: *The science and politics of IQ.* New York: Wiley.

Karmel, L. J. and Karmel, M. O. 1978: *Measurement and evaluation in the schools,* 2nd edn. New York: Macmillan.

Krathwohl, D. R., Bloom, B. S. and Masia, B. B. 1964: *Taxonomy of educational objectives Handbook II: The affective domain.* New York: McKay.

Lewis, D. G. 1974: *Assessment in education.* London: University of London Press.

Lien, A. J. 1976: *Measurement and evaluation of learning.* Dubuque, Iowa: Wm C. Brown.

Livingston, S. A. 1972: Criterion-referenced applications of classical test theory. *Journal of Educational Measurement*, 9, 13–26.

Lord, F. M. 1957: Do tests of the same length have the same standard error of measurement? *Educational and Psychological Measurement*, 17, 510–21.

Lord, F. M. and Novick, M. 1968: *Statistical theories of mental test scores.* Reading, Mass.: Addison-Wesley.

Lucas, A. M. 1971: Multiple marking of a matriculation biology essay question. *British Journal of Educational Psychology*, 41, 78–84.

Marshall, M. S. 1968: *Teaching without grades.* Corrallis, Oregon: Oregon State University Press.

Marjoram, T. 1977: Patience rewarded – a report on the progress of the Assessment of Performance Unit. *Times Educational Supplement*, 14 October 1977.

Medley, D., Schluck, C. and Ames, N. 1969: Assessing the learning environment in the classroom. *A manual for users of OSCAR 5.* Princeton, N.J.: Educational Testing Service.

Mehrens, W. A. and Lehmann, I. J. 1978: *Measurement and evaluation in education and psychology*, 2nd edn. New York: Holt, Rinehart and Winston.

Merton, R. K. 1957: *Social theory and social structure*. Glencoe: The Free Press.

Meskauskas, J. A. and Webster, G. W. 1975: The American Board of Internal Medicine recertification examination process and results. *Annals of Internal Medicine*, 82, 577–81.

Messick, S. 1965: Personality measurement and the ethics of assessment. *American Psychologist*, 20, 136–42.

Metfessel, W. S., Michael, W. B. and Kirsner, D. A. 1969: Instrumentation of Bloom's and Krathwohl's taxonomies for the writing of behavioral objectives. *Psychology in the Schools*, 6, 227–31.

Miller, G. E. 1976: Continuous assessment. *Medical Education*, 10, 81–6.

Moseley, D. 1976: *Helping with learning difficulties*. Milton Keynes: Open University Press.

McClelland, D. C. 1966: The measurement of human motivation: an experimental approach. In A. Anastasi (ed) *Testing problems in perspective*. Washington, D.C.: American Council on Education.

Nash, R. 1972: *Classrooms observed*. London: Routledge and Kegan Paul.

Newcomer, P. L. and Hammill, D. D. 1975: ITPA and academic achievement: a survey. *Reading Teacher*, 28, 731–41.

Nisbet, J. D. 1955: English composition in secondary school selection. *British Journal of Educational Psychology*, 35, 51–4.

Payne, D. A. 1974: *The assessment of learning*. Lexington, Mass.: D. C. Heath and Co.

Phillips, G. E. 1948: The marking of children's essays. *Forum of Education*, 7, 19–29.

Pipho, G. (ed) 1978: Minimum competency testing. *Phi Delta Kappan*, 59, 585–629.

Pumfrey, P. D. 1977: *Measuring reading abilities*. London: Hodder and Stoughton.

Ripley, W. H. and Blair, T. R. 1979: *Reading diagnosis and remediation*. Chicago: Rand McNally.

Rosenthal, R. R. and Jacobson, L. 1968: *Pygmalion in the classroom*. New York: Holt.

Rowley, G. L. 1974: Which examinees are most favoured by the use of multiple-choice tests. *Journal of Educational Measurement*, 11, 15–23.

Rowntree, D. 1977: *Assessing students: How shall we know them?* London: Harper and Row.

Rutter, M. and Madge, N. 1976: *Cycles of disadvantage*. London: Heinemann.

Rutter, M., Maughan, B., Mortimore, P. and Ouston, J. 1979: *Fifteen thousand hours*. London: Open Books.

Satterly, D. J. and Brimer, M. A. 1971: Cognitive styles and school learning. *British Journal of Educational Psychology*, 41, 294–303.

Schmuck, R. A. and Schmuck, P. A. 1974: *A humanistic psychology of education*. Palo Alto, Calif.: National Press Books.

Seashore, H. G. and Ricks, J. H. 1950: Norms must be relevant. *Test Service Bulletin 39*. New York: The Psychological Corporation.

Sperry, L. (ed) 1972: *Learning performance and individual differences: Essays and readings*. Glenview, Ill.: Scott Foresman.

Stalnaker, J. M. 1934: The validity of the University of Chicago qualifying examination. *English Journal (Coll. Ed.)*, 23, 384–8.

Start, K. B. and Wells, B. K. 1972: *The trend of reading standards*. Windsor: NFER Publishing Co. Ltd.

Stevens, S. S. 1946: On the theory of scales of measurement. *Science*, 103, 677–80.

Stones, E. 1979: *Psychopedagogy: psychological theory and the practice of teaching*. London: Methuen.

Sumner, R. 1975: *Tests of attainment in mathematics in schools*. Windsor: NFER Publishing Co. Ltd.

Thorndike, R. L. 1967: 'Overachievement' and 'underachievement' as psychological concepts. In B. P. Komisar and C. J. B. Macmillan (eds) *Psychological concepts in Education*. Chicago: Rand McNally.

Thorndike, R. L. 1968: A review of Pygmalion in the classroom. *American Educational Research Journal*, 708–11.

Thorndike, R. L. (ed) 1971: *Educational Measurement*, 2nd edn. Washington: American Council on Education.

Tinkelman, S. N. 1971: Planning the objective test. In R. L. Thorndike (ed) *Educational Measurement*, 2nd edn. Washington: American Council on Education.

Vernon, P. E. 1979: Intelligence testing and the nature/nurture debate 1928–1978: What next? *British Journal of Educational Psychology*, 49, 1–14.

Vernon, P. E. and Millican, G. D. 1954: A further study of the reliability of English essays. *British Journal of Statistical Psychology*, 7, 65–74.

Vincent, D. and Cresswell, M. 1976: *Reading tests in the classroom*. Windsor: NFER Publishing Co. Ltd.

Wertheimer, M. 1945: *Productive thinking*. New York: Harper.

Wesman, A. G. 1971: Writing the test item. In R. L. Thorndike (ed) *Educational Measurement*, 2nd edn. Washington: American Council on Education.

Wesman, A. G. 1972: Testing and counseling: fact and fancy. *Measurement and evaluation in guidance*, 5, 397–402.

Whitehead, A. N. 1950: *The aims of education and other essays*. London: Williams and Norgate.

Willmott, A. S. and Fowles, D. E. 1974: *The objective interpretation of test performance*. Windsor: NFER Publishing Co. Ltd.

Wood, R. 1976: Inhibiting blind guessing: the effect of instructions. *Journal of Educational Measurement*, Winter, 297–307.

Wood, R. and Napthali, W. A. 1975: Assessment in the classroom: what do teachers look for? *Educational Studies*, 1, 151–61.

Wood, R. and Skurnik, L. S. 1969: *Item-banking*. Slough: NFER Publishing Co. Ltd.

Wright, B. D. 1968: Sample-free test calibration and person measurement. *Proceedings of 1967 International Conference on Testing Problms*. Princeton: Educational Testing Service.

Wright, B. D. and Panchapakesan, N. 1969: A procedure for sample-free item analysis. *Educational and Psychological Measurement*, 29, 23–48.

Young, M. 1961: *The rise of the meritocracy 1870–2033*. London: Thames and Hudson.

Appendix

z-scores (column 1) and areas from mean to z-score in curve of normal distribution (column 2). Reproduced by arrangement with Holt, Rinehart and Winston – New York, from *Experimental design in psychological research*, 3rd ed. by A. L. Edwards, 1968.

1	2	1	2	1	2	1	2	1	2
0.00	0.0000	0.70	0.2580	1.40	0.4192	2.10	0.4821	2.75	0.4870
0.01	0.0040	0.71	0.2611	1.41	0.4207	2.11	0.4826	2.76	0.4971
0.02	0.0080	0.72	0.2642	1.42	0.4222	2.12	0.4830	2.77	0.4972
0.03	0.0120	0.73	0.2673	1.43	0.4236	2.13	0.4834	2.78	0.4973
0.04	0.0160	0.74	0.2704	1.44	0.4251	2.14	0.4838	2.79	0.4974
0.05	0.0199	0.75	0.2734	1.45	0.4265	2.15	0.4842	2.80	0.4974
0.06	0.0239	0.76	0.2764	1.46	0.4279	2.16	0.4846	2.81	0.4975
0.07	0.0279	0.77	0.2794	1.47	0.4292	2.17	0.4850	2.82	0.4976
0.08	0.0319	0.78	0.2823	1.48	0.4306	2.18	0.4854	2.83	0.4977
0.09	0.0359	0.79	0.2852	1.49	0.4319	2.19	0.4857	2.84	0.4977
0.10	0.0398	0.80	0.2881	1.50	0.4332	2.20	0.4861	2.85	0.4978
0.11	0.0438	0.81	0.2910	1.51	0.4345	2.21	0.4864	2.86	0.4979
0.12	0.0478	0.82	0.2939	1.52	0.4357	2.22	0.4868	2.87	0.4979
0.13	0.0517	0.83	0.2967	1.53	0.4370	2.23	0.4871	2.88	0.4980
0.14	0.0557	0.84	0.2995	1.54	0.4382	2.24	0.4875	2.89	0.4981
0.15	0.0596	0.85	0.3023	1.55	0.4394	2.25	0.4878	2.90	0.4981
0.16	0.0636	0.86	0.3051	1.56	0.4406	2.26	0.4881	2.91	0.4982
0.17	0.0675	0.87	0.3078	1.57	0.4418	2.27	0.4884	2.92	0.4982
0.18	0.0714	0.88	0.3106	1.57	0.4429	2.28	0.4887	2.93	0.4983
0.19	0.0753	0.89	0.3133	1.59	0.4441	2.29	0.4890	2.94	0.4984
0.20	0.0793	0.90	0.3159	1.60	0.4452	2.30	0.4893	2.95	0.4984
0.21	0.0832	0.91	0.3186	1.61	0.4463	2.31	0.4896	2.96	0.4985
0.22	0.0871	0.92	0.3212	1.61	0.4474	2.32	0.4898	2.97	0.4985
0.23	0.0910	0.93	0.3238	1.63	0.4484	2.33	0.4901	2.98	0.4986
0.24	0.0948	0.94	0.3264	1.64	0.4495	2.34	0.4904	2.99	0.4986
0.25	0.0987	0.95	0.3289	1.65	0.4505	2.35	0.4906	3.00	0.4987
0.26	0.1026	0.96	0.3315	1.66	0.4515	2.36	0.4909	3.01	0.4987
0.27	0.1064	0.97	0.3340	1.67	0.4525	2.37	0.4911	3.02	0.4987
0.28	0.1103	0.98	0.3365	1.68	0.4535	2.38	0.4913	3.03	0.4988
0.29	0.1141	0.99	0.3389	1.69	0.4545	2.39	0.4916	3.04	0.4988
0.30	0.1179	1.00	0.3413	1.70	0.4554	2.40	0.4918	3.05	0.4989
0.31	0.1217	1.01	0.3438	1.71	0.4564	2.41	0.4920	3.06	0.4989
0.32	0.1255	1.02	0.3461	1.72	0.4573	2.42	0.4922	3.07	0.4989
0.33	0.1293	1.03	0.3485	1.73	0.4582	2.43	0.4925	3.08	0.4990
0.34	0.1331	1.04	0.3508	1.74	0.4591	2.44	0.4927	3.09	0.4990
0.35	0.1368	1.05	0.3531	1.75	0.4599	2.45	0.4929	3.10	0.4990
0.36	0.1406	1.06	0.3554	1.76	0.4608	2.46	0.4931	3.11	0.4991
0.37	0.1443	1.07	0.3577	1.77	0.4616	2.47	0.4932	3.12	0.4991
0.38	0.1408	1.08	0.3599	1.78	0.4625	2.48	0.4934	3.13	0.4991
0.39	0.1517	1.09	0.3621	1.79	0.4633	2.49	0.4936	3.14	0.4992
0.40	0.1554	1.10	0.3643	1.80	0.4641	2.50	0.4938	3.15	0.4992
0.41	0.1591	1.11	0.3665	1.81	0.4649	2.51	0.4940	3.16	0.4992
0.42	0.1628	1.12	0.3686	1.82	0.4656	2.52	0.4941	3.17	0.4992
0.43	0.1664	1.13	0.3708	1.83	0.4664	2.53	0.4943	3.18	0.4993
0.44	0.1700	1.14	0.3729	1.84	0.4671	2.54	0.4945	3.19	0.4993
0.45	0.1736	1.15	0.3749	1.85	0.4678	2.55	0.4946	3.20	0.4993
0.46	0.1772	1.16	0.3770	1.86	0.4686	2.56	0.4948	3.21	0.4993
0.47	0.1808	1.17	0.3790	1.87	0.4693	2.57	0.4949	3.22	0.4994
0.48	0.1844	1.18	0.3810	1.88	0.4699	2.58	0.4951	3.23	0.4994
0.49	0.1879	1.19	0.3830	1.89	0.4706	2.59	0.4952	3.24	0.4994
0.50	0.1915	1.20	0.3849	1.90	0.4713	2.60	0.4953	3.30	0.4995
0.51	0.1950	1.21	0.3869	1.91	0.4719	2.61	0.4955	3.40	0.4997
0.52	0.1985	1.22	0.3888	1.92	0.4726	2.62	0.4956	3.50	0.4998
0.53	0.2019	1.23	0.3907	1.93	0.4732	2.63	0.4957	3.60	0.4998
0.54	0.2054	1.24	0.3925	1.94	0.4738	2.64	0.4959	3.70	0.4999
0.55	0.2088	1.25	0.3944	1.95	0.4744	2.65	0.4960		
0.56	0.2123	1.26	0.3962	1.96	0.4750	2.66	0.4961		
0.57	0.2157	1.27	0.3980	1.97	0.4756	2.67	0.4962		
0.58	0.2190	1.28	0.3997	1.98	0.4761	2.68	0.4963		
0.59	0.2224	1.29	0.4015	1.99	0.4767	2.69	0.4964		
0.60	0.2257	1.30	0.4032	2.00	0.4772	2.70	0.4965		
0.61	0.2291	1.31	0.4049	2.01	0.4778	2.71	0.4966		
0.62	0.2324	1.32	0.4066	2.02	0.4783	2.72	0.4967		
0.63	0.2357	1.33	0.4082	2.03	0.4788	2.73	0.4968		
0.64	0.2389	1.34	0.4099	2.04	0.4793	2.74	0.4969		
0.65	0.2422	1.35	0.4115	2.05	0.4798				
0.66	0.2454	1.36	0.4131	2.06	0.4803				
0.67	0.2496	1.37	0.4147	2.07	0.4808				
0.68	0.2517	1.38	0.4162	2.08	0.4812				
0.69	0.2549	1.39	0.4177	2.09	0.4817				

Glossary of Assessment Terms

Academic aptitude. A combination of abilities and skills, whatever their origin, on which learning in school depends. An *aptitude test* is one made up of items which predict success in later academic work but are minimally dependent, if at all, on the effects of instruction. Thus such tests attempt to measure the elusive property of potential for learning.

Accountability (in education). An explicit or implicit responsibility on the part of schools for bringing about certain educational objectives in a cost-effective way. The processes by which schools and local authorities justify the expenditure to the taxpayer.

Achievement test. A test which is designed to measure how much a child has acquired as the result of specific teaching. The acquisitions are usually of information, knowledge or skills which schools have made a deliberate intention to teach.

Affective test. A test of non-cognitive classroom characteristics of pupils, such as motivation, interests, attitudes and aesthetic awareness.

Age-equivalent score. The average score of a group of children of specified age. This average is usually obtained either by direct observation or estimated using other tests (singly or in combination) which are known to correlate with the score in question.

Age norms. Sets of average scores for successive age groups.

---

[7] Some definitions are based on *A glossary of measurement terms* published by CTB/McGraw-Hill, Monterey, California 93940. Reproduced by permission of the publisher. Copyright © 1959 by McGraw-Hill, Inc. All rights reserved. Printed in the United States of America.

Arithmetic mean. Usually abbreviated to 'mean' it is the value obtained when the sum of a set of scores is divided by the number of scores. Mathematically it is that value about which the sum of the deviations (q.v.) is zero.

Average. A vague way usually of specifying the arithmetic mean but sometimes loosely employed to indicate the median (q.v.) or the mode (q.v.).

Baseline measures. Measurements obtained to indicate levels of performance before the intervention of an educational or other programme against which to assess change (compare pre-test).

Bivariate chart (sometimes called a 'scatter diagram'). A diagram defined by two axes (x and y) in which tally marks are made to show the scores of a group of individual, on two tests. A useful device for checking on the shape of the relationship between two tests prior to the calculation of a correlation coefficient (q.v.).

Ceiling. The top score or upper limit of ability or achievement that can be measured by a test. A test is said to have a 'low ceiling' if it fails to differentiate a group of children whose overall performance exceeds or reaches the highest level at which it can discriminate.

Central tendency. A single score or value which provides a suitable summary of the properties of the complete set of scores. The three most commonly used are the mean (q.v.), median (q.v.), and mode (q.v.). For some sets of scores one or other of these may not provide a meaningful index of central tendency: for example, in a distribution of scores where each score occurs the same number of times.

Check list. A list of behaviours or characteristics of children's work drawn up to aid systematic observation. The rater responds by ticking 'yes' when he or she has decided that the characteristic in question has occurred to his or her satisfaction but leaves the item blank or records otherwise in the absence of this.

Certification. The use of assessment data to make a formal attestation to a learner's competence or performance, especially the level of success in an examination or as a licence to practise a profession or trade or to gain entry to it.

Class interval. The size of the divisions of a frequency distribution bounded by upper and lower score values. For example, a test of 100 items where the scores are cast into divisions which correspond to 40–4, 45–9, 50–4, etc. has a class interval of five.

Continuous assessment. Where all learning activities or assignments (or a selected combination of these) taken throughout the course provide the only data for certification (see *terminal assessment*).

Control group. A group of children who do not receive an educational programme that an investigator wishes to evaluate, as contrasted with an experimental group who do.

Covariance. The average of the product of the deviations of separate pairs of scores from their respective means. Thus if the deviation of an x score for a child is $(x - \bar{x})$ and the y score for that same child is $(y - \bar{y})$, then $\Sigma(x - \bar{x})(y - \bar{y})/n$ is said to be the covariance of x and y (where Σ = the sum of).

Completion item. A type of test question which requires the respondent to complete a phrase or sentence where one or more gaps have been left.

Composite score. A score which is obtained by the combination of several other scores. This is usually done by addition though different weights are often applied to the contributing scores to increase or decrease their contributions to the whole.

Concurrent validity. The strength of the relationship – usually expressed as a correlation coefficient (q.v.) between scores on a given test and another criterion of the same ability or characteristic obtained at or near the same time. For example, scores on a test of personality with estimates of adjustment, or scores on an end of term test with teacher ratings of achievement.

Construct validity. The extent to which a test measures an underlying, usually abstract, psychological trait. For example, the extent to which a test of verbal ability correlates with the property common to other verbal tests identified through factor analysis (q.v.).

Content validity. The extent to which a test represents a balanced sample of the outcomes the programme of teaching or instruction was designed to achieve: for example, a test would have poor content validity for a course in *mathematics* if it consisted solely of problems in arithmetic. The balance is best achieved by using a specification table (q.v.).

Correction for guessing. A device for reducing scores in tests where right answers can be obtained by chance. In a true/false question a formula sometimes used is $(R - W)$, but all are based on the assumption that guessing in an objective test will yield a number of wrong answers that is proportional to the number of alternative responses to each item. The usefulness of this device is, however, questionable.

Correlation. A general term which refers to the relationship between two sets of scores or measures. The fact that high scorers on one test achieve high scores on the other (and vice versa) does not necessarily indicate a causal relationship between the abilities measured.

Correlation coefficient. A precise mathematical index of the strength of the relationship between two sets of scores which can range from +1.0 (perfect positive agreement) to -1.0 (perfect negative agreement) with zero indicating a complete lack of relationship. The most common type of coefficient is the Pearson product-moment correlation (symbolized r) but other types are often calculated.

Criterion-referenced test. A test used to ascertain the degree of correspondence between the performance or learning by an individual and a precise definition of the behaviour exhibited by a 'successful' learner of a well defined objective for learning. Most commonly, such tests cover relatively small units of content and the scores are interpreted as showing *what* the individual learner can do rather than as a comparison with other individuals (contrast standardized tests). See also 'mastery test'.

Cross-sectional data. Results of assessments made on representative samples of children chosen from age groups which span a number of years. Often adopted as an economical substitute for longitudinal data (q.v.).

Culture-fair test. A test which is said to provide an equal opportunity of success to all respondents irrespective of culture and experiential background. Its content must, therefore, contain only that material which is common to all cultures — probably an impossibility to attain in practice — or material which is equally novel for all cultures.

Culture-free test. A test which is said to be free from the effects of cultural experience and reflects only that part of ability which is hereditary. Such claims are seldom if ever made for contemporary tests.

Decile. An example of a quantile (q.v.). One of the nine score points which divides a distribution into ten equal parts.

Deviation (d). The difference between any one score and a reference score. Most frequently a deviation score is the amount by which the score x_{ij} differs from the mean of the group of scores to which it belongs ($\bar{x}$). Thus $d = (x_{ij} - \bar{x})$. Deviation scores can also be found from the median or mode (q.v.) of a group of scores.

Deviation IQ. An index of general mental ability most commonly used in the Wechsler tests of intelligence. It is based upon the deviation of a person's score from the typical or average score for persons of the same chronological age. Deviation IQs are usually standard scores with the mean of 100 and standard deviation 16.

Diagnostic test. A test which analyses an individual's performance in order to locate its strengths or (more commonly) its weaknesses. Wherever possible diagnostic tests suggest the cause of the difficulties either by providing subscores on components identified by a formal analysis of the intellectual skill (e.g. reading) or, less formally, by discovering the nature of the difficulty during ordinary classroom performance.

Difficulty index. The difficulty of a test item measured by the proportion (or percentage) of children in a given age group who answer that item correctly.

Difficulty value. The difficulty of a test item as measured by the Rasch method of objective measurement (q.v.).

Discrimination index. An index which expresses the effectiveness of a single item to differentiate children who are high scorers from those who are low scorers on the overall test result. Most commonly it is obtained by finding the number who 'pass' the item in the highest 27% of scorers and in the lowest 27% of scorers and taking the difference between them.

Distracter. One of the plausible but incorrect options in a multiple-choice test.

Distribution. A table of scores showing the number of children who obtain each score or have a score within each score interval.

Domain-referenced test. A test which consists of a representative set of items drawn from a clearly defined area of knowledge or competence. For example, a test consisting of 50 items measuring knowledge (recall) of chemical symbols drawn at random from the domain of chemical elements, listed in the Periodic Table.

Equivalent scores. Where there are two or more forms of a test each measuring the same ability, equivalent scores are a means of translating the scores on one form into units on the other form.

Error of measurement. One of a number of statistical devices for estimating the size of the error present in a given score (see *standard error*).

Evaluation. Using assessment data to arrive at a judgment of the value or effectiveness of something. For example, the scores obtained by children to decide whether or not a programme of instruction has been 'successful'.

Expectancy table. A two or multi-way table which shows the relationship between scores on a predictive test and a criterion: for example, one which compares scores on a criterion-referenced test with a second judgment of mastery of a given skill.

Face validity. A weak form of validity in which a test 'appears to measure' what it claims to measure but in the absence of any evidence beyond that appearance.

Factor. A hypothetical trait which is assumed to underlie and affect performance on two or more (usually mental) tests. Thus a factor is the theoretical construct responsible for correlations between tests. It is identified by factor analysis (q.v.).

Factor analysis. A family of statistical methods for isolating a more parsimonious number of underlying traits by which to account for the overlap (correlations) among a number of mental tests. It shows how much of the variance (q.v.) in the original tests is associated with each factor.

Flotation technique. A method of reaching an assessment in which the teacher is recommended to record the most salient characteristics of a child; that is those which 'float to the top' of the teacher's recollections. Recommended by Marshall (1968) as an alternative to the use of check lists or any other set of criteria presented in advance and of universal application.

Formal assessment. Assessment conducted in situations which have been set up solely for that purpose (see *informal assessment*) usually using well validated tests or other instruments.

Formative evaluation. The use of assessment data by which to obtain knowledge of the effects of teaching and learning during its development. The general aim is to provide information to modify a programme of education (contrast *summative evaluation*).

Frequency polygon. A line graph joining the number of individuals who obtain each score, or who occur within a given score interval.

Goal card. Charts showing the objectives of learning, the

criteria of passing those objectives and incorporating a space for self-recording of progress. Useful in individually-guided learning.

Group test. A test designed to be taken by a number of individuals simultaneously and administered by a single examiner.

Idiographic assessment. Assessment designed to understand the individual in his own right without comparison with others.

Individual test. A test designed to be administered to one person at a time.

Informal assessment. Assessment conducted while pupils are carrying on with normal classroom activities (see *formal assessment*).

Intelligence quotient (IQ). Originally the ratio of a person's mental age (q.v.) to his chronological age expressed as a percentage but now replaced by a standardized score (q.v.) which takes the individual's raw score and age into account. The mean IQ for a group is 100 with a standard deviation (q.v.) of 15 or 16. The IQ is often interpreted as a general measure of a person's 'brightness'.

Item. A single question or exercise in a test.

Item analysis. A set of methods for examining an item to determine its difficulty, discrimination and validity.

Item bank. A collection of items classified by content and level of difficulty for purposes of test construction.

Item (or matrix) sampling. A method used in test construction in which subgroups of respondents take subgroups of items thus avoiding the need for all pupils to take all items.

Kuder–Richardson formulae. A family of formulae for estimating reliability (q.v.) by studying the internal consistency of a test.

Leptokurtic curve. A distribution of scores which rises more steeply to a peak than a normal, or mesokurtic, curve (contrast *platykurtic*).

Longitudinal data. Results of repeated assessment of the same children, usually over a considerable period of time (contrast *cross-sectional data*).

Mastery test. A test designed to determine whether a pupil has mastered a given objective of instruction or a unit of knowledge or skill. Differs from criterion-referenced testing (q.v.) in its goal, which is to label pupils as master/non-master of any objective which needs to be attacked before more difficult work can be undertaken.

Matrix sampling. A method of dividing a long test into shorter subtests and of administering each subtest to samples of children chosen by random from a population. If properly carried out reliable estimates of total scores can be obtained, thus saving time in administration and scoring.

Mean. See *arithmetic mean*.

Measurement. Assigning numbers to objects or characteristics.

Median. The 50th percentile (q.v.) or middle score in a group which divides the distribution into two equal parts such that half the scores are above and half below the median.

Mental age. The age for which a given score in a test of mental ability or intelligence is average. Thus if the average score of a large group of children aged seven years nine months is 65 then any child receiving that score is said to have that mental age irrespective of his chronological age. Mental ages are especially difficult to interpret among children older than about 11 years of age.

Mesokurtic curve. A distribution of scores which is normal or near normal.

Mode. The score which occurs most frequently in a distribution. Any distribution may have more than one mode.

Monitoring. Regular and systematic assessment of basic attainments of representative groups of children to establish changes in typical performance over a period of time (e.g. in the maintenance of standards).

Multiple choice test. A test composed of items in which the task is to select one or more correct answers from a number of options.

Nomothetic assessment. Assessment of individuals with a view to making comparisons among them or to generalize to larger populations.

Normal distribution. A distribution in which scores are symmetrically distributed about the mean with most scores concentrated near it but decreasing in frequency with increasing distance from it as described by a particular mathematical function. In a normal distribution (sometimes called a Gaussian curve) mean, median and mode coincide. The assumption that psychological, educational and other phenomena are normally distributed is a widely accepted model in the statistical description and interpretation of scores.

Normalized standardized scores. Scores manipulated to conform to the normal curve having a known mean and standard deviation. (For example, *T*-scores have a mean of 50 and SD of ten.)

Norms. Tables of scores describing the average performance of large, often representative, groups of children to provide an interpretive frame of reference by which to give meaning to the scores of individuals. The most common norms in education are IQ and verbal reasoning in standardized score form, percentile ranks and stanines. Norms only represent average, not desirable, performances and to be of value should have been obtained from groups similar to those to whom interpretation is to be extended.

Norm-referenced test. A test explicitly designed to be used to make comparison among individuals (contrast *criterion-referenced test*) with norms (q.v.) for interpretation.

Objectives. Narrow definitions of children's behaviour or performance which are indicative of the goals of teaching (see *goal cards*).

Objective measurement. A term applied to the approach developed by Rasch. The scale of difficulty values is independent of the sample on which the items have been scored and the ability measures are on a scale which expresses the odds of a respondent's success on items of known difficulty.

Objective test. One whose scoring is unaffected by the opinions of different scorers. Thus criteria of 'correctness' are set up in advance and consistently applied by a number of markers.

Platykurtic curve. A distribution of scores which is flatter than that of a normal or mesokurtic curve (contrast *leptokurtic*).

Percentiles. An example of quantiles (q.v.). The division of a ranked distribution into 99 groups each composed of the same percentage of scores. Thus the 40th percentile (P_{40}) is the score which separates the 'top' 60% from the 'bottom' 40% of scores.

Placement. Using assessment data to classify an individual for the purposes of matching him with one of an alternative number of educational programmes either as an individual or member of a group.

Post-test. A test administered at the end of an educational programme designed to evaluate the effectiveness of that programme by comparison with the pre-test (q.v.).

Power test. A test designed to be taken with no time limit, or a very generous one to measure ability or performance unconstrained by the demand of quick responding.

Practice effect. The effect of a previous experience with a test on a later administration of the same or similar test.

Predictive validity. The claim that a test is valid based on its correlation between it and scores on a criterion at a later time.

Pre-test. A test designed to obtain information about children before a programme which is to be evaluated is administered (contrast *post-test*).

Product-moment correlation. See *correlation coefficient*.

Profile. A graphic representation of an individual's or group's scores on several tests when such scores have been presented in terms which make them comparable (e.g. as standard scores or percentiles). This method of presentation affords easy identification of the strengths and weaknesses (compare *goal cards*).

Protocol. A record of the actual words used by a child when answering questions during problem solving or learning. The protocol is usually transcribed and later analysed for its significance in providing information about the processes of thought involved, e.g. for research or diagnostic purposes.

Questionnaire. A set of printed questions designed to elicit information from respondents by self-report.

Quantiles. A family of techniques for dividing a distribution of scores into equal groups (e.g. quartiles, deciles, percentiles).

Quartile. One of three points which divide a distribution into four equal-sized groups. Thus Q_1 separates the 'lowest' quarter of the group from the top three quarters.

Random sample. A set of individuals (or items on a test) drawn from the population in such a way that every member of that population has an equal chance of being selected. The sample is drawn in such a way as to preclude bias and so that certain statistical techniques for estimating population values are appropriate. Sometimes the population is divided into special subgroups before random selection from within them: this is *stratified random sampling*.

Range. The difference between highest and lowest raw score on a test.

Raw score. The actual scores obtained on a test (in education usually the 'number right').

Readiness test. A test which claims to measure the extent to which an individual has acquired the skills or knowledge required to learn some new task successfully.

Recall item. An item which requires the respondent to supply the correct answer from his memory.

Recognition item. A test item which requires the respondent to recognize or select the correct answer from among two or more alternatives.

Regression effect (regression to the mean). A consequence of imperfect correlation, it is the tendency of a predicted score to be nearer the mean of the predicted scores than was the score from which it was predicted from the mean of its series. Thus children who are very high scorers on the predictor, though above the mean on the criterion or on a second administration of the same test, are nevertheless nearer the mean on the latter. The converse is true of very low scorers on the predictor.

Reliability. The extent to which a test is consistent or dependable in measuring whatever it is that it measures.

Reliability coefficient. The coefficient of correlation between two forms of a test, between scores on two administrations of the same test taken a week or so apart or between halves of the same test after Spearman—Brown correction (q.v.). An alternative type of reliability coefficient is provided by the Kuder—Richardson formulae (q.v.).

Representative sample. A sample which accurately reflects the population from which it was drawn with respect to certain defined characteristics.

Response set. A habit or temporary disposition that causes a person to respond to test items in a particular manner.

Side-effects (of assessment). The unintended (positive or negative) results of assessment.

Simulation. An attempt to set up conditions that represent 'real life' in order to make an assessment of behaviour or performance.

Skewed distribution. A distribution of scores which departs from symmetry or balance around the mean. A distribution for which the average of the z-scores (q.v.) raised to the third power (i.e. z^3/n) is negative is said to have 'negative skew', one in which z^3/n is positive has 'positive skew'.

Sociometry. Measuring aspects of the inter-personal relationships among members of a group, usually the patterns of friendship, by asking respondents to identify the individuals they would be most likely to choose in a variety of social settings.

Spearman—Brown formula. A formula most commonly used to estimate the reliability of an entire test from a correlation between the two halves. Generally it expresses the relationship between the reliability of a test and its length.

Speed test. A test where performance is measured by the number of items correctly 'passed' in a given time. Items are usually on a similar level of difficulty within the test.

Specification table. A two-way grid (or table) summarizing the objectives of teaching and the content of the course. Entries in the grid specify the importance of the various topics and the relative importance to be allotted to them in the construction of the achievement test.

Split-half reliability coefficient. The estimate of reliability obtained by correlating scores for a given group of respondents obtained on the two halves of a test corrected by application of the Spearman—Brown formula. Comparable halves are commonly obtained by splitting the test into totals on odd- and even-numbered items. This type of coefficient is sometimes referred to as an internal consistency coefficient.

Standard. A level of requirement, degree of excellence or attainment set as a goal for pupil effort.

Standard deviation. A linear measure of the dispersion or 'scatter' of scores in a distribution, obtained by finding the square root of the size of the average squared deviation from the mean. In a normal distribution approximately two-thirds (68.3%) of the scores occur within the range from one standard deviation below the mean to one standard deviation above the mean.

Standard error of estimate. An estimate of the error inherent in predicting a criterion score from a test with which it is correlated (a predictor). It is the standard deviation of the criterion times the square root of one minus the square of the correlation coefficient.

Standard error of measurement. A statistic applied to a single obtained score to estimate the amount by which that score differs from the hypothetical 'true score' (q.v.). The larger the standard error the greater the amount of error contained in the score. The standard error of measurement is the standard deviation of the test times the square root of one minus the reliability coefficient.

Standard score. A general term describing a variety of scores transformed to make them comparable. The simplest kind is the 'z-score' in which each is the ratio of the difference between the raw score and the mean to the standard deviation of the scores: $z = (x_{ij} - \bar{x})/\sigma_x$. Since these scores range from positive to negative formulae are sometimes used to remove this undesirable feature (see *T*-scores).

Standardization sample. The sample of individuals or schools selected in order to provide norms for the interpretation of test scores.

Standardized test. A test containing a balanced set of items designed to be taken under prescribed conditions, scored objectively and interpreted in norm-referenced terms. A commercially published standardized test should present details of item analysis, reliability, validity and the nature of the standardization sample on which the norms are based.

Stanine (short for standard-nine). Usually normalized standardized scores, stanines have values from one to nine with a mean of five and standard deviations of two. Stanines two to eight inclusive have a width of half a standard deviation.

Statistical significance. A score or a result of an analysis which is unlikely to have occurred by chance. Thus 'significant at the 0.05 level' means it has been calculated that the obtained result could have occurred by chance five times (or less) in 100.

Summative evaluation. Use of assessment data to determine the effectiveness of a learning episode, unit of study, course or programme at its completion.

T-scores. A normalized, standardized set of scores constructed to have mean 50 and standard deviation ten.

Taxonomy. A principle for the classification of educational objectives.

Terminal assessment. Where assessment of work done throughout the course is not taken into account but is subordinated to the results of assessment (usually examinations or tests) taken at the end of a course or school career (see *continuous assessment*).

Test-retest reliability coefficient. A type of reliability coefficient which measures the stability of a test by correlating scores obtained by the same sample of children on two administrations of the test.

Test-wiseness. A state of readiness by a respondent to profit from previous experience of similar tests. Differential test-wiseness within a group of children is a source of invalidity in scores.

True score. Hypothetical but average score that would be expected if a child took the same test on a large number of occasions (assuming no practice effect or change in the ability being measured).

Unobtrusive assessment. Observations made with little or no awareness on the part of the assessed, usually during normal classroom practice.

Validity. A general term which describes the extent to which a test performs the function claimed for it (see *content, concurrent* and *predictive validity*).

Variance. The average of the squared deviations from the mean: the square of the standard deviation.

z-score. A type of standard score formed by dividing the deviation by the standard deviation (i.e. $z = (x_i - x)/\sigma_x$). Thus z-scores have a mean of zero and standard deviation of one.

Index